Brahms and the German Spirit

BRAHMS

AND THE

GERMAN SPIRIT

Daniel Beller-McKenna

HARVARD UNIVERSITY PRESS
Cambridge, Massachusetts
London, England

Library of Congress Cataloging-in-Publication Data

Beller-McKenna, Daniel.
Brahms and the German spirit / Daniel Beller-McKenna.
p. cm.
Includes bibliographical references and index.
ISBN 0-674-01318-2 (alk. paper)
1. Brahms, Johannes, 1833–1897—Criticism and interpretation.
2. Brahms, Johannes, 1833–1897—Political and social views.
3. Music—Germany—19th century—History and criticism.
4. Nationalism in music.   I. Title.
ML410.B8B42 2004
780′.92—dc22   2004040503

Designed by Gwen Nefsky Frankfeldt

To my parents,
Anne Scott Beller
and
E. Kuno Beller

Contents

Preface *ix*

1 Introduction: Brahms and the German Spirit 1

2 Religion, Language, and Luther's Bible 31

3 *Ein deutsches Requiem,* Op. 45, and the Apocalyptic Paradigm 65

4 The *Triumphlied,* Op. 55, and the Apocalyptic Moment 98

5 *Gebet einer König:* National Prayers in the *Fest- und Gedenksprüche,* Op. 109 133

6 Beyond the End 165

Appendix: Longer Musical Examples *195*

Notes *209*

Index *239*

Preface

This book highlights the intersection of religion and nationalism in the music of Johannes Brahms, particularly as it manifests itself in his large-scale sacred choral music. Although nationalism is a subject that arises more commonly in discussions of his contemporary Richard Wagner, Brahms's musical style, his aesthetic, and his compositional choices were also strongly determined by his identity as a German. This view runs counter to the traditional understanding of Brahms's place in music and cultural history; Brahms's music has long been valued for its classicizing detachment from its cultural milieu. Accordingly, his instrumental compositions are deemed models of "absolute" music, whose meaning is self-derived, independent of its time and place, while his vocal works—especially the more public large-scale choral works—are ascribed universal meaning in nearly all accounts by modern writers. This book challenges the universality of these pieces, arguing instead for their German-ness.

In comparison to the overtly nationalistic element in Wagner's musical legacy, the German elements in Brahms's style have been easy to overlook and, I argue, have been deliberately downplayed since the second third of the twentieth century. But nationalism comes in many guises, and the lack of an overt political agenda on Brahms's part does not obviate the need to understand how nationalism affected his works. For Brahms, nationalism is expressed more clearly in cultural terms, and this point emerges most poignantly in three large-scale choral works on biblical texts: *Ein deutsches Requiem*, op. 45; the *Triumphlied*, op. 55; and the *Fest- und Gedenksprüche*, op. 109. Using these three works as a core repertoire, I focus on the neglected intersection of nationalism and spirituality in Brahms's music. To be sure, many other works are adduced along the way in support of my arguments, and the pieces on which I have chosen to focus should be understood only as the most fruitful case studies. Rather than providing the final word on the subject, with this book I hope to build on the significant work already done by scholars such as Leon Botstein and Margaret Notley toward bringing the discussion of Brahms's music more closely into the context of late-nineteenth-century politics. If my own work shifts the focus away from Vienna toward Germany, it is intended only as a complementary point of view, not as a contestation.

The intersection of religion and nationalism was one topic of my doctoral dissertation, "Brahms, the Bible, and Post-Romanticism" (Harvard, 1994). Some material from that study reappears in Chapters 2 and 5 of this book. Other previously published material appears here in Chapter 6, which incorporates the essays "The Rise and Fall of Brahms the German" (*Journal of Musicological Research* 10 [2001]: 1–24) and "Revisiting the Rumor of Brahms's Jewish Decent" (*American Brahms Society Newsletter* [Autumn 2001]: 5–6). Also, portions of my article "How *deutsch* a Requiem? Absolute Music, Universality, and the Reception of Brahms's *Ein deutsches Requiem*, op. 45," *Nineteenth-Century Music* 22 (1998): 3–19, are scattered throughout.

Any book that takes as long to reach fruition as this one did accrues numerous debts along the way. On the material side, financial assistance has come in various forms, including a Music & Letters Award in 1996, a College of Liberal Arts Summer Research Stipend, and a Vice President's Discretionary Grant from the University of New Hampshire in 1999, a summer stipend from the National Endowment for the Humanities in 2000, and a fellowship from the American Council of Learned Societies in 2001. I am also grateful to the Handschriftensammlung of the Wiener Stadt- und Landesbibliothek for permission to reproduce a page from Brahms's notebook of biblical excerpts in Chapter 2 and to the Archive of the Gesellschaft der Musikfreunde in Vienna for access to many items from Brahms's library that are referred to throughout this book.

More important, I have been blessed with many teachers, colleagues, friends, and family members who have contributed to this project in ways great and small. Many thanks to the staff at Harvard University Press: to Peg Fulton, who saw the project through its many fallow and dormant stages but never failed to be encouraging; to Mary Ellen Geer for her excellent work on production; and to the two outside readers. Thanks also go to Christopher Gantner, who proofread the musical examples, and to my friend and fellow chorister Peter Schmidt, who applied his German expertise and keen editing eye to many passages in German throughout the book.

Among the many teachers to whom I am indebted for shaping my thinking and writing skills over my years as a student, I can only single out two: Mildred Parker, my master's thesis adviser at Temple University, whose unwavering standards in all things intellectual helped me to raise my own; and Reinhold Brinkmann, who served as a model dissertation adviser to me at Harvard University and who has continued to be an inspiration and role model in my professional life. Among musicologists I have worked with over the past ten years, I thank Marilyn McCoy, Keith Polk, Mary Rasmussen, Peter Urquhart, and "honorary musicologist" Robert Eschbach at the University of New Hampshire for support and assistance of various kinds. Special thanks go to Georgia Cowart, my friend and former colleague at the University of South Carolina, who encouraged this project at its earliest stages. Among other friends and colleagues who have helped me throughout this endeavor, I owe many thanks to Carl Leafstedt, who closely read and constructively critiqued Chapter 3 and to Rose Mauro, who read the entire manuscript and made numerous valuable suggestions. I am also grateful for the warm support I have received from several Brahms scholars, including Walter Frisch, David Brodbeck, George Bozarth, and Virginia Hancock (without whose pathbreaking work on Brahms's choral music my own research would scarcely seem possible). I particularly wish to thank Margaret Notley, whose work on Brahms and German politics has often directly inspired and enlightened my own studies and whose friendship I have valued over the years. One friend and Brahms scholar who sadly will not see this book is John Daverio, whose untimely death in 2003 robbed many of us of a trusted friend and an esteemed colleague. He is sorely missed.

No one has lived through this book with me more than the members of my family, and to them I am immensely grateful. My parents, to whom this book is dedicated, provided me early on with an intellectually stimulating environment. My brother Paul served as a model for devoting one's life to music and introduced me to most of the music that I have continued to value since childhood. Margaret G. McKenna, my mother-in-law, has long been a beacon of sense and has made the balancing act of life possible for the Beller-McKennas. My daughter Lydia's own budding love and talent for music is a joy to me, and her zest for life is my constant source of energy. Finally, my greatest thanks go to my wife, Kitty Beller-McKenna, who has helped me write this book in ways too numerous to count. I never could have followed through on this and my other professional endeavors without her love and support and without the love of music that she and I have shared for nearly two decades.

Brahms and the German Spirit

Introduction: Brahms and the German Spirit

Rediscovering the German Brahms

On 3 April 1898, the first anniversary of Johannes Brahms's death, the Johannes Brahms-Denkmal Comité in Wien published an *Aufruf* (Appeal) calling for the construction of a Brahms monument in his adopted city.[1] Just as the Viennese authorities had arranged that Brahms be "laid to eternal rest between Beethoven and Schubert," so too, the committee argued, should the city erect a permanent artistic rendering of Brahms as it had for these earlier composers. In this way, all peoples and all ages might "take account of the inseparably close solidarity that binds the deceased with his great predecessors and the city of their travels and activities."[2] Linking Brahms with Beethoven and Schubert through Vienna's reputation as a home to musical genius is a familiar ploy to readers today. As in his own day, Brahms's music-historical identity is still largely defined by his preservation of his artistic forbears' accomplishments, especially in the instrumental genres and in song. Indeed, the committee carefully enumerated these genres (symphony, concerto, songs, etc.) in the third and final paragraph of the *Aufruf*: "A Brahms-Monument in Vienna cannot remain a matter that is limited to the sphere of the city or circumscribed by the borders of the country; it must be made a general affair of all thankful friends of music."[3] When the committee broadens its appeal beyond Vienna and Austria to "all thankful friends of music," the first pieces mentioned are not the instrumental genres of Beethoven and Schubert but rather Brahms's best-known works for chorus and orchestra:

Where the assuaging tones of the *German Requiem* proclaim their heavenly message; where the *Triumphlied* renews the memory of mighty times; where *Songs of Destiny and Fate,* the *Rhapsody,* and *Nänie* sweeten with angels' voices the bitter fate of those who suffer and endure; where the four symphonies [sound their battle of the spirits]; where concertos, serenades, chamber music, and solo pieces form the center of an elevated social dialogue; where hundreds of soulful lieder cause eyes to swim in tears of bliss and longing— to all those places our call insists on common cause and open hearts and hands![4]

Choral works, especially larger pieces with orchestra, produced a community-building effect in nineteenth-century Germany—even more directly than the symphony, to which that function is often assigned by modern commentators.[5] With this in mind, it is hardly surprising to our eyes that the committee chose to begin its list with *Ein deutsches Requiem*, op. 45, Brahms's largest and most successful opus, and one with ostensibly broad appeal "beyond the sphere of the city" and "the borders of the country."

What follows, however, might surprise us today. Preceding the *Schicksalslied, Gesang der Parzen, Alto Rhapsody,* and *Nänie*—that is, Brahms's well-known single-movement choral pieces—comes the *Triumphlied,* which "renews the memory of mighty times." Brahms's *Triumphlied,* op. 55, is a nearly forgotten work today, but during his lifetime it ranked among his most popular works and was often compared favorably to the *German Requiem*.[6] He began composing the *Triumphlied*—a three-movement piece for double chorus, baritone soloist, and orchestra—during the patriotic fervor of the Franco-Prussian War of 1870–71. Like the *Requiem* of 1868, op. 55 sets biblical texts. But whereas in the earlier work Brahms taps the Bible's philosophical and reflective vein, in the *Triumphlied* he celebrates the establishment of the long-awaited *Kaiserreich* by drawing his text from Revelation, the primary apocalyptic book of the Bible, and specifically from chapter 19, which thanks God for ushering in the "New Kingdom." It is no secret why so open a union of nationalistic sentiment with Scripture lost its appeal in the twentieth century. Such patriotic sentiments already seemed inappropriate (at best) following the German defeat in the First World War. After the nightmare of National Socialism in the 1930s and 1940s, giving fresh voice to the aggressively patriotic feelings expressed in the *Triumphlied* was out of the question.

The Brahms-Monument Committee, unburdened as they were by that historical perspective, identified Brahms with his two most overtly German works. While the *Triumphlied* announces itself as nationalistic by evoking the *Gewalt* of Germany's political and national ascendance, *Ein deutsches Requiem* is less obviously "German" (ironically, given its title). Yet the latter piece speaks directly to a German audience through its use of Luther's translation of the Bible—a core document of German literature. Even the most conservative and apolitical assessments of the social meaning of op. 45 explain the "deutsch" in Brahms's title as a reflection of the work's German (rather than Latin) text. This assessment was not lost on the committee; at the end of his century, Brahms's supporters recognized a centrally German element in his music, and one that was integrally bound to religious content. If we no longer hear that connection in Brahms's music today, it is worth exploring how and why that understanding of the composer and his art has mutated over the past hundred years. Approaching such an understanding will be a main focus of this book.

Our modern concept of Johannes Brahms as a composer owes much to Arnold Schoenberg's "Brahms the Progressive." Schoenberg first delivered his views on Brahms in a Berlin radio address bearing this title during the Brahms centennial birthday month of May 1933. In 1947, the fiftieth anniversary of Brahms's death, Schoenberg revised his remarks in a similarly titled essay.[7] Brahms, as we have come to know him through Schoenberg, is a harbinger of modernism; his flexible phrase structure and supple use of forward-looking harmony led more strongly to the emancipation of the dissonance and free prose style of the early twentieth century, according to Schoenberg, than did the musical style of Brahms's more ostensibly progressive contemporary Richard Wagner. Recent observers have noted that Schoenberg turned to Brahms "as the legitimizing model of history for the radical innovations of modernism."[8] Thus, he effected an ironic reversal of the conservative image that had defined Brahms since his own lifetime, and which had intensified during the three and a half decades after his death. Since the end of World War II (and hence, since about the time Schoenberg published his essay), we have been only too happy to embrace this subversion of the accepted wisdom concerning Brahms's and Wagner's roles in nineteenth-century music history. Wagner suffers in the comparison and is toppled from his position as the progressive musical force of his time. I am not suggesting that the Brahms-Wagner dichotomy is wrong or misguided. Indeed, it endures because it still rings true just as it did in the late nineteenth century, when both composers were active. Much separates these two figures, both as men and as composers. Yet much is lost when we view Brahms as part of a simple duality. First and foremost, we are disinclined to appreciate the extent to which Brahms's identity as a German (both to himself and to his audience) affected his music, and the degree to which that German identity was integrally connected to religious issues. I hope to demonstrate throughout this book how Brahms's music is deeply colored by the interpenetration of the two, despite the tendency over the past fifty years to ignore or deny their significance for his artistic output.

Cultural Nationalism and Religion

Linking spirituality and nationalism in nineteenth-century Germany is nothing new of course: although other European nations (England in particular)

joined Germany in claiming God-given authority for their existence, scholars have long noted the special quality of a perceived spiritual determinism
that runs throughout the rise of German nationalism after 1815. Koppel S.
Pinson signaled this strain of thought in 1934 (i.e., before the dangers of
National Socialism had manifested themselves fully in the Western psyche)
with his influential *Pietism as a Factor in the Rise of German Nationalism.*[9]
More recently, many writers have added to and refined Pinson's argument,
most notably Liah Greenfeld, pointing out the role played by religion in Romanticism at the turn of the nineteenth century and in the nationalist movement that sprang up in Germany shortly thereafter.

At a glance, Brahms's output might appear to be a likely vehicle for an examination of how religion and nationalism were expressed in German music
of the nineteenth century. Brahms was an ardent patriot and a devoted ad-
mirer of Chancellor Bismarck (on both counts this made him typical among
German liberals in the last third of the century). And even if we should
rightly draw a distinction between "patriotism" and "nationalism," it is not
uncommon for one to lead to or coexist with the other. Brahms also set
more sacred texts than any other composer of his stature during the nineteenth century (save Bruckner). Most of these were texts from Luther's Bible, indicating his interest in the core document of German Protestantism.

Despite these potential reasons to explore nationalism (or even merely patriotism) and religion in Brahms's music, neither has received much currency
within Brahms scholarship. Instead, Brahms scholars have focused on aspects of his musical style that separate him from, rather than relate him to,
the culture in which he lived. The primary strategy for this critical stance has
been to claim the power of universality for Brahms's music. Universalistic
assessments of Brahms's music normally fall within one of two closely related paradigms: Brahms as a classicist and composer of absolute music versus the symbolic and programmatic music of Wagner, Liszt, and the New
German School; or Brahms as the historicist, engaging more completely
with music of the past than had any of his predecessors. Each of these paradigms connects Brahms's music to issues beyond the time and place of its
origin. Classicism relates Brahms's music to the instrumental tradition of
Haydn, Mozart, and Beethoven, which had already achieved canonical status by the second half of the nineteenth century and had developed an attendant ideology of transcendence. Historicism, by contrast, speaks mainly to
Brahms's sacred choral music and a handful of instrumental works in archaic genres, providing a means of evaluating pieces that might otherwise
appear regressive against the prevailing musical aesthetics of Brahms's time.

Both approaches stem from a common impulse—to distance Brahms's
music from the context of Germany in the second half of the nineteenth century. They are thus an outgrowth of the Brahms-Wagner dichotomy that has

powerfully shaped our conception of western European music history since the late nineteenth century. In keeping with the need to maintain the strong opposition between these two figures, Brahms's music has often been dissociated from the political and philosophical issues of its milieu, in contrast to Wagner's music, which is so inextricably bound to them. Wagner himself had already set the tone for such comparisons between the two composers in 1862 by remarking of Brahms's *Handel Variations* (op. 24) that a good deal could still be done using the old forms, provided one knew how to use them. Wagner's left-handed compliment neatly summarized the polar view shared by many contemporaries: that Brahms maintained the traditional forms of the recent past while Wagner pursued the music of the future. Brahms's and Wagner's music provided enough support for that paradigm to explain its continued persistence into the twenty-first century.

Encouraged by Eduard Hanslick's idealist aesthetic as well as by Wagner's polemics (his later criticisms of Brahms were more openly hostile), this polarized late-nineteenth-century judgment of the two composers has left an indelible impact on the modern view of Brahms. Even Schoenberg's revisionist essay "Brahms the Progressive" maintains the centrality of the classical tradition for Brahms's style. Schoenberg merely turns the tables on Wagner by crediting Brahms with the creation of a new technique, "developing variation," out of the classical style, thereby implying a superhistorical role for Brahms, who connects the eighteenth and twentieth centuries and thus transcends his own time. This account, widely adopted by music scholars since the middle of the twentieth century, resonates strongly with the long-standing focus on Brahms's instrumental compositions as "absolute" music whose meaning is self-derived, independent of its time and place. As I will outline at the end of this book, Schoenberg's revision, while making no attempt to de-Germanify Brahms, prepared the way for others to effect just such a critical turn after World War II, and this constitutes a major subtext for my own approach to the topic of this book; in light of the tragic political history of Germany in the twentieth century, we prefer to see Brahms as a representative of the good and noble in German musical art in distinction to Wagner, whose ideology dovetails too neatly with—and was so eagerly embraced along with his music by—the National Socialists. The critical tradition has found no better way to salvage Brahms the German than to downplay his Germanness, but in doing so, we risk losing sight of the spirituality and nationalism that his music conveys.

In the last fifty years we have, I believe, turned the very real classicizing tendencies in Brahms's art into a tool for denying a central aspect of his music, the interpenetration of spirituality and nationalism, and for driving an unreal and misguided wedge between Brahms and the nineteenth-century German world in which he lived and composed: "unreal" because Brahms was very much a product of his milieu, not only in terms of musical style, but also in terms of the political and social forces that informed his music; "misguided" because it is a wedge driven from an unfounded fear—the fear that in acknowledging and examining Brahms's Germanness, we might see traces of incipient fascism akin to the glaring signposts we recognize in Wagner's rhetoric and (for some) in his music.

To be sure, some scholars have worked effectively in recent years to locate Brahms within the culture of his time, though—for the most part—without reference to Brahms's positive identity as a German. Rather, such efforts have focused on Brahms almost exclusively within the context of Vienna and largely around the issue of anti-Semitic politics there. Peter Gay had already paved the way for this approach in his 1978 collection of essays, *Freud, Jews, and Other Germans,* where he politicizes German culture of the late nineteenth and early twentieth centuries in order to deconstruct the late-twentieth-century apologia of "the apolitical German." Yet, whereas Gay focuses on Wilhelmine Germany at many points in that book, he is largely drawn to fin-de-siécle Vienna—as the presence of Freud in the book's title suggests. Wagner's strongly anti-Jewish polemics directly influenced Viennese intellectuals in the 1880s and 1890s, at the same time that anti-Semitic politicians were gaining ground in the city. Gay, however, never addresses the potential importance of those political developments for the reception of Brahms's music. Rather, this has been a vital point in Leon Botstein's and Margaret Notley's fine literature on Brahms as a Viennese liberal.[10] Through a variety of essays, both scholars have convincingly demonstrated how Brahms's conservative musical principles (particularly in the realm of chamber music) adhered to a politically inclined aesthetic stance among the cultural elite of Vienna, who sought to maintain the rational, intellectual character of liberalism in the face of growing right-wing conservatism, irrationalism, and anti-Semitism (much of Brahms's Viennese circle was Jewish).

Groundbreaking though this work has been, however, it has downplayed Brahms's self-identification with northern Germany and has avoided (if not refuted) the question of how Brahms relates to nineteenth-century German nationalism. Indeed, surveying Brahms scholarship generally, one finds that his name has become sequestered from the stigmatized term *nationalism.* That separation stems from our negative associations with nationalism as a movement that has long since served its usefulness in political terms (though it has hardly left the world stage) and has been widely condemned in liberal political theory for over thirty years. Yet this is to consider only the repugnant extremes to which twentieth-century societies carried nationalistic thinking. For most of the nineteenth century, nationalism in Europe was integrally connected to the modern liberal state form of government, as an antipode, that is, to dynastic rule. The rise of nation-states such as Germany and Italy, as well as the political modernization of the governments of England and France, stemmed from a new national consciousness that, in the words of Liah Greenfeld,

> locates the source of individual identity within a "people," which is seen as the bearer of sovereignty, the central object of loyalty, and the basis of collective solidarity. The "people" is the mass of a population whose boundaries and nature are defined in various ways, but which is usually perceived as larger than any concrete community and always as fundamentally homogeneous, and only superficially divided by the lines of status, class, locality, and in some cases even ethnicity.[11]

The variety of ways in which a people's boundary and nature may be defined has permitted nationalism to take on many forms over the past two hundred years. (Greenfeld refers to the "conceptually evasive, protean nature of nationalism and the cause of the perennial frustration of its students.")[12] Scholars on this subject generally agree, however, that a common denominator among modern varieties of nationalism has been the sharing of a distinguishable national culture, a communal bond that demonstrates itself most clearly for some nations through a common language. This was most certainly the case for Germany during the nineteenth century.[13] The development of a "High German" literary style allowed the language to become fixed in a lasting form, thereby historicizing the word and granting an illusion of antiquity and rootedness in a distant past. Some writers single out the German experience of language identity as a special case, specifically because of Germany's historical political impotence. Adrian Hastings has pushed this argument most strongly; if his is perhaps an extreme formulation of the thesis, it is nevertheless useful for making clear the importance of language in German nationalism:

> If the idea of Germanness as a continuing reality could hardly be grounded in political facts—as it could in England or France—or even in terms of a clearly delimited territory (for the borders of the German-speaking community were extremely confused and there was much intermingling particularly with Slavs) then it had little more than language left, language imagined as a legacy of ethnic origins. An idea of nation dependent on language seems necessarily to push the claim back beyond language to an assumed genetic identity, the identity in this case of the *Volk*. One's ethnic identity becomes primary but manifested through linguistic identity. The German predicament—consciousness of nationhood, absence of a state, strength of German as a literary language—made the particular form which German nationalism would take almost inevitable, the nationalism of *jus sanguinis*, the most dangerous of all nationalism's forms. . . . It was certainly the nineteenth century which produced German nationalism, but it could only do so—one must once more insist—out of the half-submerged reality of a medieval nation.[14]

Given that language is central to this formulation of nationalism, an important distinction must be drawn between the particularized Germanic medieval nation, which Hastings rightly sees as the inspiration for German nationalism, and the generalized Romantic fascination with the medieval era as an epoch of Christian purity in Europe. For all his infatuation with mystical Romantic literature, Brahms did not equate spirituality with Catholicism and never subscribed to the pan-European neo-Catholicism of a Novalis or an Eichendorf; even when he was inclined to set medievalist texts by such authors, Brahms shied away from any direct associations with Catholicism. This raises a critical point for understanding the connection between spirituality and nationalism in Brahms's music; Brahms's sacred music and spiritually informed secular works are strongly marked by his German identity and, with early and increasing emphasis, his Protestant upbringing. Whereas Brahms was never dogmatic toward religion, he was also not pantheistic or a universalist in his approach to things spiritual. As I seek to demonstrate throughout this book, Brahms's music (especially but not only sacred) frequently presents a spiritual element that is distinctly informed by his identity as a German Protestant.

Focusing on Brahms's texted sacred works is merely the most direct and convenient means by which to understand the impact of cultural nationalism on his music. Cultural nationalism is a more complicated force, however, and it would be wrong to assume that we can recognize it only in works that contain overtly religious and/or nationalistic texts. Brahms's very focus on traditional instrumental genres from the Viennese classical period cannot be separated from the pride Germans felt in that tradition, as expressed by countless German musicians. Take, for example, Robert Schumann's oft-repeated statement from an article on new symphonies of 1839, in which he identifies the Beethoven symphonies as a national treasure comparable to "Italy's Naples, France's Revolution, and England's navigation."[15] To be sure, Schumann made that remark first and foremost as a musician. Yet the nationalizing impulse in his formulation cannot be easily dismissed. German-speaking lands were deeply invested in a push toward national political unity during the first half of the nineteenth century, and the popularity of instrumental music by German composers of the preceding century offered an obvious place to begin developing a sense of national pride. As early as the 1820s in Berlin, the music critic Adolf Berhnhard Marx had championed the repeated performances of Beethoven's symphonies as a means of inculcating in German audiences an appreciation for the philosophical depth of the Austro-German symphonic tradition.[16]

Both Schumann and Mendelssohn contributed symphonic works with more or less specific Germanic meaning (Mendelssohn's Symphony no. 5 ["Reformation"] of 1830, Schumann's Symphony no. 3 ["Rhenisch"] of

1850). But it was not through such programmatic gestures that the specifically Germanic associations of the entire genre were to lie, but rather with the perception that the Beethovenian symphonic tradition was philosophically and spiritually elevated in a manner that was peculiarly German. Thus, when Franz Brendel sought to replace the label *Zukunfstmusik* to describe the progressive school of Liszt, Berlioz, and Wagner, he arrived at the equally provocative moniker "Neudeutsche Schule." In attempting to justify the inclusion of two non-German composers at the head of this school, Brendel constructed a lineage from the music of the German past:

> [Berlioz and Liszt] would never have become what they are today had they not from the first drawn nourishment from the German spirit and grown strong with it. Therefore, too, Germany must of necessity be the true homeland of their works, and it is in this sense that I suggested the denomination Neo-German School for the entire post-Beethovenian development. . . . Protestant church music up to and including Bach and Handel has long been known as the Old German School. The Italian epoch of the Viennese masters is the period of Classicism, of the equal supremacy of idealism and realism. Beethoven once more clasps hands with the specifically Germanic North and inaugurates the Neo-German School.[17]

At the historical moment Brendel was uttering his words (during his inaugural address to the first meeting of the Allgemeine Deutscher Musikverein in Leipzig on 1–4 June 1859), Brahms was busily backpedaling from his earliest attempts to compose a symphony in the Beethovenian (*cum* Mendelssohn *cum* Schumann) manner, a project he had undertaken as early as 1856. Instead, he invested his energies in smaller forms of chamber and choral music through the 1860s, gradually aspiring to larger choral-orchestral works by the end of the decade.

Brahms's orientation toward the political position of the Beethoven symphonic tradition must be taken into account to explain his choice of genres during the 1860s. By the time Brendel made his famous *Neudeutsche* formulation, Wagner had long since claimed Beethoven's Ninth Symphony and late string quartets as the springboard for progressive style in German music. In such works as *Das Kunstwerk der Zukunft* (1849) and *Oper und Drama* (1851), Wagner united the mystical Romantic tradition (via E. T. A. Hoffmann, Ludwig Tieck, et al.) of assigning absolute instrumental music the power to express the verbally inexpressible spirit world with a belief in the ur-spirit of the German *Volk*, all in the guise of a super-Christian Germanic religion of the future.[18] Whatever the musical issues (e.g., his stated insecurity about composing in the genre after Beethoven), Brahms's reluctance or inability to complete his First Symphony between 1856 and 1876 was probably influenced by the historical role of the genre in the cultural nationalism that surrounded musical debates during these very years.

We know that Brahms felt strongly about Wagner's and Brendel's appropriation of the classical Viennese legacy; in 1860 he helped pen a declaration against the *Neudeutscher* in which he took issue with Brendel's claim, as Brahms and his co-authors saw it, that "generally, especially in North Germany, the argument for or against this so-called Music of the Future has been fought out and decided in its favor." On the contrary, the declaration asserts that "the products of the leaders and students of the so-called 'New German' school, who put these ideas partly into practical application and partly into the formation and imposition of ever newer and outrageous theories, can only be condemned and deplored as contrary to the innermost essence of music."[19] Through means that have never been made clear, the manifesto was leaked to the unsympathetic journal *Signale der musikalische Welt* and caused Brahms and his three co-signatories more embarrassment than fame. Brahms's choice of choral and chamber music, however, did nothing to sidestep the issue of cultural nationalism. Chamber music, whose heyday was seen to lie well in the past, remained a bastion of absolute music and was rarely taken up by the *Neudeutscher.* By distinction, Brahms's persistence in this area displayed his eagerness to maintain his identity as a *Schumannianer* and thereby secured his position as an opponent of the "North German music of the future." The place of choral music in the equation was just as significant. Although Liszt, Berlioz, and many followers of Wagner contributed to choral music in the mid-nineteenth century, Brahms's deep emersion in contrapuntal rules of the sixteenth through eighteenth centuries set him apart as a traditionalist from the grand and effusive choral style of the *Neudeutscher.*

Brahms moved on from a cappella or lightly scored choral works to larger works for chorus and orchestra during the years 1866–1872—significantly, the very years during which Prussia emerged as the leader of the *klein Deutschland* solution to national unity. The texts of Brahms's large choral works at this time further emphasize his traditional stance, on the one hand, and his adherence to the heritage of great German literature, on the other: two are on biblical texts (*Ein deutsches Requiem,* op. 45, 1868; and *Triumphlied,* op. 55, 1872); two are on texts by Goethe (*Rinaldo,* op. 50; and *Alt-Rhapsodie,* op. 53, both 1869); and one is on a text by Hölderlin (*Schicksalslied,* op. 54, 1871).[20] These were also the works, as noted at the outset of this chapter, that fixed Brahms's place at the forefront of German music around 1870. The confluence of Germany's emergence as a powerful political state, Brahms's emergence as a major figure, and the culmination of his early period in large works on great German literature cannot be overemphasized. Brahms chose to reach out to larger audiences with masses of assembled performers, singing the words of Luther's Bible, Goethe, and Hölderlin at the very moment in German history when a nation was transforming its identity from that of a culture to that of a state. Add to this the religious underpinnings of German cultural nationalism, and the direct connections between Brahms's sacred vocal music and German nationalism become clear.

The Role of the Volk

Behind claims of a spiritual content in German music is the belief in the *Volk* as a source of all German culture—high and low. Recognizing the centrality of the *Volk* in this formulation is a necessary step toward evaluating Brahms's relationship to German nationalism and, furthermore, the place of religion in that relationship. Again, our modern perception might be blurred by the distinct brand of *völkisch* nationalism that emerged from new racist theories and ideologies during the late nineteenth century and helped form the philosophical underpinnings of Hitler's Germany. Scholars of the Third Reich have traced this strand of nationalism back in many ways to the Pietistic and Romantic traditions in German culture.[21] To the extent that both of those earlier movements were reactions against urbane modernisms of their own ages (the early eighteenth and early nineteenth centuries), they established the paradigm for attributing to the *Volk* a spiritual, quasi-Christian authority. Those qualities fueled a belief in the revival of an idealized medieval German nation as a God-given inevitability. Although these ideas persisted through the middle of the century, they were overshadowed at that time by the more real drive toward a unified German political state, a goal that appeared attainable for the first time in the 1860s after many false starts in the previous two decades.

After 1871, during the period Eric Hobsbawm labels the "Transformation of Nationalism," the adulation of the *Volk* that the Romantics had bequeathed needs to be distinguished from a new, racially tinged form of *völkisch* thought that came to drive a more virulent nationalism. The new nationalism emerged as an expression of nondogmatic spirituality after the newly founded *Kaiserreich* (1871) proved too materialistic and democratic to provide a vehicle of political expression to a mythically conceived people. In a reaction against the prevailing rationalism and scientific bent of modernism, *völkisch* ideology of the Wilhelmine era celebrated the Romantics' mystical and spiritual image of the *Volk*, who were idealized as the true embodiment of the German nation. As a cult of irrationality, *völkisch* nationalism fit hand in glove with the aesthetic, philosophical, and political writings of Richard Wagner, which gained ever-increasing currency from the 1870s to the end of the century. Wagner's complicity in the new *völkisch* program was evident early on through his focus on race as a distinguishing national characteristic in writings such as "Das Judenthum in der Musik"

(1848) and "Was ist Deutsch?" (1865).[22] Race, in fact, was the decisive factor in tipping the scales of nationalism toward its "murderous virulence" (in Ernest Gellner's formulation) at the turn of the twentieth century. Gellner adds: "The community was to be not merely culturally, but also biologically distinctive: it was not merely to defend and protect its own cultural specificity; it was to affirm it politically with an aggressiveness which was more of an end than a means."[23]

Brahms, a city dweller all his life, also maintained a romanticized and distanced ideal of the *Volk*, yet he represents a distinct brand of nationalistic interest in folk song as compared to the *völkisch* movement of the late nineteenth century. He is best connected to the *Volk* through his numerous settings of and his lifelong interest in German folk song, for which he left a substantial paper trail: he compiled over two hundred pages of folk song texts, incipits, and tunes (replete with annotations concerning sources and their locations), and he set no fewer than 106 separate folk songs, many more than once. Aesthetically, these settings place Brahms artistically apart from the *völkisch* nationalists. His music adheres to rational principles of harmonic and formal organization as opposed to the more experimental "prose" style of the New German school. Brahms's published settings maintain a clear sense of the melodic style of German folk song, including (when called for) modal nuance and rhythmic flexibility, all the while maintaining a relatively staid harmonic idiom. Thus he avoided two musical-stylistic extremes to which a more aggressively *völkisch* bent might have led him: overly simple chordal harmonizations, on the one hand; and, on the other, the speechlike patterns of Wagner and Liszt that made their claim to the *Volk* legacy only in a mystical, spiritual way while making no attempt to approximate the actual sound of folk song.

Nevertheless, Brahms displays clear elements of nationalism in his approach to folk song, as I will elucidate presently. Furthermore, if one peruses the folk texts and melodies that Brahms chose to work with, one finds a preponderance of religious themes. Brahms likely did not set out to couple religion and folk song: that relationship had existed historically, as a cursory glance at the interrelationship of Lutheran chorales, German-Catholic hymns, and German folk songs as far back as the fifteenth century attests. More immediately, German Romantics had raised both folk culture and religion of the distant past to iconic status at the turn of the nineteenth century. Many of Brahms's early choral works speak to the Romantic tendency to bind veneration of the *Volk* with religion. Most prominent among these works are the seven that Brahms set as the *Marienlieder*, op. 22 (1859–1861), which he described as "somewhat in the style of old German church and folk songs."[24] Brahms originally composed them in June or July 1859

Example 1.1   Horn fifths motive in Brahms, op. 22: (A) no. 1, "Der englische Gruß"; (B) no. 2, "Marias Kirchgang."

for the women's chorus he conducted in Hamburg during that summer and the next. As with dozens of folk song settings and a few sacred choruses, the *Marienlieder* were partly intended as repertoire for his fledgling choir.

Musical gestures that symbolize folk song, old church music, or both abound throughout these strophically set choruses. For example, Brahms begins the first two numbers in the set (no. 1, "Der englische Gruß," and no. 2, "Marias Kirchgang") with a stereotypical high-art evocation of folk style, the so-called "horn fifths" motive (actually a 6–5–3 progression; see ex. 1.1 A and B). This interval pattern was commonly used in the nineteenth century to evoke nostalgic distance and separation (consider the opening of Beethoven's "Abschied" Sonata or the end of the piano prelude in Schubert's "Lindenbaum"). Most commonly that separation involved a pastoral or village setting, as the horn's symbolic function is dependent on such locales: the open road on which the postman blows his horn, the woods in which the hunter's horn sounds, or the valleys in which the horn echoes. Distance takes the form of time in the opening of these two choruses, an effect that is supported by the equally stereotypical archaisms in each: the

Example 1.2   Horn fifths motive in Brahms, op. 22, no. 4, "Der Jäger": bars 9–19.

(mock-) imitative polyphony that begins no. 1, and the jarring open fifths in no. 2.

Romantic longing, pastoral imagery, and religious symbolism combine most notably in the fourth chorus of the set, "Der Jäger." The "hunter" of the title is none other than the archangel Gabriel with his horn. German and Swiss art as far back as the thirteenth century depicts Gabriel as the hunter, and the folk text Brahms sets here is merely a late (i.e., fifteenth-century) literary offshoot of that iconographic tradition.[25] In the middle section (bars 9–33; ex. 1.2) of this A B A, modified strophic song, at the words "The angel blew his little horn, it rang out loud and clear" (bars 9–13), and again at the parallel phrase "Greetings to you Maria, you fine noble maiden" (bars 17–21), the familiar horn fifths of nos. 1 and 2 return, thereby recalling the opening words of the set, "Gegrüßet Maria," that were also set to horn fifths, while evoking in musical form the verbal mention of Gabriel's horn. Verses one through four of this chorus, provided here, are worth considering, for they serve as a fine example of how intertwined Christian imagery can become with the *Volk,* in this case through the medium of the landscape.[26]

Es wollt' gut Jäger jagen,	A good huntsman went a-hunting,
Wollt' jagen von Himmelshöhn;	hunting from the heights of heaven;
Was begegn't ihm auf der Heiden?	Whom should he meet upon the moor
Maria, die Jungfrau schön.	but the beauteous Virgin Mary?
Der Jäger, den ich meine,	The huntsman whom I mean
Der ist uns wohl bekannt;	is well known to us;
Er jagt mit einem Engel,	He hunts with an angel—
Gabriel ist er gennant	Gabriel is his name.
Der Engel blies sein Hörnlein,	The angel blew his little horn,
Das laut' sich also wohl,	it rang out loud and clear:
Gegrüßt seist du, Maria,	"Hail to thee, O Mary,
Du bist aller Gnaden voll!	thou art full of grace!
Gegrüßt seist du, Maria!	"Greetings to you Maria,
Du edle Jungfrau fein!	You fine noble maiden!
Dein Schoß soll hegen und tragen,	Thy womb shall cherish and bear
Ein Kindlein zart und klein.	an infant small and tender."

Of course, there were no moors in Judea, and the huntsman is much more believable as a Germanic figure than a biblical one. Mary and Gabriel have been localized (or, one might say, "nationalized") in this folk imagery: a common device in Christian folk literature (and art) from around the world. Blending the home culture (in this case northern European) with the Semitic religious icons of Christian Scripture leaves little room to separate out the religious from the nationalistic. Essentially, they are one and the same; one cannot speak of how nineteenth-century Germans idealized the *Volk* without addressing the religious component therein.

Brahms was especially drawn to the rich vein of German Marian poetry from the fifteenth through seventeenth centuries as evidenced by his seven settings of such texts for chorus in the *Marienlieder,* op. 22, as well as by his "Ave Maria," op. 12, and "Regina Coeli" (no. 3 of the *Geistliche Chöre,* op. 39), both for women's chorus.[27] Mary also serves as the underlying persona of both the sung and unsung texts in op. 91, no. 2 (to be discussed at length later on). References to the Christ child and heavenly figures are not uncommon in lullabies. Brahms himself set other lullabies with these qualities. Best known among these is the so-called "Brahms Lullaby," the *Wiegenlied,* op. 49, no. 4, of 1868. Whereas most listeners are familiar with the purely secular folk text of the song's first verse ("Gute Abend, gut Nacht, mit Rosen bedacht . . .") which is drawn from Arnim and Brentano's *Das Knaben Wunderhorn,* fewer know the second verse by Georg Scherer (printed below), which Brahms added to his original composition in 1874, six years after its original publication as a one-stanza song:

> Guten Abend, gut Nacht,
> Von Englein bewacht,
> [Good evening, good night,
> Watched over by angels,]
> Die zeigen im Traum
> Dir Christkindleins Baum:
> Schlaf nun selig und süß,
> Schau im Traum 's Paradies.[28]

Although these lines were modern, the poet appears to have fashioned them with the preexisting folk song in mind: hence the matching opening text and scansion. Scherer expands the passing reference to God near the end of the original stanza ("Morgen früh, wenn Gott will, / Wirst du wieder geweckt"), thereby creating a miniature religious scene where angels guard the sleeping child in the name of the baby Jesus. A similar sentiment is contained in the text of the four-voice setting of the folk song "Ach lieber Herre Jesu Christ" (see ex. 1.3). Brahms composed this arrangement in 1863 as one of fourteen *Deutsche Volkslieder* for the Wiener Singakademie, which he directed during the 1863–64 season and to whom he dedicated the set.[29] Most of the arrangements in the set display the same homorhythmic style as "Ach lieber Herre Jesu," yet none display such a rigid half-note chordal motion as Brahms used here. In fact, there is hardly any sense of tension, shape, or progression in this piece: it is entirely diatonic and has virtually no rhythm and little melodic character to speak of. "Ach lieber Herre Jesu" is a singularly bland composition from the pen of Brahms. By presenting the original in as unadorned a style as possible, Brahms focuses our attention on the abstract religious quality of the text, and specifically on a naïve sentiment appropriate for this paean to the infant Jesus. But the appearance of purity here is also an evocation of the folk origins of the text. These two lullabies are only the most blatant illustrations of how deeply the *Volk* ethos was imbued with a strong dose of Christian religiosity in Brahms's Germany.

In all of the settings I have mentioned, pastoral imagery and religious symbolism are couched in either a nineteenth-century Romantic sense of longing or a feigned naïve faith. We may assume, therefore, that the religiosity and the *Volk*-ness of Brahms's setting are a Romantic affectation. Much of the *Marienlieder,* and for that matter much of Brahms's youthful early sacred settings for chorus (i.e., those before 1864), should be heard in this way. As with many Germans of his time, Brahms's fascination with folk song grew out of the same early-nineteenth-century Romantic idealization of the past that also led, through other channels, to Wagner's reactionary ideology. What separates Brahms from Wagner on this score is the lack of an *overt* political agenda in Brahms's music; Brahms's interest in folk song

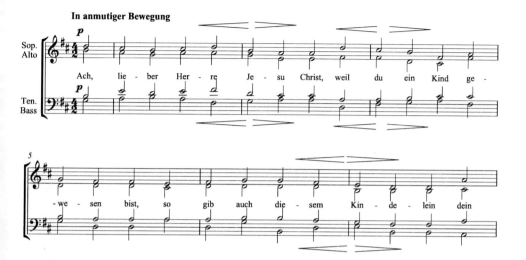

Example 1.3   Brahms, WoO 34, no. 6, "Ach lieber Herre Jesu Christ": bars 1–8.

is nationalistic, but it is a cultural brand of nationalism that may or may not be put to political ends (in Brahms's hands it was not). But one should not underestimate the political potential in such music; simply because Brahms did not consciously intend for his folk song settings to have political meaning, or understand them to have such meaning, did not negate their potential to be heard that way. And whereas no one would confuse the style of Brahms's folk song settings with, say, that of Wagner's chorus of the people in the final act of *Die Meistersinger,* it is nevertheless difficult to hear Brahms's Romantic inclination to celebrate the *Volk* in a spiritual guise without being reminded that it was precisely at this moment in German history that the adulation of the *Volk* moved perceptibly and undeniably toward the nationalist ideology that gripped Germany in the second quarter of the twentieth century.

The years leading up to World War II proved that it was possible to interpret Brahms's engagement with folk song as nationalistic, and many whose agendas stood to gain from such an interpretation did just that. I reserve a thorough treatment of that chapter in Brahms reception history until the end of this book, but it is worth outlining some important points in that story here. Brahms's love of folk song was already well documented during his lifetime, a legacy that led several commentators to seek the roots of Brahms's artistic (and mostly instrumental) idiom in folk music. In part, this gambit was intended to rescue Brahms from the frequently leveled accusation that his music was too academic and elitist—too "modern." Tracing Brahms's high-art style back to the *Volk* helped to unify two separate strands of cultural national pride among Germans: the purity of the *Volk* and the supremacy of the Viennese "absolute" music tradition. That pairing proliferated in Brahms literature during the first few decades of the twentieth century, so much so that it remains an unchallenged truism in much present-day Brahms scholarship.

A brief example from Wilhelm Furtwängler's keynote address to the 1933 Brahms centennial festival in Vienna, an essay more rife with nationalistic rhetoric than is usually acknowledged, abundantly illustrates the point. Brahms, writes Furtwängler, had "the special ability to live out and to feel the great supra-personal community of the *Volk*." And Furtwängler points specifically to Brahms's melodic style as evidence thereof: "Brahms . . . had the ability to write melodies that were unmistakably his, down to the last detail, and which yet sounded like folk songs. . . . Brahms . . . *was* the *Volk*, *was* the folk song."[30] In this formulation, Brahms's affinity with German folk song is a reflection of his belonging to the German nation. Given the timing of Furtwängler's remarks, one cannot separate cultural from political nationalism in this case. Following World War II, perhaps in response to prewar essays of this type, writers moved to reinterpret Brahms's love of German folk song as a strictly academic endeavor. Werner Morik's comprehensive study *Johannes Brahms und sein Verhältnis zum deutschen Volkslied* (1965) serves as a monument to that trend. Reading through the impressive compilation of well-analyzed data there, one could easily forget that folk song carried with it strong political connotations only a few decades earlier, much less that there had been highly politicized literature about Brahms and folk song during those years.[31]

A Case in Point: Brahms's "Geistliches Wiegenlied"

To buttress the preceding argument, I turn now to consider a much admired but little discussed song by Brahms, the "Geistliches Wiegenlied," op. 91, no. 2, one of two songs for alto with viola obbligato that Brahms published in 1884. In myriad ways, this song raises the various issues I have exposed thus far: vernacular translations, folk song, absolute music, spirituality, and cultural nationalism. Brahms sets in play in this song a number of borrowed elements, and in the interactions among those musical and textual elements we may observe the influence of religiosity and German cultural history on his musical style. Pursuing that line of inquiry leads me to the hazy middle ground between reception and intention, that is, between the perception of a Germanic element in Brahms's music, on the one hand, and the direct cultural influences to which Brahms may have been responding in his music, on the other. This is a gray area, but one that must be traversed before I undertake the primary work of this book: a discussion of religion and nationalism in Brahms's music.

Example A.1 in the Appendix includes bars 1–93 of "Geistliches Wiegenlied." The song sets Emanuel Geibel's German translation of Garcia Lope de Vega's sixteenth-century cradle scene, in which Mary calls on the blowing winds and rustling treetops to still themselves for the child Jesus. Intertwined with this song setting for alto and piano is the most notable feature of "Geistliches Wiegenlied," the obbligato viola and the archaic German hymn tune it plays, "Josef, lieber Josef mein." The text of that "altes Lied" also invokes the Virgin and child in a more homey scene that originated in late-fifteenth-century church dramas, where the new German text borrowed the tune but dropped the Latin text of the still older (fourteenth-century) hymn "Resonet in Laudibus." Brahms uses this tune to initiate the song, which proceeds as a large tripartite structure (A B C A B; see fig. 1.1) in which the viola returns with this melody four times in part or in full. Each appearance of the old hymn tune in the viola closes one of the song's A or B sections, which are marked by ever-increasing levels of dissonance, both harmonic and rhythmic. Musically, the tune of "Josef, lieber Josef mein" acts as a mollifying device, constantly stabilizing the song and bringing it back to its peaceful starting place. Both melodically and rhythmically, the tune is well suited to this role: the rocking, siciliana-like 6/8 rhythms and many skips by chord tone are conducive to the lullaby of the text, in which Mary rocks the infant Jesus to sleep amidst howling winds that rustle the treetops.

This is most clearly heard at the end of the song's B section (bars 40–73). In distinction to the F major opening section A, in which the alto sings largely in arpeggios, Brahms begins his setting of stanza two in A minor with the alto emphasizing scalar motion. By the middle of stanza two, the alto gradually returns to singing arpeggios, and concludes (not coincidentally) with a downward arpeggiation of F major (bars 54–56). How she progresses from those scalar passages to that F major arpeggio is worth examining, for it is in that process that the basic dynamic of the song (dissonance and tension relieved by the melody of "Josef, lieber Josef mein") manifests itself. In stanza two, Brahms sets the final word of verses one through seven to appoggiaturas. Upon its second appearance, on "windes *brau-sen*" (bluster) in bar 43, the appoggiatura turns particularly dissonant as the B natural ornamental pitch creates a tritone against the F in the bass of the deceptive cadence there (V^7 to VI in A minor). Thereafter the downbeats of bars 45 ("Heute") and 47 ("sausen," howl) continue to produce tritones, as the appoggiatura is inverted and embedded within a pair of rising chromatic lines. None of this chromaticism on the surface deflects the basic harmonic

Prelude ("Josef, lieber")	A	(R) Refrain	B	(R)	C	A	(R)	B	(R)	Postlude ("Josef, lieber")
1–12	13–22	23–39	39–57	58–73	74–89	90–99	100–116	117–134	135–145	145–157
		Stanza 1		Stanza 2		Stanza 3			Stanza 4	
F major			A minor- F major		F minor/ D-flat major	F major		A minor- F major		

Texts

Stanza 1

Die ihr schwebet	You who hover
Um diese Palmen	About these palms
In Nacht und Wind,	In night and wind
Ihr heiligen Engel,	You, holy angels
5 Stillet die Wipfel!	Silence the treetops!
Es schlummert mein Kind.	My child is slumbering.

Stanza 2

Ihr Palmen von Bethlehem	You palms of Bethlehem
Im Windesbrausen	In the roar of the wind
Wie mögt ihr heute	How can you today
10 So zornig sausen!	So angrily rustle !
O rauscht nicht also	Do not make so much noise
Schweiget, neiget	Be quiet, bow yourself down
Euch leis und lind;	softly and mildly;
Stillet die Wipfel!	Silence the treetops!
15 Es schlummert mein Kind.	My child is slumbering.

Figure 1.1   Outline of Brahms's "Geistliches Wiegenlied," op. 91, no. 2.

course of this phrase, which, after all, ends up with a half cadence to E7, the dominant of A minor. But now, at the very moment when Mary implores the treetops to stop rustling, a sharp musical disjuncture occurs. As the bass re-introduces the descending thirds motive in octaves on its way back to A in bars 48–51 (albeit displaced by an octave), the alto line begins to smooth itself out: the appoggiatura is returned to its descending direction in bar 50 (where B natural has a much softer effect against the first-inversion A major chord than it had previously had against F major in bar 43) and is absorbed back into a straight descending line in bars 52–53. Although the alto line in these bars melodically resembles the initial subphrase of bars 40–41, the melodic gap between D and B natural in bar 52 signals the return of the familiar descending major-triad arpeggio, now on G. And as the alto sings the words "leis und lind" in bars 54–56, she returns to the familiar F major descending arpeggio to begin the bridge back to the refrain, which returns in bar 58.

Stanza 3

Der Himmelsknabe	The heavenly infant
Duldet Beschwerde;	is suffering hardships;
Ach, wie so md er ward	Ah, how he has been wearied
Vom Leid der Erde.	by the earth's sorrows
20 Ach, nun im schlaf ihm	Ah, now in sleep,
Leise gesänftigt	softly soothed ,
Die Qual zerrint.	His agony dissolves.
Stillet die Wipfel!	Silence the treetops!
Es schlummert mein Kind.	My child is slumbering.

Stanza 4

25 Grimmige Kälte	Cruel coldness
Sauset hernieder;	rushes down
Womit nur deck ich	With what now shall I cover
Des Kindleins Glieder!	the little child's limbs!
O, all ihr Engel,	O all you angels
30 Die ihr geflügelt	Who wander
Wandelt im Wind,	winged in the wind;
Stillet die Wipfel!	Silence the treetops!
Es schlummert mein Kind.	My child is slumbering.

Hymn

Josef, lieber Josef mein	Josef, my dearest Josef
Hilf mir wieg'n mein Kindlein fein	Help me rock our charming baby
Gott der wird dein Lohner sein	God will be the rewarder
Im Himmelreich	In the heavenly realm
der Jungfrau Sohn,	The Virgin's son
Maria, Maria	Maria, Maria

Figure 1.1   (continued)

During this reemergence of more abstracted material from "Josef, lieber Josef mein" in the alto line of bars 48–56, the viola had already returned to motives from the lullaby's tune, passing through various harmonic stages (A–G–F) along the way. Only gradually, however, did its own arpeggios and return figures begin to line up with those in the alto part, finally connecting at bar 53 when the viola plays D–E–D against the alto's figure A–G–G. Although this is a seemingly minor surface detail, the gradual rapprochement between the two performers is, in fact, highly significant, since the eventual reconciliation between the viola and the alto in these bars epitomizes the shift from relative instability to stability that has occurred here—all through the medium of the "altes Lied."

"Josef, lieber Josef mein" derives its capacity to comfort—at least in part—from its religious identity; both as a medieval hymn tune and as a lullaby to Jesus, the melody of this Germanicized devotional song evokes an idealized German-Christian cultural history. Brahms prepares us to hear the tune this way from the outset, designating the viola's opening ritornello "altes Lied" and thereby calling attention to the tune's remote historical identity. For the listener (privy neither to this cue nor to the text of "Josef, lieber" that is printed beneath the viola's notes), distance is implied by the echo-like texture of the accompaniment, which does not enter with the viola but follows instead at the half phrase (as in bars 2–4 and 5–6). Even within the piano part itself, the hands echo each other at these points, as the right hand follows at one metrical unit (a dotted quarter note) with similar figures to those with which the left began.

Distance here refers to a remote religious era, and the largely diatonic setting Brahms provides for the tune once again suggests the Romantic conception of spiritual purity in an age of medieval, pan-European Christianity. But part of the tune's power to console within "Geistliches Wiegenlied" lies in its specifically German identity. Not only was the original Catholic hymn from which the tune derives ("Resonet in Laudibus") Germanic in its origins, but also the contrafactum of the hymn into the vernacular marks it as an actively German piece of cultural capital. Translation in "Geistliches Wiegenlied" is more than a necessity of genre; it is integral to the hymn text, the alto's sung lyric, and the song's entire *Entstehungsgeschichte*. On 13 April 1863 Brahms wrote to his soon-to-be married friend Joseph Joachim: "In good time [*Seinerzeit*] I will send to you a wonderful old Catholic song for use at home. You will have recourse to no prettier lullaby."[32] Judging from the correspondence that followed over the course of the next year, Brahms apparently was referring to the Renaissance German Christmas hymn "Josef, lieber Josef mein," set to the melody of the medieval German Catholic hymn "Resonet in Laudibus."[33] Brahms had copied both texts (eleven stanzas of the German) and the corresponding melody out of David Gregor Corner's *Groß-Catolischem Gesangbuch* of 1631 and Karl Severin Meister's *Katholische Kirchenlied* of 1862.[34] About a year and a half later (in the fall of 1864), Brahms sent another version of this old song to the Joachims. Now the melody constituted a viola obbligato amidst a setting of Lope de Vega's sixteenth-century "Cantarcillo de la Virgen," in an 1852 German translation by Emanuel Geibel titled "Geistliches Wiegenlied." It is in this form that the song was published twenty years later (in 1884) as the second of Brahms's *Zwei Gesänge für eine Altstimme mit Bratsch und Pianoforte*, op. 91.

In the texts of "Geistliches Wiegenlied" we encounter a modern-sounding facade (Geibel's poem) that is nevertheless informed by an iconically pious German background ("Josef, lieber"). The Romantic character of the alto's text partly results from its translation into German. Geibel, while faithful to some aspects of his Spanish original—its irregular rhyme, the free meter and line lengths of the verses, the refrain that ends each stanza—writes in a distinctly modern and Romantic German style. For example, "Nacht und Wind" and "leis und lind," two rhyming pairs of archetypal nineteenth-century German Romantic poetic imagery, are Geibel's own inspiration; nothing in Vega's original calls for these phrases. Likewise, his frequent vocative exclamations ("*Ihr* heilgen Engel," "*O* rauscht nicht also," "*O* all ihr Engel") do not appear in Vega's sixteenth-century Spanish original.

In 1864 Brahms had only recently developed a Germanic inclination in his musical output, as a further consideration of his encounter with "Josef, lieber Josef mein" illustrates. George Bozarth has demonstrated how Brahms encountered the familiar German hymn "Josef, lieber Josef mein" upon arriving in Vienna for the first time in 1862.[35] As had been his wont since his late teens in his native Hamburg, Brahms set about scouring Vienna's libraries shortly after he arrived there. As usual, his penchant was for early music and folk song, and he was quickly rewarded by his discovery of Corner's seventeenth-century songbook in the Nationalbibliothek at Vienna. Brahms copied all or part of seventy-six melodies and texts from Corner's book on two separate double folios, copiously annotating them and listing cross-references with Meister's modern collection (a newly acquired copy of which he had brought with him from Hamburg). Within two years Brahms had used five of these folk songs and hymns in his two volumes of *Deutsche Volkslieder* set for chorus, published in December 1864. As with many of the earlier folk song settings that he had composed for choirs he directed in Detmold and Hamburg, Brahms composed the fourteen German folk song settings of 1864 for the Vienna Singakademie, which he conducted in the 1863–64 season. And like his earlier settings, the texts of the 1864 settings, beyond those from the recently discovered Corner collection, were drawn largely from Andres Kretzschmar and Anton Wilhelm Zuccaglmalgio's *Duetsche Volkslieder mit Ihren Original-Weisen* of 1838–1840.

Note that all of these text sources deal primarily or exclusively with German songs. Brahms had not always shown such a Teutonic bent. The two Corner bifolios represent only a small portion of the many manuscript collections Brahms maintained from his late teens until the last decade of his life, comprising hundreds of miscellaneous pages that contained folk songs, early music, canons, and of course the famous "Octaves and Fifths."[36] Brahms's earliest efforts to collect folk song concentrated specifically on *non*-German (albeit exclusively Nordic) folk song. Indeed, one such collection, believed by Max Kalbeck (Brahms's primary biographer) to have been compiled in the late 1840s before Brahms left Hamburg (in which case it would be the earliest extant exemplar of this sort), contains fifteen folk songs from such diverse northern European locales as Ireland, Scotland, Denmark, Lapland, Finland, and France—and only one from Germany.[37] Brahms's first securely datable collection of folk songs was completed in June 1854 at Düsseldorf, a group of thirty-seven settings that he presented to Clara Schumann. Although this collection includes a much higher proportion of German songs, the set is still relatively pan-European in its makeup: Swedish, Hungarian, Danish, and Polish songs appear here as well.[38]

By the time Brahms copied the texts from the Corner anthology in 1864, however, a significant shift had taken place concerning his attitude toward his native culture. One most easily observes this transformation in his approach to religious texts during the intervening years. Brahms had begun setting sacred texts in conjunction with an intense study of classic contrapuntal techniques that he undertook between 1856 and 1860.[39] Initially he selected traditional Catholic Latin texts ("Ave Maria," op. 12; *Drei geistliche Chöre*, op. 37; *Missa Canonica*, WoO 17–18) probably reflecting the main sources he was studying at the time: Palestrina, Hassler, and other composers from the late sixteenth through early seventeenth centuries. By the end of the 1850s, however, Brahms preferred to set sacred texts that were by and large German, including both Catholic and Protestant hymns, as well as passages from Luther's Bible (*Begräbnisgesang*, op. 13; *Marienlieder*, op. 22; Psalm 13, op. 27; *Zwei Motette*, op. 29; *Geistliches Lied*, op. 30). After this period, Brahms set no more Latin texts, concentrating almost exclusively on biblical texts in his sacred music. His emphasis on German folk songs and "geistliche Lieder" in Corner and other anthologies during the mid-1860s, therefore, comes as no surprise. Rather, that emphasis continues the general gravitation toward specifically German cultural materials that Brahms was already displaying in his sacred settings of the late 1850s.

I invoke Brahms's sacred choral settings of this period specifically to raise the religious issues that attend Brahms's approach to folk song. As was true of many nineteenth-century Germans, his fascination with folk song was closely related to an idealization of the past. German Romantics cherished not merely *das Volk*, but rather the idea of a German cultural past for which the *Volk* stood. Associated with that past were many things, including an idealized Christianity. One reads this initially in much literature from the early nineteenth century: the novels of Novalis, the stories of Kleist, and (slightly later) the poetry of Eichendorf—to name but a few prominent representatives. Idealized Christianity also infuses the previously mentioned patriotic literature of the period by Arndt, Fichte, and others, where it is closely linked with a trumpeting of *völkisch* values. Thus, Brahms's inclusion of several sacred hymns and quasi-sacred folk songs in these hand-copied collections is not unusual but rather is part of a broad cultural linkage at the time between spirituality, the *Volk*, and German history. The ambiguous status of many such items—somewhere between *Volk* and sacred song—illustrates how difficult it is to separate the religious element from this veneration of German folk song.

In its overall textual makeup, "Geistliches Wiegenlied" is heavily Germanic, in both a historical and a modern Romantic sense. One does not hear the text of the old hymn, of course. But the song begins with a complete statement of its first strain played as an instrumental prelude by the viola. (And there the performers are privy to its first line of text from "Josef, lieber Josef mein," which Brahms directed his publisher to print beneath the viola's opening melody, where it is labeled "altes Lied.") Whether or not Brahms's audience recognized the "altes Lied" and conjured up its text for themselves, the simplicity of the borrowed melody and Brahms's transparent presentation of it convey a *volkstümlich* purity and grace, which Brahms can then bring into a dialectic relationship with his more artful melodic setting of Geibel's translated poem.

The interaction of these two texts becomes manifest in the melodic duet of the alto and solo viola. Brahms's Geibel setting and its companion piece in op. 91, a setting of Friedrich Rückert's "Gestillte Sehnsucht," are the only two obbligato lieder he composed.[40] The talents of the *Ehepaar* Joachim likely inspired the duet-like texture of "Geistliches Wiegenlied." Amalie Joachim gave up a promising career on the operatic stage when she married Joseph in 1863 but continued to perform in oratorios and lieder recitals thereafter. Joseph, of course, maintained an active career as one of Europe's leading violin virtuosos throughout the second half of the nineteenth century. If, as is generally believed, the song was composed in 1864 for the birth of the Joachims' first child (named Johannes after Brahms, his godfather), it may have been conceived as a "lullaby" for the new baby, to be jointly performed by the new parents. By the time the op. 91 songs were published in 1884, however, the Joachims' marriage had long since collapsed. Brahms sent a copy of the songs to Joseph Joachim, who was finalizing divorce proceedings against Amalie, from whom he had been estranged since 1880. The songs were something of a peace offering to Joseph; Brahms had sided with Amalie two years earlier in a letter, which she later used during the divorce proceedings, causing a decisive rift between Brahms and his friend of thirty years. One supposes that Brahms intended to bring about reconciliation between the Joachims through these songs, perhaps imagining a performance together (Amalie did perform the songs, but never with Joseph on the viola). If so, the particular disposition of the alto and viola lines would have enhanced the conciliatory effect: in each song the viola leads with a preludial melody that furnishes the motivic material for the vocal part that follows.

Conciliation, or, more generally, pacification, is a primary characteristic in both songs of op. 91, most notably in the "Geistliches Wiegenlied."

On the surface, constant return of "Joseph lieber" in the viola calms the ever more dissonant episodes (at least through the middle of the song before the initial material is recapitulated). But there is also a deeper level at which the mollifying effect of the "Joseph, lieber" tune is inherent in the very essence of Brahms's song. In large part that role for the "alte Lied" is developed through the subtle interrelationship between the alto's sung line and the viola's obbligato part. The viola states "Josef, lieber Josef mein" as the prelude before the voice enters with material that more loosely develops motives from the old Christmas song. Some of the motivic connections between the two parts are relatively blatant, as when the alto begins by inverting the F major triad and borrowing the neighbor note D, two figures that initiate "Josef, lieber." Some less conspicuous elements of the "cantus firmus," however, permeate Brahms's newly composed melody as well. First among these is the return figure from "Josef lieber" (marked R in example 1 in the Appendix): C–D–C in the first strain, B♭–C–B♭ to begin the second, and inverted as G–F–G near the end of the tune. This last form of the return figure appears prominently in the alto part of Brahms's song. It is present in an extended form in the alto's opening phrase and more notably in the sequence-forming motive beginning at bar 23. There, Brahms isolates the extended form of the return figure from the end of "Joseph, lieber" ("der Jungfrau Sohn"), adding poignancy to Mary's pleas to the "holy angels" to still the treetops by adding a modal inflection to the sequence with the minor dominant (C minor) segment in bar 25. And as the first strophe comes to a complete cadence in bar 33, the viola reiterates the initial phrase of the instrumental prelude, ending with a prolonged neighbor-note figure (C–D–C) in bars 37–38 that once again evokes the return figure from the hymn.

Each of these motivic relationships (the F major arpeggio and the return figure) is fairly audible and apparent. More interesting, however, are the *implicit* qualities of "Josef, lieber Josef mein" that manifested themselves not only in Brahms's newly composed alto part but throughout the accompaniment as well. Some of these amount to generalized characteristics. For instance, the alto line immediately presents a chorale-like melodic profile with its relatively longer note values in a deliberately unfolding arch contour (bars 13–16).[41] Beneath this melody, however, the block chords in the right hand of the accompaniment suggest separate associations with the borrowed tune. Most readily perceptible is the very character of the accompaniment; the barely adorned major and minor chords in the right hand represent a familiar style in the music of Schumann and Brahms, which Jonathan Bellman has labeled "chivalric." Bellman notes that in the Romantic fascination with the age of chivalry, "two discrete but related themes found voice . . . : emergent nationalism and nostalgia for a mythical German Golden Age."[42] Nowadays we might quibble with the historical accuracy of such associations, but to the nineteenth-century Romantic mind, "Josef, lieber Josef mein" carried the same general sense of a German cultural past that inspires the use of a chivalric tone in the alto voice here. Bellman also points to the use of this musical style in two works of the early 1860s whose texts have strong medieval and/or knightly connotations: the solo *Romanzen* on Tieck's *Magelone*, op. 33; and the cantata *Rinaldo*, op. 50, on Goethe's translation of Tasso's *Gerusalemme liberata*.[43]

Beyond these generalized characteristics, however, some abstract motivic qualities of "Josef, lieber Josef mein" penetrate deeply into the musical fabric of "Geistliches Wiegenlied." "Josef, lieber Josef mein" is largely triadic, beginning as it does by outlining an F major triad four times (with the additional neighbor note D). Triadic melodies automatically present thirds as significant motives. With this in mind, the context in which the F major triad is developed in this melody can be heard as the catalyst for chains of thirds that develop after the voice enters in bar 13. Right away, as the alto inverts the F major triad from the viola's cantus firmus, the keyboard left hand in bar 13 (maintaining the lilting rhythm of "Josef, lieber") extends the descending triad in that melody by arpeggiating in direct succession the triads I, vi, and IV. When heard as an extension of the motive C–A–F (as sounded by the left hand against the voice's entry in bar 13), that root progression (F–D–Bb) creates a thirds chain, C–A–F–D–Bb.[44] The alto then articulates a series of unfolding thirds (bars 23–26) before launching a prolonged descent by thirds herself from E to D in bars 27–32, articulated on the downbeats of a long descending-scale passage over a six-bar dominant pedal. Simultaneously, the right hand of the piano part (doubled in figuration by the viola) supplies a matching descent that is rich with thirds, both vertical and horizontal. By this point in the song (the end of the first stanza), the descending thirds that are implicit in the descending triadic arpeggiation of "Josef, lieber" have thoroughly saturated Brahms's setting.

Amid the consonance that this triadic abundance provides, two poignant chromatic inflections in Brahms's setting of stanza one stand out. As I have already mentioned, the melodic E-flat of bar 25 and the supporting C minor harmony add a tinge of modal inflection to Brahms's setting. Modality forms yet another implicit characteristic of the viola's borrowed tune. Note that the melody of "Josef, lieber" never lands on the pitch E, and thereby leaves itself open to a mixolydian modal rather than a major interpretation. The E-flat in bar 25, then, can be understood as a coloration in the modern setting that was inspired by the aura of the old Christmas song. Chromaticism of a completely different stripe occurs in the previous phrase, at bars 19–20. There, A-flat and D-flat form a dissonant intrusion on what had been strictly diatonic material (save a secondary dominant in the accompaniment at bar 6). Hardly modal, these inflections would appear to be spurred by the previously mentioned Romantic imagery of the text ("Nacht und Wind"). The distinctly different impetus for these two separate chromatic inflections within six bars of each other is critical, for Brahms establishes a paradigm for the entire song in which modern elements in the poem and its musical setting are quelled by the reintroduction of characteristic elements from "Josef, lieber" and, inevitably, by the viola's ritornello, which occurs in this instance beginning at bar 34. That is to say, the modern-inspired chromaticism of bars 19–20 is softened by the modally, archaically inspired chromaticism of bar 25.

I have already argued for the pacifying role of the reemergent hymn tune at the end of the song's B section, Brahms's setting of the poem's second stanza (bars 39–57). Patterns of tension and release emerge most baldly in the setting of the third (middle) stanza, where Brahms's treatment of Geibel's poem deviates formally from his approach in the rest of the song. Brahms separates off the first four verses of the stanza for treatment as a distinct musical unit (see fig. 1.1) and sets the remaining five verses with the same music he had used to set stanza one (the penultimate verse, "Stillet die Wipfel," is repeated now in place of "Ihr heilgen Engel," the "extra" verse that preceded it in the opening stanza). Brahms could hardly have set the two halves of this stanza more differently. For the verses expressing the Christ child's suffering, the 6/8 lilting meter of the previous stanzas shifts abruptly to a sarabande-like 3/4, while a constant welter of contrary-motion scale fragments and several chromatically descending lines in the viola perch perilously above a harmonic fluctuation between the keys of the parallel minor (F) and its submediant (D-flat). Conversely, Brahms sets the ensuing verses, in which the child's torment melts away as he sleeps, to the same tender 6/8 strains he used to set stanza one. In stanza three, then, rather than effecting a gradual purification through the reintroduction of the viola cantus firmus, Brahms starkly juxtaposes a stormy setting for Jesus' sorrows with a blissful setting for his comforting sleep. Whereas the means may differ, the effect is the same: a dissonant musical diversion is assuaged by a return to the cantus firmus–informed material.

When the remainder of the song effects a large-scale recapitulation of bars 1–73, an A B A form is established with the tumultuous beginning of stanza three (i.e., bars 74–89) at its epicenter. Such recapitulatory forms are fairly common in Brahms's song output and frequently reflect dramatic unfoldings like that of "Geistliches Wiegenlied," in which the high point of tension in the lyric lies at its center. (Indeed, "Gestillte Sehnsucht," the first song in op. 91, follows just such a trajectory.) Thus, one should apply caution in reading too much into the ternary form of "Geistliches Wiegenlied." Nevertheless, it is hard to ignore the profound image at the center of this song. The Christ child's hardship of assuming "[das] Leid der Erde" can easily be understood as a prefiguration of his adult crucifixion. Sparing any chiastic interpretation of the song's form, it is no stretch to read religious significance in the central (and dissonant) place these culturally loaded poetic images occupy in the song. It is also Christ child imagery that supplies relief in the form of the "altes Lied," which is, after all, a lullaby sung by Mary to Joseph over the sleeping Jesus.

In a commentary on Brahms's five lieder, op. 49, Leon Botstein notes that the lengthy and intensely melancholic and nostalgic last song in the set, "Abenddämmerung," on a poem by Brahms's contemporary Friedrich von Schack, stands in stark distinction to the gentle and reassuring "Wiegenlied" which immediately precedes it. He further notes that in op. 48, another song set published in 1868, Brahms follows a similar ending strategy by preceding a setting of Schack's "Herbstgefühl" (another essay in gloom) with a setting of the old German Renaissance folk song "Vergangen ist mir Glück und Heil." From all this Botstein discerns "a nascent philosophy of history. Contemporary texts . . . are juxtaposed to more archaic poetry and folk-like sentiments. The contemporary and the modern emerge as the bearer of the profoundly sad, the melancholic, and the pessimistic."[45]

In these cases it is "archaic poetry and folk-like sentiments" that set the present in tragic relief. A similar opposition drives "Geistliches Wiegenlied." But there the archaic and the *völkisch* cannot be separated from the religious. That which is old and *völkisch* (and in all of these instances under discussion, the *Volk* in question are unambiguously the *German Volk*) is imbued with a spiritual aura. "Josef, lieber Josef mein" derives its power to console and heal not merely from the fact that it is old, but from the innocent religious character of the idealized German past as seen through nineteenth-century German eyes.

Brahms's attraction to this melody no doubt stemmed partly from his aesthetic predilections, that is, from purely musical considerations. Yet there was just as likely a measure of cultural sentimentality in his choice of "Josef, lieber." This was a German song that Brahms documented in a German source from a seminal period in German history (the time of the Reformation). The medieval Catholic origin of the tune (as the Gregorian hymn "Resonet in Laudibus") in no way diminishes its Germanic identity for Brahms and his nineteenth-century audience. In fact, as a cultural translation, so to speak, the hymn tune is suited in op. 91, no. 2, to Geibel's literal translation of Vega's poem from the original Spanish into German. All is at once German and sacred in the "Geistliches Wiegenlied," regardless of its origins.

Another way to articulate the relationship between old and new material in op. 91, no. 2, is to identify "Josef, lieber" as a "healing" element. A half century later, the need for healing in the face of modernism was frequently stressed by reactionary German cultural critics (a theme to which I return in the final chapter). Sources of healing included various elements from the German past, the ancient *Volk* among them. Brahms, composing in 1864, still drew his cultural impressions of the *Volk* and his veneration of chorales from Luther's time from his Romantic predecessors. His employment of "Josef, lieber" as a healing agent in his "Geistliches Wiegenlied" therefore bears little if any of the anxiety and pessimism that would mark the pervasive (and extremist) adulation of the *Volk* a few decades later. Rather, it echoes an earlier Romantic milieu in which Brahms's concept of *Volksthumlichkeit* was forged.

Yet it is impossible to draw a distinct boundary between Romantic *Sehnsucht* and fin-de-siècle anxiety, between nostalgia and melancholy, between a healthy historicism and an irrational adulation of a mythical past. To revisit briefly a main thesis of this chapter and of this book, modern listeners fear such gray areas in the relationship of Brahms's music to the culture of his times. Ours is a fear occasioned by a knowledge of where the modern extremes of those dualities might lead, and how their musical associations (Wagner) can raise troubling questions about the social power and responsibility of music beyond its claims to autonomy. This fear has caused Brahms's image to be drawn too narrowly, too far on the politically safe side. I do not mean to imply that there is a "dangerous" side of Brahms that we have missed. Rather I would suggest that there is a political complexity to this composer and his music that is commensurate with the other dualities that scholars normally ascribe to him: musically, as a Romantic "classicist" and as a historically obsessed modernist; personally, as a "solitary altruist"; and philosophically, as a pessimistic progressive.[46] In the remaining chapters of this book I explore that complexity in Brahms and consider as well the impact of religion on political meaning in his music.

Religion, Language, and Luther's Bible

Brahms's Religious Outlook

In a published reminiscence from 1910, Joseph Suk recalled a conversation among Brahms, Antonín Dvořák, Dvořák's wife, Anna, and himself in Vienna on March 26, 1896:

> Then faith and religion were discussed. Dvořák, as everybody knows, was full of sincere, practically childlike faith, whereas Brahms's views were entirely the opposite. "I have read too much Schopenhauer, and things appear much differently to me," he said. . . . Dvořák was very reserved on the way back to the hotel. Finally, after a very long time he said: "Such a man, such a soul—and he believes in nothing, he believes in nothing!"[1]

Dvořák's overreaching assessment aside, Brahms's faith was, no doubt, far more complicated than his own.

Pinning down Brahms's religious orientation is famously difficult. Clara Simrock, wife of Brahms's publisher (and friend) Fritz Simrock, recalled that "Brahms was no churchgoer, yet he was of a deeply religious nature."[2] This observation reflects Brahms's private versus his public relationship to religion. On the one hand, Brahms was raised in a traditional North German Lutheran household, and his continued interest in religious texts (Luther's Bible in particular) suggests that he privately maintained throughout his life some measure of the Christian outlook on the world with which he was raised. Even if we take into account a variety of pessimistic and secularizing comments from his later years, there is nothing to suggest that Brahms ever betrayed that formative religious training. Brahms was nevertheless a typical product of the post-Romantic secularization of German culture. By the end of the eighteenth century, the Enlightenment had eroded the moral authority of the Lutheran Church in Germany, and subsequent generations of intellectuals—Romantics (many of whom were trained for the church) and others—had turned as strongly against Lutheran dogma as against rationalism itself. The upshot of this revolution was twofold. Outside the church it led to various forms of secular religion, including two manifestations that bear directly on Brahms's music: the new quasi-sacred setting of the concert hall and the ritual celebration of the state. Each of these themes will be taken up in the course of this book. Within the church, Romanticism had spurred a dramatic theological transformation, most prominently manifested at the beginning of the century in Schleiermacher's 1799 address to "Religion's Cultured Despisers." Here Schleiermacher had evoked religious feeling not only to counter the logical component in idealist philosophy but also to liberate the believer from traditional Christian dogma. As a result, Brahms and his German contemporaries inherited a culture in which it was possible to be "religious" in a broad, nondogmatic sense, without holding to the particular tenets of Christianity. For German artists and intellectuals, Lutheranism became as much a cultural tradition as a system of faith.[3] Whatever his beliefs in a deity, Brahms strongly identified with this secularized and cultural brand of Lutheranism.

For the Romantics, however, the abandonment of dogma did not mean a renunciation of religion or, necessarily, of Christianity. Indeed, several scholars have argued convincingly that Romanticism was shaped specifically by a Judeo-Christian understanding of God and of our relation to God. The endless striving toward the unattainable in Romanticism is, in this account, an expression of Christian doctrine on a mortal's incapability to reach the divine. All of these ideas may be subsumed under the rubric of striving for the "Ideal." Such thinking explains the fascination with medieval Christianity and even the Catholic conversion of Friedrich Schlegel and other early German Romantics, writes Frederick C. Beiser:

> If we carefully examine the chief documents regarding the Romantics' early flirtation with the Medieval church—Novalis' *Christianity or Europe,* Schlegel's *Fragments,* and Wackenroder's *Effusions of an Artloving Monk*— then we find many reasons for their sympathy for it. The Medieval church gave people a sense of community; it represented the highest spiritual values; it taught, and to some extent even practiced, an ethic of love, the noblest moral philosophy; and above all it inspired and gave pride of place to art. . . . The early Romantics' sympathy for the Catholic Church was primarily a love for the medieval *ideal,* not an approval of still less a conversion to, the actual historical institution.[4]

As writings such as Novalis's *Christianity or Europe* make clear, part of medieval Christianity's appeal for the Romantics was its universal nature and its capacity to build a common community among the separate nations of Europe. One of the more complicated connections between Romanticism and nationalism as they unfolded in Germany during the nineteenth century has to do with the way in which the universalizing tendencies of Romanticism could be channeled into the particularity required of any nationalism. Germans saw themselves as uniquely poised to lead all of Europe in further-ing the development of humanity as a modern successor to Greco-Roman civilization. With regard to religion, the Romantics' call for a return to an idealized unity of faith in Europe provided the basis for later rhetoric of a new German-Christian religion that would supersede the old Catholic and Protestant divisions.

Perhaps nothing so strongly separates Brahms's sense of his Germanness from the radical side of nationalism in the later nineteenth century as does his sacred vocal music and the manner in which he engages with Luther's Bible. Whatever his historicizing tendencies as a musician, Brahms ap-proached Bible reading, scholarship, and setting as part of a living and con-tinuous tradition within Lutheranism—not as a throwback but as a natural outgrowth of his upbringing. Brahms was raised in a fairly conventional North German Lutheran tradition of faith. As with most Hamburg children of his day, his schooling included the Lutheran catechism and confirmation, both of which would have exposed him at an early age to the Bible and tra-ditional religious thought in a systematic way.[5] Brahms also was influenced heavily by his mother, Christiane Brahms (née Nissen), who came from a long line of Lutheran pastors and was by all accounts a pious woman. One sees this in her letters to Johannes, where she frequently admonishes him to trust in God or to pray, although these comments are usually perfunctory additions to more substantive, down-to-earth advice on practical matters both personal and professional. The effects of his mother's piety may best be reflected in a notebook of proverbs, *Deutsche Sprichwörter,* which Brahms compiled in 1855 while living in Düsseldorf near the Schumann home. Sev-eral pious religious maxims appear near the beginning of the collection. Most of the entries do not stem from any known *Sprichwörter* collections of the time, suggesting the likelihood that Brahms knew them from an oral tra-dition (i.e., in the home).[6] The first three entries in the *Sprichwörter* serve to illustrate:

> Wer Gott nicht hält,
> Der fällt.
> [He who holds not with God / will fall.]

> Das Herze ist das allerbest,
> Das sich allzeit auf Gott verläßt.
> [That heart is the best of all / that always trusts in God.]

> Frisch und fröhlich zu seiner Zeit[,]
> Fromm und treu in Ewigkeit
> [Fresh and cheerful in the present, / pious and faithful in eternity.][7]

Hans Christian Stekel, who has compiled the most complete assessment of the composer's religious attitudes, observes that a transformation took place in Brahms's religious thought sometime shortly after he compiled these proverbs. Stekel attributes that change to Brahms's new relationships with more cosmopolitan friends outside Hamburg, most notably the Schumanns and Joseph Joachim. In particular, Brahms had lost his earlier piety to a "freethinking" approach to religious issues.[8] Just what this new freethinking on Brahms's part might have entailed is unclear, and here scholars wishing to assess his religious attitudes have been left to rely mostly on secondary evidence: scattered comments by Brahms in his letters or as recalled in the reminiscences of his friends, and (more frequently) his musical settings of sacred texts. The picture that emerges from these sources is one of a humanistic approach to theological issues that is, again, entirely in keeping with post-Romantic German intellectualism. As we will encounter in the next chapter, that perception of Brahms and religion centers on his largest work, *Ein deutsches Requiem*, op. 45.

Long after Brahms's encounters with the Schumanns and others had loosened his religious attitudes, some of his comments abandon piety all together, and this might lead one to believe that his youthful faith had disappeared entirely. During the early 1880s Brahms expressed his desire to find "heathen" texts in the Bible, as in a letter of 14 July 1880 to Elisabet von Herzogenberg: "I would love to compose some motets or any sort of choral music (or otherwise compose nothing at all), but try to see if you can find me some texts. . . . There is nothing heathen enough in the Bible. I've bought a Koran but find nothing in there either."[9] And two years later (8 August 1882) he writes to her: "From all the new works I have only received the Psalm [Heinrich von Herzogenberg's setting of Psalm 116, op. 34]. . . . But I must always expend such an effort to begin a Psalm that has so little heathen about it as this one."[10] To these comments may be added Brahms's frequent reference to the "godless" nature of his biblically based *Vier ernste Gesänge*, op. 121 of 1896.[11] Those songs, like the earlier biblical motets "Warum ist das Licht gegeben dem Mühseligen?" op. 74, no. 1 (1878), and "Ich aber bin elend," op. 110, no. 1 (1889), demonstrate Brahms's increasing use of sacred texts to probe philosophical issues and to question the very nature of life and the human condition. In all of these biblical settings, the mention of Christ is conspicuous by its absence.

In a continuation of the second letter to Elisabet Herzogenberg quoted above, Brahms wrote, "I have just written such a piece [as Heinrich von Herzogenberg's Psalm] that thoroughly suffices so far as the heathen are concerned, and I think that it has also made my music somewhat better than usual."[12] Stekel identifies the Brahms composition in question as the *Gesang der Parzen*, op. 89, for chorus and orchestra (1883), and points out that "in his texts Brahms continually dealt with the basic questions of human existence, with death, fate, and suffering." A cursory glance at the texts of

Brahms's secular choral-orchestral works (*Alto Rhapsody*, op. 52, 1869; *Schicksalslied*, op. 54, 1871; *Nänie*, op. 82, 1880; and the *Gesang der Parzen*) bears this out. Stekel then rightly asserts that Brahms sought out the same difficult questions in the Bible (especially in works like the *Vier ernste Gesänge* and *Ein deutsches Requiem*) in order to "legitimize" them.[13] But there is also an inherent expression of ambivalence in the act of seeking answers to secular questions (or at least formulations of those questions) in Judeo-Christian Scripture. Brahms opened his religious horizons upon leaving his boyhood home in Hamburg, and he developed a keen interest in the scientific and philosophical tenor of the age, but he was never able to leave behind completely his initial religious upbringing. If he was not satisfied by the dogma of the church, neither was he content with the answers he found in the material world or in the secular poetry of German humanists and Romantics: Goethe (op. 52 and op. 89), Schiller (op. 82), and Hölderlin (op. 54). Little wonder, then, that in his copy of Jacob Grimm's *Kleinere Schriften,* Brahms underlined the following aphorism: "Science only believes what it knows, the church only knows what it believes."[14]

Another avenue toward assaying Brahms's religious views, and one that has only recently begun to be explored, lies in the various "comments" he made in the form of underlinings and other marginalia in his baptismal 1833 Luther Bible and in two related documents: a handwritten pocket notebook of biblical passages, and his 1859 eleventh edition of Gottfried Büchner's popular Bible concordance.[15] Although I discuss the two former sources more thoroughly later in this chapter, it is initially worth surveying the broad picture of Brahms's religious views offered by markings and entries in all three documents. First it must be noted that the mere presence of these documents partly confirms the standard view of Brahms's religious attitudes; Brahms was more of a religious *thinker* than a *practitioner.* Owning a Bible concordance and copying texts into a notebook show more of an interest in ideas—and, significantly, how those ideas are preserved in literate form—than in dogmatic adherence to a particular faith or in church attendance. (Although, to be fair, a literate religious bent is inherently part of the Protestant faith in which Brahms was raised, and thus itself may be interpreted as faith-based.)

More so than in his musical settings of sacred texts, Brahms's biblical annotations suggest that he was just as likely to find interest in purely theological issues as in philosophical ones. A list of the entries he marked in the Büchner Bible concordance illustrates the point (the numbers in parentheses refer to the page numbers in Büchner where Brahms made a marginal annotation or mark): "Apostel" (69), "Bauen" (129), "Christus" (224, 228–229, 231), "Comödien" (234), "Dreieinigkeit" (267, 268), "Erde" (332, 335), "Hölle" (595), "Jesus" (621), "Judas" (630), "Jude"

(631), "Kohle" (662), "Mose" (746), "Psalm" (799–800), "Taufe" (954), "Vernünftig, Vernünftiglich" (1048), "Volk" (1064), "Weib" (1083). Standard religious fare ("Apostle," "Baptism," "Christ," "Jesus," and "Trinity") intermingles in this list with potentially more mundane topics ("Comedians," "Earth," "Coals," and "Sensible"). Some of the passages he marked fit well with the image of Brahms seeking out things irreligious within Scripture. For example, we may not be surprised to find that under the entry "Erde," the composer of the *Vier ernste Gesänge*, underlined: "Through sin, man is no longer the lord of beasts and nature, in that it brought him to his Fall; his nature and individuality were thereby divided into countless types."[16] Removing human beings from their place of preeminence in God's creative hierarchy is also the theme of op. 121, no. 1, which begins with the words of Ecclesiastes 3:18, "For the fate of humans and the fate of animals is the same; as one dies, so dies the other."

Nevertheless, one is struck by the preponderance of purely religious and distinctly Christian concerns evinced by Brahms's markings. For a composer whose sacred music displays a noticeable lack of dogma, Brahms's interest in the entries "Apostle," "Christ," "Trinity," "Jesus," and "Baptism" is surprising. He hardly seems to have been seeking any philosophical, much less "Gottlos," undertones in these passages. Rather, he appears to have been genuinely interested in basic questions of the Christian faith as the Bible could shed light on them. Thus, in Büchner's entry "Christus," Brahms's two annotations get to the heart of Christ's theological identity and meaning. First, Brahms brackets and marks the initial entry with a *nota bene* ("NB"):

Christus

§1. This is the official name of our savior, and means as much as Messiah, an anointed one, for in accordance with his human nature he has been anointed with the Holy Spirit's oil of gladness in unlimited measure, and has the greatest royal dignity. Ps. 4:8. Hebrews 1:9. Isaiah 61:1.

Four pages later Brahms draws a marginal line next to all of subsection 4a, which addresses the most basic theological issue in Christianity: Was Christ god or man? Not surprisingly, Büchner argues for Christ's divinity. Brahms underlines several lines in Büchner's argument, indicating his keen interest in the fine points of the debate. And on page 231, under a discussion of Christ's birth, Brahms again marks a passage that grapples with Jesus' human versus divine nature:

§12. How the eternal birth took place we do not know, Isaiah 45:15. Ps. 139:6. . . . This much is for certain, that the existence [*Sein*] of the Son was not something random, but rather something that is essentially founded in God and therefore eternal. <u>As concerns his human incarnation,</u> or his human birth, this occurred through supernatural means so that he could be born pure of all sinful implications and could enlighten all as the one holy and innocent being of our race, the second spiritual Adam.

Brahms's annotations and underlining here do not tell us where he came down on these questions: such is the tantalizing yet frustrating nature of such evidence. But it is highly revealing that he was interested in these matters at all. Whatever the philosophical implications of such musings, the issues addressed here are decidedly theological. Brahms's interest in them, however liberal and undogmatic his religious inclinations, shows that part of his attraction to the Bible was simply a matter of religion. Likewise, for all of his explicit aversion to dogma and his avoidance of distinctly Christian themes in his later sacred music, Brahms marked numerous passages in his 1833 Luther Bible that are utterly unambiguous in their Christian meaning. For example, he marked Hebrews 11, verses 1 ("Now faith is the assurance of things hoped for, the conviction of things not seen") and 6 ("And without faith it is impossible to please him. For whoever would draw near to God must believe that he exists and that he rewards those who seek him"). To be sure, such unabashed Christian doctrine is overwhelmed by the numerous passages Brahms marked (including those in the New Testament) which could be read as philosophical, nondenominational, or downright "heathen." But it would be misleading to suggest that Brahms showed no penchant for purely Christian sentiments in the Bible.

Brahms and the Bible: Faith and Language

Brahms's familiarity with the Bible is a commonplace of music history and was well known among his circle. He himself liked to show off how well he knew his way around the *Heilige Schrift,* either by pointing out finer theological points in his settings of bibilical texts to his friends, or by assuming a mock-biblical tone in letters.[17] His pride and satisfaction over his Bible knowledge is nowhere more in evidence than in his famous exchange with Karl Reinthaler in the fall of 1867, when the Bremen conductor was preparing his cathedral choir for the premiere of *Ein deutsches Requiem* there the following spring. Brahms answers Reinthaler's complaint that the *Requiem* lacks a distinctly Christian core by stating: "I also avoid knowingly and intentionally passages such as John 3:16. Occasionally, I have taken much liberty because I am a musician, because I had use for it, because I couldn't argue away or erase a 'henceforth' from my venerable poets."[18] (This exchange is discussed more thoroughly later in the chapter.) Although this remark gives evidence of Brahms's undogmatic religiosity, it also reveals his pride and satisfaction over his ability to cite chapter and verse when explaining his choice of biblical texts. Brahms makes the point more explicitly in a letter to Otto Dessoff concerning the "Warum" motet (1877), where he writes, "I enclose a trifle, for which perhaps—my Bible knowledge is to be praised. Moreover, it preaches much better than my own words."[19] And in a letter to Joseph Widmann, himself a former theology student, Brahms asks whether his friend has noted a subtle irony in the second of the *Fest- und Gedenksprüche*, op. 109 (1889), where Brahms takes Jesus' description of the devil as "ein starker Gewappneter" out of context: "Have you completely missed the theological, Jesuitical sophistry in no. 2 of the *Sprüche*? (Or merely kept silent about it.) I always wanted to ask you earlier whether something like this is really permissible."[20]

These statements are frequently reprinted in the Brahms literature. Ultimately, however, Brahms's reputation as a Bible reader is based on another pair of quotes that have been put to great use in making the case for his biblical expertise. One, involving Brahms's study of the Bible as a youth, is recalled by Richard Heuberger:

> Brahms praised the manner in which young Protestants learn, or learned. He said: "We learned the Bible by heart, without understanding any of it. Should a light ignite in one later, then one already has all of the material which then suddenly comes to life. As a lad I was always fanciful and a daydreamer. Thank God none of my teachers cared, and I had to learn notwithstanding my *Schwärmerei*. Children cannot understand all that they have to learn."[21]

This is—to my knowledge—Brahms's only direct statement about his early reading of the Bible. Whereas his comments leave little doubt that he read the Bible as a youth, they do not suggest a lifelong interest in or a serious study of Scripture. On the contrary, Brahms makes it quite clear that, although he became familiar with the words of the Bible at an early age, he had no interest in their meaning until later. We must conclude then, that at some point in Brahms's adult life a "light" was ignited in him that inspired his appreciation of the Bible.

A second reported statement by Brahms, as recalled by Rudolf von der Leyen, begins to explain the nature of that inspiration. In his recollections, *Johannes Brahms als Mensch und Freund,* Leyen writes:

> On one occasion we spoke about Robert Schumann, Brahms's great and most beloved friend, and specifically about the sad time of his sickness in Endenich. Brahms told me that Schumann longed for the Bible there, and that this desire was understood by his doctors to be a new symptom of his mental illness and was, for the most part, denied. "People just don't understand," said Brahms, "that we North Germans crave the Bible and do not let a day go by without it. In my study I can pick out [*herausgreifen*] my Bible even in the dark!"[22]

Brahms criticizes the doctors for not recognizing Schumann's request for the Bible as a legitimate need. At face value, then, Brahms seems to be downplaying the seriousness of Schumann's mental illness, or at least asserting that Schumann's request had led his physicians to overestimate his condition. Yet Brahms was acutely aware of how badly Schumann's mind had deteriorated during his hospitalization at Endenich; Brahms visited him there in 1856 during the last weeks of Schumann's life, when the older composer was barely lucid. Brahms's comments, therefore, have less to do with his opinion of Schumann's mental condition than with his desire to identify with Schumann as a fellow North German Bible reader. Consequently, Leyen's story implicates Schumann as a significant figure for Brahms's interest in the Bible as an adult. Another, more obscure anecdote supports that contention, and suggests an even stronger impetus. Arthur M. Abell, writing in 1931, recalls meeting Brahms near the end of the composer's life, when he asked Brahms to what he owed his deep interest in the Bible. Brahms, according to Abell, replied that "it was Schumann who first aroused my deeper interest in the Holy Writ (*Heilige Schrift* were his words). Schumann always was quoting the Bible. Then the death of my mother gave my studies of the scripture a new impetus." If Abell's recollection is as trustworthy as Leyen's, Schumann played a significant role in Brahms's adult appreciation of the Bible.[23]

Whereas the remark quoted by Abell is little known or repeated, those cited by Leyen and Heuberger account for a good deal of Brahms's reputation as a Bible expert. Countless later writers repeat one or both of the kernel ideas from each, that is, that Brahms had studied the Bible since childhood (Heuberger), and that he could find his Bible in the dark (Leyen). A typical conflation appears in Walter Niemann's popular Brahms biography from 1920, when he refers to Brahms as having "confessed to his friend Rudolf von der Leyen that like a true North German, he longed for the Bible every day, never let a day go by without it, and could lay his hand on the Bible in his study, even in the dark—who from his childhood upwards was a devoted believer in the Bible."[24] Like most other writers, Niemann retains Brahms's reference to "we North Germans" from Leyen, which resonates strongly with the mention of "young Protestants" in Heuberger. Niemann thereby elevates the importance of Brahms's North German Protestant heritage for his reputation as a Bible expert: Brahms—the thinking goes—set so many biblical texts because he was an avid reader of the Bible, and he was an avid reader of the Bible because he was a North German. It is true that his Protestant heritage did play a role in his biblical settings, since, as Brahms himself points out, memorizing texts from the Bible as a youth provided the raw materials for his later interest in the Bible. Nevertheless, the catalyst for Brahms's productivity as a composer of biblical texts was not his childhood education but Robert Schumann. Omitting Schumann from the transmission of Leyen's quotation, as most later writers do, obscures the role that the older composer played in sparking the necessary light in Brahms after his youthful *Schwärmerei.*[25]

Schumann's influence on Brahms's biblical interests manifests itself in Brahms's first great success as a composer, *Ein deutsches Requiem*, op. 45, completed in 1868. Despite the date of its completion, twelve years after Robert Schumann's death, the influence of the older composer on the *Requiem* can hardly be overemphasized. Opus 45 is Brahms's first large work for "the powerful masses of the choir and orchestra," for which Schumann called on him to compose in "Neue Bahnen," the seminal 1853 essay in which the older composer presented Brahms to the German music world.[26] Schumann also encouraged Brahms's study of past masters, an endeavor that is reflected in the various seventeenth- and eighteenth-century compositional techniques that permeate this work, such as the a cappella, suspension-laden choral entrances at the beginning of the first movement and the fugues that end the third and sixth movements. Christopher Reynolds has even suggested very pointed compositional references to Robert Schumann in the *Requiem*, asserting direct motivic links between op. 45 and works by Schumann such as *Das Paradies und die Peri*, Symphony no. 1 in B-flat, and a chorale setting from his *Album für die Jugend.*[27]

An even more direct set of relationships are those suggested by John Daverio between Brahms's op. 45 and a variety of Requiem-related works by Schumann: his Requiem, op. 148; the third ("Cathedral") scene from Goethe's *Faust;* and the *Requiem für Mignon.*[28] While Daverio hears the influence of these works across a wide range of Brahms's choral and orchestral music (including many specific imprints on op. 45), his most significant insight on this matter concerns "the consolatory tone that pervades much of Schumann's and Brahms's choral-orchestral writing and that served to embody" what Daverio labels "the Requiem idea." Brahms learned from Schumann not only to read the Bible, but also to use Luther's text to rise above narrow religious dogma and express a decidedly modern, humane view of the weightiest questions, in this case mortality. Daverio points especially to Schumann's *Requiem für Mignon* as a strong model in this regard. In comparing this piece to Brahms's *Deutsches Requiem*, one might be struck by the distinctly separate musical language employed by the mentor and the student (Schumann's choral style sounds much closer to Mendelssohn than to Brahms). Yet both works exhibit "not a morose lament for the dead but rather an exhortation to the living to cease mourning and cultivate their own innate abilities instead."[29] It is also significant that such a comparison could hold up between works which draw their texts from great secular literature (Goethe's *Wilhelm Meister*) and from Scripture (Luther's Bible), respectively; although Brahms certainly did not discount the religious meaning of the Bible (no matter how carefully he controlled the meaning he extracted from his chosen passages, as I shall illustrate presently), he nevertheless sought out meaning in Luther's Bible that would resonate with great German literature. For Brahms the Bible was but one more great work in the German literary tradition he revered, and could be used to express a highly individualistic religious attitude. In this way Brahms displays his great cultural debt to Romantic attitudes toward Christianity as transmitted through Schumann, beyond any musical quotations or stylistic overlaps we may or may not hear between those two composers' choral-orchestral music.

The *Requiem* is in any event a favorite testing ground for determining where Brahms stood on faith, as it invites diverse interpretations around the axis of its religious meaning. Whereas its fifteen separate biblical texts carry many central articles of Christian belief, nowhere is Jesus Christ or his resurrection mentioned. Thus, op. 45 is alternately open to a Christian, a more generally religious, or even a secular interpretation. A typical clash arose in a pair of articles from 1949, when Robert Hernried and Rudolf Gerber, working primarily from the texts of the *Requiem* and Brahms's own comments about them (to be discussed presently), arrived at separate conclusions about where Brahms stood in relation to Christianity. For Hernried, "[Brahms] remained his entire life closely bound to the fundamental moral laws of the New Testament," and "Brahms's attitude toward Christianity was deeply affirmative; it was just secularized." Gerber, who begins his essay by quoting Hernried's conclusions, challenges Hernried for identifying Brahms's beliefs as specifically "Christian," as opposed to a more general label like "religious." Gerber, along with many others, echoed Max Kalbeck, who had already taken an ecumenical approach to the work in his 1908 biography:

> Brahms called his mourning music [*Trauermusik*] *A German Requiem*, in distinction to the Latin death mass for use in the Catholic Church. His *Requiem* is not merely German in the sense that it would be a translation or re-texting [*Umdichtung*] of the old Latin text, which it does not try to be; it is German according to its character, as it expresses through the reflective, scholarly choice of its texts. One could also say the *Requiem* is Protestant, if one more broadly defines Protestantism than the orthodox conceive it, and counts the free study in the Holy Writ among its primary features. The German fought with his blood for the right of Bible freedom for the laity, and thereby wrested from the priestly powers their strongest weapon; the German artist, therefore, requires only his good Protestant right when he allows himself freely to read and combine texts from the Old and New Testaments, as they seem suitable to his own purposes. Before him hover human ideas, worthy of a worldly philosophy, which permits peace and rest not to the dead, but rather to the living. This idea

is secular [*weltlich*], however, not irreligious, it is philosophical, yet it is pious and beautiful, and it is thoroughly anti-dogmatic.[30]

Perhaps the key word in Kalbeck's assessment is the last: "anti-dogmatic." Brahms was ever mistrustful of anyone who claimed to hold the key to understanding any system or doctrine (religious, musical, or otherwise), especially those who further lorded their supposed superior knowledge over others. It was probably this quality in the rhetoric of the New Germans (Liszt above all) that repelled Brahms relatively early in his career. Throughout his life he maintained great musical respect for Wagner, and one could make the argument that, early on, Liszt was an important influence as well. But the lofty rhetoric of both men rankled Brahms in the same way that any dogmatic approach to faith earned his enmity.[31] As Kalbeck states, Brahms's approach to religious texts is deeply rooted in the German Protestant tradition of personal discovery through Bible reading. It is not irreligious, nor even un-Christian; it simply allows the ideas of the Christian tradition (in this case the Bible) to be treated more freely and to be put to one's own purposes.

As I have indicated, Brahms's remarks about religion and dogma are rarely direct and usually leave open a dual interpretation, which probably reflects ambivalence on his own part. His comments to Carl Reinthaler about the *Requiem* provide a classic case in point. Reinthaler had written:

> My thought was this: you stand in the work not only on religious but on completely Christian ground. Already the second movement alludes to the prophecy of the Lord's return, and in the penultimate [movement] the mystery of the resurrection of the dead, "and that not all will be put to sleep," is thoroughly dealt with. It lacks, however, for the Christian consciousness the point upon which everything revolves, namely, the redeeming death of the Lord. "Had Christ not arisen, thus would your faith be in vain," said Paul in connection with the passage that you have dealt with. Perhaps at the passage "Death, where is your sting," etc., the point could be found, either briefly within the movement itself before the fugue or through the construction of a new movement. Anyhow, you say in the last movement: "Blessed are the dead, who die in the Lord from now on"; that can only mean, after Christ has brought his salvation work to completion.[32]

Brahms responded immediately to Reinthaler's suggestion: "As concerns the text, I must admit, I would very happily also omit the 'German' and simply put 'Human'; I also avoid knowingly and intentionally passages such as John 3:16. Occasionally, I have taken much liberty because I am a musician, because I had use for it, because I couldn't argue away or erase a 'henceforth' from my venerable poets."[33] With this brief paragraph (the rest of his response to Reinthaler concerns preparations for the performance), Brahms disavows two separate possible readings of his work: first, he distances himself from the word "deutsch" in the title of the piece; and second, he denies a strict theological purpose to the work.

Brahms's reference to the word "deutsch" in the *text* is curious: he is responding to a criticism, or a question, that Reinthaler never lodged. The conductor's comments concern neither the title of the work nor the language of its text but rather its religious nature. Brahms's comment, therefore, draws attention to the importance of language in his thinking on the *Requiem* and may betray his own awareness of, and sensitivity to, the religious and/or nationalistic implications raised by the word "deutsch" in his title. For whatever else Brahms may have intended by the unusual title of his piece, ostensibly at least the word "deutsch" refers to the substitution of the familiar Latin with the German vernacular. To write a "German" *Requiem*, after all, is to supplant a foreign text, a willful replacement of Latin with German and of Catholic with Lutheran. The German language becomes the unifying element among the various issues raised in Reinthaler's letter and in Brahms's response. Here Brahms echoes a well-developed impulse among nineteenth-century Germans to place their language at the center of culture and, by extension, at the center of what it meant to be German. It was no coincidence that Brahms displayed this attitude toward language in conjunction with the biblically based op. 45: Luther's Bible was often understood as the cornerstone of the modern German language.

If German Romantics saw the *Volk* as the font of the German language (see Chapter 1), the ensuing generations saw that language as an object of veneration and pride. Throughout the nineteenth century, German artists and intellectuals rallied around their language as a unifying element in the face of their otherwise politically fractious identity. Language had formed a central part of German identity for Romantic nationalists in the two generations before Brahms. Ernst Moritz Arndt made his ideas about the German nation and its language widely known during the wars of liberation from France through his various writings and his widely popular patriotic songs. The best known among these was his "Gesang des Vaterlands," where he spells out the relationship between language and homeland quite clearly. "Where is the German Fatherland?" each verse begins, before listing various German-speaking regions, only to reject each in turn with the words, "Oh no! No! No! His Fatherland must be larger." Finally, in the sixth and last verse, Arndt answers his question: "Wherever the German language is heard, Praising God in heaven, there shall it be!"

Although it would be anachronistic to hold Brahms to the nationalistic view of language expressed in the Napoleonic era, it would be equally unreasonable to think that none of that patriotic veneration of the German language had filtered down to him, especially given his strong attachment to Luther's Bible. Brahms owned at least one book by Arndt, *Meine*

Wanderungen und Wandelungen, in which he marked the following passage concerning the German military victories of 1814: "After a five-hundred-year-long sad, snore-filled sleep, a morning dream of a resurrected German nation and kingdom is gradually dawning on the Germans."[34]

Arndt's contemporary Johann Gottlieb Fichte, writing in 1807 from French-occupied Berlin, largely dedicated the fourth of his *Reden an die deutsche Nation* to the importance of language as a defining element of the German people. Early on in this address, Fichte observes that the Germans are already distinguished from the "Gauls, Cantabrians, etc." for having remained in their ancestral territory. "More important, however," Fichte writes, "is the change of language. Here . . . it is not a question of the special quality of the language retained by one branch or adopted by the other: on the contrary, the importance lies solely in the fact that in the one case something native is retained, while in the other case something foreign is adopted."[35] As a result, according to Fichte, German is a "living" language, having maintained an innate connection to its roots, while Latinate languages (especially French) are "dead." He goes on to develop an argument that German is better able to represent "supersensuous" ideas, and concludes:

> What an immeasurable influence on the whole human development of a people the character of its language may have—its language, which accompanies the individual into the most secret depths of his mind and will and either hinders him or gives him wings, which unites within his domain the whole mass of men who speak it into one single and common understanding . . .—how different the results of this influence may prove to be where the relation is as life to death, all this in general is easily perceived.[36]

In order to preserve their national identity, Fichte implores Germans to root out foreign words, placing him in consort with contemporary German linguistic purists such as Joachim Heinrich Campe and Carl Gustav Jochmann. Although these authors eschewed directly nationalistic argumentation, their interest in removing xenologisms from German was fueled by a desire to make the language more accessible and productive for average users (i.e., those outside the literati or intelligentsia) across all social strata.

As the nineteenth century progressed, the people who inhabited these strata (especially the economically lower, less educated ones) would come to be identified more and more with the historical German *Volk*. It is little surprise, then, that the ensuing generation of grammarians who worked in the aftermath of German Romanticism pursued the history of the German language and its role in defining the German people. "Earlier stages of the German language," writes the modern linguist Michael Townson, "were seen to represent a 'golden age' of unity and youthful vigor in which 'language and

people were one,' but which now no longer obtained, and the political motives behind the study of German-language history were to evoke that spirit
of the Golden Age to remind the Germans of that unity which they now
were lacking."[37] Townson proceeds to focus on the "emancipatory political
activity of Jacob Grimm" and the stamp of Romantic cultural nationalism
that infused the work of Grimm and his brother Wilhelm.

At face value, the work of the Grimms and their successors does not
appear to be politically motivated. And the rational, scientific method
through which they investigate the German language and its history seems
less prone to subjective nationalistic sentiment. Yet the scholarship of the
Grimms and others in their Berlin circle of influence was often openly nationalistic and directly invoked the same mystical adulation for the German
Volk as had their Romantic predecessors. Brahms had entrée into these cir-
cles through his friendship with Joseph Joachim and the latter's close-knit
associations with the Grimms. Among Jacob Grimm's students in Berlin was
Wilhelm Scherer, whose *History of German Literature* was one of the most
widely read surveys on German literature during the late nineteenth century.[38] Brahms knew Scherer, possibly through the Grimm circle or through
Scherer's connection to Theodor Billroth and the Vienna-based patriotic
German club Silesia.[39]

Scherer's nationalistic rhetoric about the German language implies an abstract bond among the Germans through *deutsche Spracheinheit,* as in the
following passage from his essay of that name:

> The history of our language is, to a certain degree, the history of our people
> itself.
>   Language is the truest reflection of nationhood [*Volksthums*]. The totality of
> all spiritual power enters therein. . . .
>   But language is more still. It is also an educational power for the life of the
> state. It is the primary connection that binds a nation and through which comes
> their consciousness of an inner unity. Language serves statisticians as the surest
> sign of nationality.[40]

Elsewhere, Scherer lauds the Bible as the ur-document of German language
and culture. By including the Bible in his *Geschichte,* Scherer clearly treats it
as literature, yet he is quick to point out its broader cultural applications:

> The translation of the Bible is Luther's greatest literary achievement, and at the
> same time the greatest literary event of the sixteenth century, or even of the
> whole period from 1348 to 1648. Here the foundations of a common culture
> for all ranks of society were laid. Not merely the general outline of biblical con-
> tent, with which all Christians had long been familiar, but rather an entire intel-
> lectual [*geistige*] world, the classical products of ancient Hebrew literature, ev-
> ery received word of Jesus Christ, the letters of his greatest apostles—all this
> was now the common property of all: an inexhaustible source of grand and edi-

fying thoughts, a treasure often worshipped to the point of superstition and abuse, and a noble, imperishable code of language.

Although the Reformation increased the divisions within the German nation, although it rent asunder Protestant Germany and Catholic Germany, yet, on the other hand, it softened the contrast between South Germany and North Germany by definitely imposing on the Low Germans a High German literary dialect. In this respect, the Reformation also laid the foundation for modern German literature and for that unity of intellectual life in which we rejoice today.[41]

Scherer not only hails Luther's Bible as "the greatest literary event of the sixteenth century" but also credits it with unifying the German language and German literature from that time forward. Later he recasts this assertion in explicitly religious terms: "Even the Catholics had use at once for Luther's Bible, indeed to oppose him. 'They steal my language from me,' he said; but it was a triumph to him to have taught even his enemies how to speak."[42]

Scherer's *Geschichte* was buttressed by a not so subtle nationalist narrative: Scherer offers the same sort of nationalist veneration to Ulfilas's fourth-century translation of the Bible from Greek to Gothic German, which he calls the "true key to German antiquity," and whose author he describes as "our guide into the mysteries of the national prehistory."[43] In Scherer's rhetoric, the religious role of the German Bible cannot be separated from its role as a national cultural icon.

Scherer also demonstrates the degree to which the *Luther-Bibel* was a primary document—a repository of the common language and a generator of the modern literary tradition. In this sense, the Bible unites Protestant and Catholic Germany through language. But Protestantism emerges in the equation as more privileged, as the catalyst for a high, unified German culture. Ernest Gellner stressed the interconnection of "Protestant-type" religions and nationalism, and the centrality of language to both. "By translating scripture into the vernacular," writes Gellner, "Protestantism elevates the vernacular into a high culture. . . . Thus Protestantism achieves for its own religious ends, that transformation of a peasant dialect into a 'real' language, codified and capable of transmitting messages in a context-free manner over a large anonymous population. That which, later, nationalism strove to do, and did, for overtly political ends, Protestantism practiced earlier."[44]

Gellner's theory has obvious ramifications for Brahms's setting of the very document that raised the German vernacular to the status of high culture (all in the name of Protestantism), Luther's Bible. Indeed, the complete title of op. 45, *Ein deutsches Requiem nach Worten der Heiligen Schrift,* without striking an overtly nationalist pose, celebrates the work's biblical lineage and makes clear the importance of the text's German-Protestant origin.[45]

Reading over Brahms's Shoulder

There is no record of Brahms ever having spoken directly to the role of the Bible in the history of German culture, yet his intellectual involvement with the Bible demonstrates his participation in that very cultural tradition. Brahms owned as many as six Bibles during his adult life. Five of these remained in his library at his death and were bequeathed to the Gesellschaft der Musik-freunde according to Kurt Hofmann's catalog of Brahms's library (referenced by the "H" numbers here).[46] In addition to his baptismal Luther Bible printed at Hamburg in 1833 (H. 61, of primary interest here), Brahms owned three separate editions of the New Testament in different languages: a 1545 copy in old German (H. 59), a 1643 French edition (H. 60), and an 1884 Italian edition (H.62). Within the last twelve years of his life he also owned a 1526 Nuremberg edition of Luther's translation of the Pentateuch, although this was not in his *Nachlass*.[47] Presumably, the specific copy of the Bible to which Brahms frequently referred was the 1833 baptismal Bible. It is a small-format, unimposing print, exactly the sort of Bible one would make frequent use of in the home. We may assume that the other Bibles he collected were merely that—collector's items. Brahms made no annotations in these Bibles, which suggests that they were not used for close study (Brahms's lack of facility in foreign languages is notorious anyway), reserving for that purpose the 1833 Luther Bible, as indicated by the marginalia in that copy.

Figure 2.1 lists all of the texts that Brahms marked in his 1833 Luther Bible. His markings cover a wide range of subject matter and prose (or poetic) style, drawing on twenty-eight separate books of the Bible, including selections from the Old Testament, New Testament, and Apocrypha. Some of the passages are as short as a single verse; others encompass over a dozen verses totaling hundreds of words. Some of the books to which Brahms turned most often are not surprising in light of the biblical texts he chose to set to music. For example, given the weighty settings of texts from Job and Ecclesiastes in the motet "Warum ist das Licht gegeben?" and the *Vier ernste Gesänge*, respectively, one is not surprised to find that Brahms marked eleven separate passages in Job and six in (the relatively brief) Ecclesiastes. The frequency with which he marked sections of the Bible, however, does not necessarily square with what we could glean about Brahms's biblical interests from his musical settings of biblical texts. His use of the Psalms in compositions versus his marking of them in the Bible illustrates the point. Of the thirty-one biblical texts that Brahms set to music between 1859 and 1896, eight (or roughly one quarter) were Psalm texts. Yet of the eighty-six passages that he marked in his Bible, just nine are from the Psalms, or roughly one tenth—far fewer than one might anticipate.[48]

Some of these inconsistencies are better understood in the context of the

---

Bold = Set to music
<u>Underscored</u> = Copied into pocket notebook of biblical texts, A-Wst HIN 55.733

Genesis 39:9
Numbers 6:22–27
Deuteronomy 11:18–19
1 Samuel 14:7–10; 15:2
2 Samuel 7:20; 22:2
1 Kings 8:27–30
1 Chronicles 17:8; 30:20, 21; 2 Chronicles 6:19
Job 3:20–23 (op. 74, no. 1): <u>25;</u> 6:26; 7:19–21; 12:6; 14:1–2; 14:7–10; 15:3; 17:1;
    <u>17:7;</u> 28:25–28; 29:3–6; 29:12–15
Psalm 1; 8; **51** (op. 29, no. 2); 104:24; 115:17–18; 116:3–8; **126:5–6** (op. 45,
    mvmt. 1); 139; 145:15–21
<u>Proverbs 4:18–19, 23;</u> 6:6–11; <u>23:26;</u> 25:11
Ecclesiastes 1:9–10:12–18; **<u>3:18–22</u>; 4:1–4** (op. 121, nos. 2 and 3); 5:12–15/6:4–9;
    8:14; 9:1:4
Isaiah 40:2–12; 43:1–2; 43:11; 43:24–25; 44:22; 45:7–8; . 49:26; 55:6–11
Lamentations 1:12; **<u>3:41–42</u>** (op. 74, no. 1)
<u>Wisdom of Solomon 9</u>
Tobit 4:5–6
Ecclesiasticus 32:5–9; **<u>41:1–4</u>** (op. 121, no. 3); 43:31–37; 50:24–26
Matthew 5:3–4:8; 6:19–34; 7:2, 13; 9:5; 10:8–10; 11:28–30; 12:36
John 13:15
Romans 1:19–20; 3:14–15; 6:12
1 Corinthians 3:16–17; **13** (op. 121, no. 4)
2 Corinthians 3:2–3:4–6; 5:1; 5. 17? 10?
Ephesians 3:13
1 Timothy 3:4
Titus 1:12–13
1 Peter 1:24–25 (op. 45, mvmt. 2)
1 John 3:16, 1; 4:16–19
Hebrews 10:26; 11:1:6; 12:11–13
James 1:12; 1:17–22; 2:14–26(?)

Figure 2.1   Passages marked by Brahms in his copy of the Luther Bible.

other biblical sources in Brahms's *Nachlass,* especially his pocket notebook
of biblical texts, one of several such notebooks he maintained that are now
owned by the Vienna Land- und Staatsbibliothek. In a few cases, an isolated
marking in his 1833 Bible may seem unimportant but gains in significance
when compared with an entry in the notebook, and vice versa. In particular,
as I demonstrate later in this chapter, the innocuously marked chapter 9 of
Wisdom of Solomon in Brahms's Luther Bible looms large in the pocket notebook, where it is the final entry (folios 18v–19r; see fig. 2.2). One quickly observes that this was a significant text for Brahms: he wrote the chapter out
nearly in its entirety, titled it "Prayer of a King," and added significant
markings in the margin that might suggest ideas for a musical setting. Moreover, as I illustrate near the end of this chapter, the texts of Brahms's *Vier*

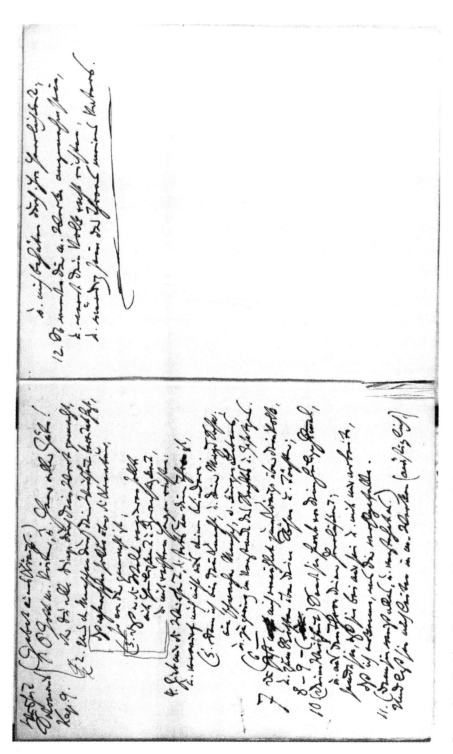

Figure 2.2 Weisheit (Wisdom of Solomon) 9: "Gebet eines Königs" as copied by Brahms into his pocket notebook of biblical texts, A-Wst HIN 55.733, folios 18v–19r.

ernste Gesänge, op. 121 of 1896, which directly precede Wisdom 9 in the notebook, may be read in a far different light when their proximity to this and the passage that precedes them in the notebook (1 Kings 6:11–12) is taken into account. None of this, however, could be gleaned from the simple blue-penciled bracket that Brahms placed around the beginning of Wisdom 9 on page 908 of his Luther Bible. All of the available evidence must be considered together in order to form a clearer picture of how Brahms dealt with the Bible.

Of that evidence, Brahms's Luther Bible is primary, not only for the marks he made in it and what these tell us about how he read the Scripture, but also for the texts' pre-formative influence on Brahms's musical settings. Namely, details of punctuation and layout particular to Brahms's edition of the Luther Bible probably directly affected both his choice of texts and the way in which he set them musically. For example, some of Brahms's careful construction of texts in *Ein deutsches Requiem* may have been suggested not only by his thorough study of the Bible, or any Bible concordance, but also by the printed cross-references to the second text in the piece, Psalm 126:5–6, as they appear on page 602 OT, where Brahms marked them with a blue-penciled stroke in the left margin.[49] That verse is presented below along with the cross-references as they appear in Brahms's Luther Bible.

> Die mit Tränen säen, werden mit Freuden ernten
> (Ps. 30.6   Matt 5.4   James 5.7–8)
> Sie *gehen hin und weinen, und tragen edlen Samen, und kommen mit Freuden, und bringen ihre Garben.
> (Acts 14.22   *Isaiah 35.10   John 16.20–22)

Four of the six cross-references here were used elsewhere in the *Requiem:* Matthew 5:4 begins movement one; James 5:7 and Isaiah 35:10 make up the middle and end of movement two; and John 16:22 begins movement five. One could not expect to find the same references in other Bibles of the day. Each printing of the Luther Bible was (and to a large extent still is) marked by the individualistic concordances supplied by these sub-posed references. My own examination of numerous German printings of Luther's Bible from the first half of the nineteenth century (including the 1818 edition by the same Hamburg firm that published Brahms's 1833 Luther Bible) finds none with this group of references for Psalm 126:5–6.

Of the texts to the first two movements of op. 45, only Peter 1:24–25 is missing from these citations; Brahms similarly marked that passage in his Bible with a blue stroke in the left margin. Thus, the artful compilation of biblical passages that makes up the text of op. 45, and for which Brahms is so often praised, may owe less to his Bible knowledge than we have previously thought. Instead, he may merely have taken advantage of the references presented to him by his own copy of the Bible. Beyond suggesting textual compilations, the layout and appearance of texts in his Bible may have

Bars:	Refrain 1	A	Refrain 2	B	Refrain 3	A'	Refrain 4
Bars:	1–4	4–20, 20–24	25–28	28–43	51–54	54–64, 64–76	77–84
Text:	"Warum"	verse 20 Agnus dei fugue	"Warum"	verse 21–22 New material	"Warum"	verse 23 Agnus dei fugue	"Warum"

Figure 2.3 Formal diagram of "Warum ist das Licht gegeben?" op. 74, no. 1: part 1 (bars 1–84).

suggested formal musical organization to Brahms as well. In two cases, where musical settings exist, we observe from his markings or his Bible's own punctuation how Brahms went about breaking down a text in the Bible with a musical form in mind. The first case concerns the most extensively marked passage in the entire book, Psalm 51. Although nearly every verse from 3 to 19 receives some sort of black pencil marking, verses 11–19 are emphasized by the stroke in the left margin. Brahms apparently uses X's in conjunction with two separate lines to divide the text into two parts: verses 11–14 and 15–19. In fact, Brahms set verses 12–14 as the motet op. 29, no. 2, part of which may have been composed as early as 1856 (the finished work was published in 1864). As far as we know, he never set verses 15–19.

The second case concerns the setting of Job 3:20–23 in the opening section of the motet "Warum ist das Licht gegeben," op. 74, no. 1. This example involves fewer markings but reflects Brahms's more detailed musical involvement with the text. To set the text (which is the first of five text passages in the motet), Brahms adapted the fugal theme of an Agnus Dei he had composed in the late 1850s as part of an unfinished *Missa Canonica*.[50] He transposed the original thorny five-voice F minor fugue from the Agnus Dei into D minor, reduced the texture to four voices (S A T B), and added the refrain-like interjections "Warum, Warum?" for op. 74, no. 1. The resulting form in the first part of the motet is represented in fig. 2.3. As indicated by the letters A B A′ in the top row of the diagram, after setting Job 20 to the Agnus Dei figure, Brahms reused that material for Job 23 in bars 54–76 (A′), following a section of newly composed material (B: bars 28–43) that sets Job 21–22.

In Brahms's particular edition of the Bible, verses 21–22 are set within parentheses, separating the two "die" clauses of those verses from the preceding verse 20 and the following verse 23. Brahms bracketed the relevant verses, Job 3:20–23, in blue pencil:

20   Warum ist das Licht gegeben dem Mühseligen, und das Leben den
      betrübten Herzen,
21   (Die des Todes warten, und kommt nicht, und grüben ihn wohl aus dem
      Verborgenen;
22   Die sich fast freuen und sind fröhlich, daß sie das Grab bekommen)
23   Und dem Manne, deß Weg verborgen ist, und Gott vor ihm denselben
      bedecket?
      [20Why is light given to one in misery, and life to the bitter in soul,
      21Who long for death, but it does not come, and dig for it more than
      for hidden treasure; 22And rejoice exceedingly, and are glad when they
      find the grave? 23Why is light given to one who cannot see the way,
      whom God has fenced in?]

Brahms's setting of these verses directly conforms to the punctuation here (see ex. 2.1); verses 21 and 22 are set to their own material (ex. 2.1B) in con-

Example 2.1   Melodic themes from "Warum ist das Licht gegeben?" op. 74, no. 1: part 1 (bars 1–84): (A) corresponds to section A in fig. 2.3: bars 1–3; (B) corresponds to section B in fig. 2.3: bars 28–33; (C) corresponds to section C in fig. 2.3: bars 52–56.

trast to the surrounding verses 20 and 23, which were set to the Agnus Dei fugue and its variation (ex. 2.1A and C). Already, then, the punctuation of a text within his 1833 Bible may have prompted Brahms's formal approach to a musical setting of that text.

Brahms marked verse 25 of Job 3 separately with a semicircular bracket in the right margin on page 509. Although he did not set this verse to music, he did include it in his notebook of biblical passages. Indeed, the "Warum?" motet marks a good place to begin an examination of that source, since the first two passages copied into it (James 5:11 and Lamentations 3:41) form the middle texts of that motet.[51] The biblical notebook was but one in a series of pocket notebooks that Brahms maintained throughout his life, and in which he wrote out texts he found suitable to musical setting, crossing out texts after he had set them.[52] Of the four notebooks that have survived, the three others are devoted to poetic texts, including those for all but twenty-six of the songs that he composed after 1877 (as well as for a few earlier songs), whereas the biblical notebook includes the texts to all of Brahms's biblical settings from 1877 on. In all four notebooks, Brahms cited the

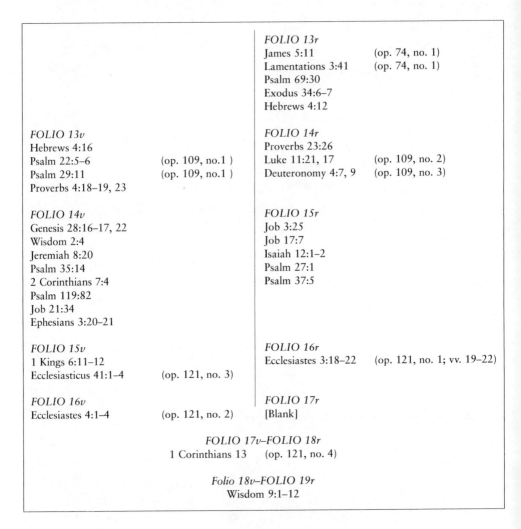

		FOLIO 13r	
		James 5:11	(op. 74, no. 1)
		Lamentations 3:41	(op. 74, no. 1)
		Psalm 69:30	
		Exodus 34:6–7	
		Hebrews 4:12	
FOLIO 13v		FOLIO 14r	
Hebrews 4:16		Proverbs 23:26	
Psalm 22:5–6	(op. 109, no.1)	Luke 11:21, 17	(op. 109, no. 2)
Psalm 29:11	(op. 109, no.1)	Deuteronomy 4:7, 9	(op. 109, no. 3)
Proverbs 4:18–19, 23			
FOLIO 14v		FOLIO 15r	
Genesis 28:16–17, 22		Job 3:25	
Wisdom 2:4		Job 17:7	
Jeremiah 8:20		Isaiah 12:1–2	
Psalm 35:14		Psalm 27:1	
2 Corinthians 7:4		Psalm 37:5	
Psalm 119:82			
Job 21:34			
Ephesians 3:20–21			
FOLIO 15v		FOLIO 16r	
1 Kings 6:11–12		Ecclesiastes 3:18–22	(op. 121, no. 1; vv. 19–22)
Ecclesiasticus 41:1–4	(op. 121, no. 3)		
FOLIO 16v		FOLIO 17r	
Ecclesiastes 4:1–4	(op. 121, no. 2)	[Blank]	

FOLIO 17v–FOLIO 18r
1 Corinthians 13   (op. 121, no. 4)

Folio 18v–FOLIO 19r
Wisdom 9:1–12

Figure 2.4   Copies in Brahms's pocket notebook of biblical texts, A-Wst HIN 55.733.

source of the text and crossed out nearly all of those that he had set to music. In biblical as well as poetic texts, he occasionally made marginal diagrams (braces and other types of vertical strokes) for himself, apparently to help organize his own thoughts about possible musical settings. The notebook, which measures 16.5 by 19.8 cm, originally contained twenty-four pages, the first twelve and last two of which have been torn out.[53] Brahms copied thirty-two passages from twenty-six books of the Bible onto twelve pages of this notebook (folios 13r–19r; fig. 2.4), leaving folios 17r and 19v through 22v blank. These texts relate to a chronologically contiguous group of Brahms's compositions between 1877 and 1896: op. 74, no. 1; op. 109; op. 110, no. 1; and op. 121. A noticeable visual distinction occurs between the texts copied on folios 13r–15r and those on the remaining pages of the notebook; the former, relatively short passages are written in pencil, several to a page; the latter tend to be lengthier, one or two to a page, and are written in ink.

The dates of the compositions in question suggest that he copied these biblical texts into the notebook relatively late. Still, the date of this source and its relationship to Brahms's markings in his Luther Bible is murky. Although the first two texts in the notebook (James 5:11 and Lamentations 3:41) relate to the remaining biblical passages in Brahms's "Warum" motet of 1877, the opening text of that piece, Job 3:20–23, is not found here.[54] It may have been copied on the preceding torn-out page, but it is also likely that the chronological connection between Brahms's biblical compositions, the marks he made in his Luther Bible, and his copying of texts into the notebook is far more complicated and unrecoverable from this evidence.

In any case, our reading of the evidence supplied by the notebook is unavoidably complicated by our knowledge of which texts Brahms grouped together in actual musical settings. The first remaining page in the notebook, folio 13r—which includes James 5:11, Lamentations 3:41, Psalm 69:30, Exodus 34:6–7, and Hebrews 4:12—provides a good example of how a group of texts familiar to us from an eventual musical setting (op. 74, no. 1, and op. 110, no. 1) may be understood to carry a quite different meaning when viewed in their context within the notebook. Absent our awareness of how the first two texts on this page were utilized in the "Warum" motet, we might be inclined to see a connection between the first and fourth texts on the page, James 5:11 and Exodus 34:6–7, through the "barmherzig" motive:

folio 13r
James 5:11   denn der Herr ist **barmherzig** und ein Erbarmer.
                         [The Lord is compassionate and merciful.]

Exodus 34:6, 7   Herr, Herr Gott **barmherzig** und gnädig
                         [The Lord, the Lord, / a God merciful and gracious]

Similarly, we might link the Exodus passage with that which follows it on the page, Hebrews 4:12, for their common "und . . . und . . . und" construction and their depiction of God as a judge:

folio 13r
Exodus 34:6–7   Herr, Herr Gott, barmherzig, **und** gnädig, **und** geduldig,
                         und von großer Gnade **und** Treue. Der du beweisest
                         Gnade in tausend Glied, **und** vergibst Missetat, Übertretung
                         und Sünde, **und** vor welchem niemand unschuldig ist.

[The Lord, the Lord, / a God merciful and gracious, / slow to anger, / and abounding in steadfast love and faithfulness, / keeping steadfast love for the thousandth generation, / forgiving iniquity and transgression and sin, / yet by no means clearing the guilty.]

folio 13r

Hebrews 4:12

[Denn] das Wort Gottes ist lebendig **und** kräftig, **und** chärfer denn kein zweischneidiges Schwert, **und** durchdringt, bis daß es scheidet Seele **und** Geist, auch Mark **und** Bein, **und** ist ein Richter der Gedanken **und** Sinne des Herzens.

[Indeed the word of God is living and active, sharper than any two-edged sword, piercing until it divides soul from spirit, joints from marrow; it is able to judge the thoughts and intentions of the heart.]

Finally, if we turn the page to the first text on folio 13v, Hebrews 4:16,[55] we find a text that relates to several of those on 13r, and could serve as a chorale-like summation of the ideas expressed in them:

folio 13v

Hebrews 4.16

[Darum] **Lasset uns** hinzu treten mit Freudigkeit zu dem Gnadenstuhl, auf daß wir **Barmherzigkeit** empfangen, wenn uns **Hülfe** not sein wird.

(from folio 13r)

(Lamentations 3:41)

Lasset uns unser Herz . . .

(James 5:11)

Der Herr ist **barmherzig**

(Psalm 69:30)

Gott deine **Hülfe** schütze mich

These texts, therefore, are apparently linked not only by their physical proximity in the biblical notebook but also by their content, which indicates that Brahms copied biblical verses as thematically linked groups into this source.

If, however, we approach folio 13r with an awareness of how he actually used these texts, we arrive at very a different interpretation of their relationship to one another. For example, as previously mentioned, the first two texts on the page, James 5:11 and Lamentations 3:41, were used—in reverse order—as the second and third sections of the "Warum" motet, while the next two texts (Psalm 69:30 and Exodus 34:6–7) were combined to form the text of the motet op. 110, no. 1. Thus, it is possible to reach a very different conclusion about the proximity of the first pair of texts on 13r vis-à-vis the second pair; that is, that their appearance on the same page is entirely coincidental, or that their relationships indicate they belong to a pool of verses from which Brahms later chose freely in constructing texts for his motets.

Several openings in the notebook contain similar text groups to those on 13r and 13v (sometimes also appearing to run over to the top of the next page as they do there). Generally, Brahms chooses passages that either in and of themselves or in juxtaposition to one another form binary oppositions. Occasionally he chose verses from a part of the Bible where such oppositions are to be expected (Psalms, parables). But more often he created them himself through his choice and ordering of particular biblical passages. Several such groups occur at the opening of folios 14v–15r. There Brahms entered a number of "negative-positive" groups in which one or more brief passages that express a pessimistic or plaintive thought are followed by one or more uplifting verses. So, for example, a set of texts on folio 14v that expresses a nostalgic sense of sorrow, characterized by words such as *dahin* and *vergangen* (Wisdom of Solomon 2:4, Jeremiah 8:20, Psalm 35:14) is followed by several texts that express the possibility of comfort; indeed, all three contain some form of the word *Trost* (2 Corinthians 7:4, Psalm 119:82, Job 21:34).[56] Similar pairings of pessimistic texts with the promise of comfort are found throughout *Ein deutsches Requiem*, as I will discuss in the next chapter. That Brahms was copying such texts into his notebook (presumably) in the 1870s or later—that is, long after the *Requiem* had been composed—suggests that he specifically sought out such patterns of binary opposition in the Bible, beyond their normal occurrence in the Psalms or other particular, more specific sections of Scripture.[57]

Solomon's House and a King's Prayer

Another type of binary opposition informs the texts on the previous opening (folios 13v–14r), but here we begin to encounter issues that may resonate beyond musical considerations to touch on political and other cultural themes. Except for the first passage on folio 13v (Hebrews 4:16), folios 13v–14r contain the four texts that make up the *Fest- und Gedenksprüche*, op. 109 (1888–89), in their composed order, along with three passages from Proverbs (not shown here) that appear between the texts to op. 109, nos. 1 and 2:

folios 13v–14r

Psalm 22:5–6	op. 109, no. 1 In you our fathers put their trust; / they trusted and you delivered them. 6They cried to you and were saved; / in you they trusted and were not disappointed.
Psalm 29:11	op. 109, no. 1 The Lord gives strength to His people; / the Lord blesses His people with peace.

Luke 11:21, 17

op. 109, no. 2

21When a strong man, fully armed, guards his own house, his possessions are safe. 17Any kingdom divided against itself will be ruined, and a house divided against itself will fall. 18If Satan is divided against himself, how can his kingdom stand?

Deuteronomy 4:7, 9

op. 109, no. 3

What other nation is so great as to have their gods near them the way the Lord our God is near us whenever we pray to Him? / 9Only be careful, and watch yourselves closely so that you do not forget the things your eyes have seen or let them slip from your heart as long as you live. Teach them to your children and to their children after them.

The patriotic bent of the eventual op. 109 texts, their most commonly discussed and widely acknowledged characteristic, manifests itself in two main categories within the *Fest- und Gedenksprüche:* the Lord's historical relationship with His *Volk* (made explicit in nos. 1 and 3), and the unity of a "house" as symbol for a nation (in no. 2). If one extends the group on 13v–14r to include the first text at the top of the following page, folio 14v, the references to "Gotteshaus" in a series of verses from Genesis 28 reinforce the words "Palast" and "Haus" from Luke 11:21, 17 (op. 109, no. 2) on folio 14r. The passage from Genesis is of the "locus iste" variety, as each line relates God to a place in a form of praise:

Genesis 28:16–17

Surely the Lord is in this place—and I did not know it! How awesome is this place! This is none other than the house of God, and this is the gate of heaven. And this stone, which I have set up for a pillar, shall be God's house.

Again, in order to appreciate the potential meanings and connections presented by this compilation, we must suspend our knowledge of how Brahms ultimately used some of the texts here (i.e., for op. 109). And once more, the suggestion of a theme in the notebook becomes less opaque when considered against similar evidence presented by Brahms's marking in his Bible. His predilection for biblical passages that contain spatial metaphors for God's kingdom led him to mark the following passages there, all of which compliment the "house" imagery on folios 13v–14v of the notebook.[58]

Exodus 39:9	He is not greater in this house than I am; nor has he kept back anything from me except yourself, because you are his wife.
Deuteronomy 11:19	And you shall teach them to your children, talking of them when you are sitting in your house, and when you are walking by the way, and when you lie down, and when you rise.
1 Kings 8:27–30	"But will God indeed dwell on the earth? Behold, heaven and the highest heaven cannot contain thee; how much less this house which I have built! / 28Yet have regard to the prayer of thy servant and to his supplication, O Lord my God, hearkening to the cry and to the prayer which thy servant prays before thee this day; / 29that thy eyes may be open night and day toward this house, the place of which thou hast said, "My name shall be there," that thou mayest hearken to the prayer which thy servant offers toward this place. / 30And hearken thou to the supplication of thy servant and of thy people Israel, when they pray toward this place; yea, hear thou in heaven thy dwelling place; and when thou hearest, forgive."
2 Corinthians 5:1	For we know that if the earthly tent we live in is destroyed, we have a building from God, a house not made with hands, eternal in the heavens.
Wisdom 9:7–8	You have chosen me to be king of your people and to be judge over your sons and daughters. / 8You have given command to build a temple on your holy mountain, and an altar in the city of your habitation, a copy of the holy tent that you prepared from the beginning.
1 Corinthians 3:16–17	Do you not know that you are God's temple and that God's Spirit dwells in you? / 17If any one destroys God's temple, God will destroy him. For God's temple is holy, and that temple you are.

Among the New Testament texts here, the metaphor of a house or temple runs along predictable Judeo-Christian theological lines, as in the equation of the individual as a vessel for God's spirit in 1 Corinthians 3:16 or of the earth as a mortal representation of heaven in 2 Corinthians 5:1 ("For we know that if the earthly tent we live in is destroyed, we have a building from God, a house not made with hands, eternal in the heavens").[59]

Some of the passages that Brahms marked in the Old Testament and Apocrypha, however, use spatial metaphors more imaginatively, namely, the related passages from 1 Kings 8 and Wisdom of Solomon 9. As books,

Kings and Wisdom are integrally related: 1 Kings is a discussion of Solomon's reign over Israel, and its early chapters focus on God's gift of wisdom, as in 1 Kings 4:29: "God gave Solomon very great wisdom, discernment, and breadth of understanding as vast as the sand on the seashore." Those words speak directly to verse 4 of Wisdom 9, "Give me the wisdom that sits by your throne," the central theme of that chapter, which Brahms labels "Gebet eines *Königs*" in his notebook. Both 1 Kings 8:27–30 and Wisdom of Solomon 9 are spoken by Solomon, and relate to the same two structures—the temple in Jerusalem and Solomon's own house in the forests of Lebanon—and in each Solomon addresses God on behalf of the Israelites. In the passage from 1 Kings 8, Solomon stands between the newly finished temple and an assembly of all the leaders of Israel whom he had summoned. After blessing the assembled, Solomon lifts his hands to heaven and prays to God. Brahms's pencil mark in his Bible begins at verse 27, the very point at which Solomon acknowledges that the temple is merely a conduit to God, not His dwelling place ("But will God indeed dwell on the earth? Behold, heaven and the highest heaven cannot contain thee; how much less this house which I have built!"). It is thus not the individual who prays to the temple in hope of forgiveness but rather the entire nation of Israel ("And hearken thou to the supplication of thy servant and of thy people Israel, when they pray toward this place; yea, hear thou in heaven thy dwelling place; and when thou hearest, forgive").

None of these passages draws a direct relationship among the temple, the individual, and the nation, but we may infer how Brahms connected these entities from his selection of passages. Clearly the temple and the individual may be equated as vessels of the Holy Spirit in the New Testament passages here. But just as a single person forms a particularized and human version of the temple, so too does the individual represent in singular the plurality of the people to whom he or she belongs, and who also pray to God through the temple. Solomon himself, in the excerpt from the passage that Brahms selected from Wisdom of Solomon 9, closely connects his identity as a leader of the nation with his divine charge to build the temple in Jerusalem. Thus, the house serves here as a metaphor for the nation and the nation as a metaphor for the individual.

Brahms's interest in Wisdom of Solomon 9 goes beyond the simple mark he made in his Luther Bible. As I noted earlier, he also copied out nearly the entire chapter on folios 18v–19r of his biblical notebook. In that source the connection between Wisdom of Solomon 9 and 1 Kings is more evident; at the top of folio 15v, the first text among those that Brahms entered in ink, is 1 Kings 6:11–12, which also refers to the building of the temple, the people of Israel, and God's promise to Solomon's father, David:

1 Kings 6:11, 12

Now the word of the Lord came to Solomon. "Concerning this house that you are building, if you will walk in my statutes, obey my ordinances, and keep all my commandments by walking in them, then I will establish my promise with you, which I made to your father David. I will dwell among the children of Israel, and will not forsake my people Israel." [12]So Solomon built the house and finished it.

Whereas the connections between this text and Wisdom of Solomon 9 are obvious, the relation of either to the texts that fall between them on folios 15v–18v in the notebook is obscure. Those texts, Ecclesiasticus 41:1–4, Ecclesiastes 3:18–22 and 4:1–4, and 1 Corinthians 13, almost exactly constitute the texts of the *Vier ernste Gesänge,* op. 121 (Brahms used all but Ecclesiastes 3:18 for the songs). In its general tone, as well as its emphasis on God's ways and promise to his people, the 1 Kings passage seems to resonate more with the op. 109 texts on 13v–14r than with those of the *Vier ernste Gesänge.* But this text most probably does *not* carry over from previous folios, as did those at the top of 13v (Hebrews 4:16) and 14v (Genesis 28:16–17, 22). Instead, it appears to serve as an opening statement that leads eventually to the last text in the notebook, Wisdom of Solomon 9:1–12 (folios 18v–19r).

At first reading, it is difficult to understand how the texts to the *Vier ernste Gesänge,* which are copied on folios 15v–18r, could belong to a composite group that begins and ends with the "Solomon as King" texts. The texts of op. 121 make no reference to rulers or laws, and seem instead to dwell on issues of life, death, and love. But a closer examination of all six texts on folios 15v–19r reveals themes—some overt, some implicit—that bind them as a unified group and create a context in which they fit conceptually between the framing texts from 1 Kings and Wisdom of Solomon. In the notebook, the texts of op. 121 are entered in the order listed above. Ecclesiasticus 41:1–2, as it leads off this arrangement, produces a decidedly different effect than it does in its eventual setting as song no. 3 of op. 121. Whereas it flows logically from the Ecclesiastes texts that precede it in those songs (and follow it here in the notebook), its focus on death seems to be introduced quite abruptly after 1 Kings 6:11–12. But the message in verses 1–2, that death can be viewed in opposite manners by the old and the young, leads in verses 3–4 to a statement on immortality: "Do not fear death's decree for you; remember those who went before you and those who will come after."

Although Brahms did not set verses 3 and 4 (nos. 5 and 6 in the Luther Bi-

ble), he cites them with an incipit after the verses that he did copy, writing:
"5. (Fürchte den Tod nicht/)." Sirach's sentiments are not far removed from
the emphasis in both 1 Kings and Wisdom of Solomon on the succession of
generations, the continuance of God's promise to his people, and the need to
follow God's path (a sentiment echoed elsewhere in the biblical passages
copied into the notebook, as we have seen). Indeed, one can understand the
remainder of chapter 41 in Ecclesiasticus to refer directly to the fate of Solomon, described throughout 1–2 Kings, as one who strays from the way of
the Lord in his old age and whose offspring suffer as a consequence.[60]
Within his Bible, Brahms marked several other passages from Ecclesiasticus,
including 43:31–33 whose last verse reads, "For the Lord has made all
things, and to the godly He has granted wisdom." Thus, whereas it may not
be immediately apparent from his selection of texts in his biblical notebook,
Brahms was certainly cognizant of the connections to the Wisdom of Solomon as a gift from God and the later chapters of Ecclesiasticus.[61] The two
passages from Ecclesiastes which follow on folios 16r and 16v continue the
theme of death raised by Ecclesiastes 41:1–4. Ecclesiastes 3:18–22 concludes that one should be happy in one's works, for these will last whereas
the flesh will not. Works carry a similar value in this passage to that borne
by a virtuous name in Ecclesiasticus 41 (as quoted in note 60).

The possibility that Brahms was considering a piece in which the Ecclesiastes texts and the "Gebet einen Königs" (Wisdom of Solomon 9) were to be
part of one composition or a unified opus is rendered still more plausible by
a citation to the latter text directly below Ecclesiastes 4:1–4 on folio 16v.
Brahms wrote that citation in pencil, unlike the main text on that page,
which is written in ink, which suggests that the two passages were not selected or copied simultaneously. Having cited Wisdom of Solomon 9 at the
bottom of 16v, Brahms left the rest of that page and the facing one (17r)
blank, and copied all of 1 Corinthians 13 onto the next pair of folios (17v–
18r) before he finally entered the Wisdom text onto folios 18v–19r.[62] It is
difficult to explain how the Corinthians text fit into Brahms's plans. One explanation could be that Brahms selected the Wisdom text after or (conceptually) concurrent with 1 Corinthians 13. In that scenario, the last two texts
may have been considered as separate possible conclusions to the larger
group. Later, perhaps around the same time he made the pencil markings in
the text of Wisdom of Solomon 9, Brahms could have made the pencil citation of that chapter below Ecclesiastes 4:1–3 on folio 16v, indicating that at
some point he was thinking of concluding the set with the Wisdom text
rather than 1 Corinthians 13. As alternate conclusions to the hypothetical
larger conception represented by the texts on 15v–19r, the Corinthians and
Wisdom texts would have imposed quite a different meaning on the texts
that preceded them. In essence the difference boils down to a faith in Wis-

dom versus a faith in Love. Further still, we can categorize these separate faiths as public versus private. In order to understand better how these distinctions might have occurred to Brahms and why he would eventually choose a private over a public faith when he composed the *Vier ernste Gesänge* in 1896, we must consider the likely time frame for his copying of these texts into his notebook.

The two "Solomon as King" texts provide a reasonable hypothesis for dating the entries on 15v–19r around 1888, the so-called *Drei-Kaiser-Jahr* which witnessed the deaths of the ninety-year-old Emperor Wilhelm I in March and of his successor, Frederick III, barely three months later. Brahms was, according to Kalbeck, deeply moved by the "tragedy" of these events and "felt the blow, which befell the royal family and house, the fatherland, and the people, more painfully than many who were closer to the monarch."[63] Wilhelm I, who had ascended to the throne in 1861, oversaw the creation of a unified German state. His grandson Wilhelm II was only twenty-nine when he took over the throne after the short reign of his father, Frederick. In light of these circumstances, it is easy to read the 1 Kings passage as pertaining to the elder Wilhelm and the Wisdom of Solomon text to the younger. Kalbeck makes the latter connection, going so far as to assign the copying of the text to about the time of the new Kaiser's first speech.[64] Wilhelm I was, after all, the king who had been made ruler of the first unified German *Kaiserreich,* and Brahms had dedicated his *Triumphlied,* op. 55, to him in 1871 upon the military victory over France which brought the state into being. To any child of German Romanticism, this could easily constitute the "establishment of my promise with you, which I made to your father" (1 Kings 6:12).

Earlier, on folios 13v–14r, Brahms had already defined his idea of national identity through the concept of a pact between God and the *Väter* of the German *Volk:* "Unsere Väter hofften auf dich . . . und sollst deinen Kindern, und Kindeskindern kund thun" (Psalm 22:5–6), words that were to become parts of the *Fest- und Gedenksprüche,* op. 109. Indeed, for reasons I take up during my discussion of op. 109 in Chapter 5, Brahms turned back to those (apparently) previously copied texts when he composed the *Fest- und Gedenksprüche* in 1888, rather than employing the texts beginning on folio 15v which he probably copied closer to that time. In op. 109 the house metaphor occurs in passing and does not reveal the depth to which this image occupied Brahms in his Bible reading. Only through considering the sources behind the scenes does the interconnectedness of politics and religion in Brahms's music emerge more clearly.

When Brahms composed his *Vier ernste Gesänge* in 1896, he discarded the more public texts on these pages, both the concluding chapter 9 of Wisdom of Solomon as well as the initial 1 Kings 6. What remained were not only the intensely personal texts of songs one and two but also the hymn to love of 1 Corinthians 13, which explicitly ranks wisdom (along with faith and hope) beneath love. Whereas both wisdom and love are attributes that may be more public at one time and more private at another, the Corinthians text lends itself far more strongly to a private and personal reading.[65] Significant for the present context is the personal nature of this statement: Brahms is commenting at least as much on his own situation near the end of his life as he is on the world around him. When Brahms composed these songs in the spring and early summer of 1896, he was unaware that he had less than a year left to live. Nevertheless, he had suffered the loss of several friends during the previous few years (and he would later unveil the *Vier ernste Gesänge* among friends gathered after Clara Schumann's funeral), losses that, one could easily imagine, caused him to consider his own mortality. By posing Christian love *(caritas)* as a balm for his grief, Brahms was acknowledging the compatibility—perhaps even the necessary interpenetration—of Romanticism and Lutheranism. Yet, in his original conception, all of these texts bound up the religious with the national. And if an older composer muses on his own life situation in the *Vier ernste Gesänge*, we should also listen for the reverberations of the nation in that music. The German *Reich* (like the Austrian Empire) was headed for troubled times, and, as we shall see, Brahms knew it.[66]

Ein deutsches Requiem, Op. 45,
and the Apocalyptic Paradigm

Comfort and the Eternal Promise of Resolution

Brahms did not hesitate to use biblical texts for political expression, as the "Gebet eines Königs" makes clear. And as I have previously argued, the very use of Luther's Bible and other German sacred texts can take on implicit nationalistic (if not necessarily political) overtones. How does *Ein deutsches Requiem*, op. 45, Brahms's largest work on biblical texts, figure into this equation? On the face of it there is nothing remotely political about this piece. Rather it is usually understood as a personal philosophical statement on the need for comfort by those who survive the dead. Perhaps a more accurate statement, one made by Malcolm MacDonald in his 1990 Brahms biography, is that Brahms's *Requiem* offers "consolatory meditation on the common destiny of the dead and the living."[1]

Reading the *Requiem* this way accords well with what is known of the work's impetus: Brahms's reaction to the death of his friend and early mentor Robert Schumann in 1856 and of Brahms's own mother in 1865. Brahms actually composed the piece over the course of fourteen years in three stages. An earlier version of movement two was composed first, in 1854, as part of a work written in reaction to Schumann's attempted suicide in that year. Brahms was unable to finish that piece and eventually reused parts of it for his Piano Concerto no. 1 in D Minor, op. 15, which he completed in 1857. The next stage of the *Requiem*'s development is difficult to trace, but appears to have been spurred by the death of Brahms's mother in 1865. Within a few months of her death, the first and fourth movements had been finished, and the third, sixth, and seventh followed over the course of the next year and a half. Only after the official premiere of the work at Bremen on 10 April 1868 (Good Friday), and a repeat performance there three weeks later, did Brahms compose the movement with soprano solo and choir, which was then inserted as the fifth movement in the complete seven-movement work that was published later that year and premiered in Leipzig on 18 February 1869.

The addition of the fifth movement strongly affected the character of op. 45 both musically and textually. Musically, it provided a more gradual progression of keys from the middle to the end of the work. After the abrupt shift to E-flat in movement four (following on the heels of D major at the end of movement three), the G major of the inserted movement five relates to the preceding key, but through a fairly distant third relationship, as opposed to the stronger, relative minor relationship of C minor in movement six (which originally followed directly from the E-flat of movement four). Textually, movement five reinjected comfort *(Trost)* as a main theme of the piece. "Trost" is presented in the opening phrase of the *Requiem:* "Selig sind die da Leid tragen, denn sie sollen *getröstet* werden." Although the baritone soloist of movement three briefly takes up the question of *Trost* in his last utterance ("Nun, Herr, wes soll ich mich *trösten?*" bars 142–144), he does so as an expression of doubt and anxiety. Only in movement five does anticipation of comfort, in fact its promised delivery, become the central theme of the work.

Brahms had turned to the theme of "comfort" several times in his selection of sacred texts. At the end of the "Warum" motet, op. 74, no. 1, for example, comfort derives from the knowledge that death is God's will: "Mit Fried' und Freud' ich fahr dahin / in Gottes Willen / *getrost* ist mir mein Herz und Sinn / sanft und stille." In the second song of the *Vier ernste Gesänge,* op. 121, by contrast, comfort eludes both those who suffer and those who inflict suffering:

Ecclesiastes 4:1	Und siehe, da waren Tränen derer, die Unrecht litten und hatten keinen **Tröster,** und die ihnen Unrecht täten waren zu mächtig, **daß sie keinen Tröster haben konnten.**
	[And see, there were tears for they who suffered injustice and had no one to comfort them, / and those who committed injustice were too strong, / [so] that they could have no one comfort them.]

In addition to these passages that found their way into musical works, Brahms copied, but never set, the series of *Trost* texts on folio 14v of the biblical notebook that I mentioned in the previous chapter. Three consecutive texts on that page form a subgroup that expresses a nostalgic sense of sorrow, characterized by words such as "dahin" and "vergangen," and the reference to sorrow for one's (presumably deceased) mother:

Wisdom of Solomon 2:4	Unser Leben fährt **dahin,** als wäre eine Wolke da gewesen. [Our life will pass away, as if a cloud had been there.]
Jeremiah 8:20	Die Ernte ist **vergangen,** der Sommer ist **dahin.** [The harvest is past, the summer is ended.]
Psalm 35:14	Ich ging **traurig,** wie einer, der Leide trägt über seine Mutter. [I went about as one who laments for his mother.]

These are followed on the same page by a second group of three texts, which, while not necessarily reversing the mood of the first three, nevertheless point toward resolution by moving the focus from sorrow to comfort *(Trost):*

2 Corinthians 7:4	Ich bin erfüllt mit **Trost,** ich bin überschwänglich in Freuden, in aller unserer Trübsal. [I am filled with comfort, I am overfilled with joy amid all our affliction.]
Psalm 119:82	Meine Augen sehnen sich nach deinem Wort, und sagen: Wann **tröstest** du mich? [My eyes long for your word (promise) and ask: When will you comfort me?]
Job 21:34	Wie **tröstet** ihr mich so vergeblich! [How you comfort me so idly!]

Although Brahms likely copied these passages into his notebook after 1877, thus long after the *Requiem* was completed in 1869, their similarities to the *Requiem* are clear.[2] Compare, for example, the Wisdom of Solomon 2:4 text above with Psalm 39:8 from movement three: "Sie gehen daher wie ein Schemen." More generally, Jeremiah 8:20 above recalls the withered grass and fall blossoms of 1 Peter 1:24 in movement two of op. 45. And, of course, the wording of Psalm 35:14 above is strikingly similar to Isaiah 66:13 in movement five ("Ich will euch trösten wie einen seine Mutter tröstet"), with the connection to that movement's text strengthened by the word "traurig," which echoes "Ihr habt nun Traurigkeit" (John 16:22).

Thereafter it is specifically the *Trost* words in the next three passages on folio 14v that relate generally to the text of op. 45. Comfort, or *Trost,* is a central theme in the *Requiem;* it appears immediately in the opening verse from Matthew 5:4 ("Selig sind, die da Leid tragen, denn sie sollen *getröstet* werden") and again in the texts from movements three and five mentioned above. These two references from middle movements of the piece seem to form a separate inner dialogue, as a solo male voice in movement three seeks comfort that is offered—with obvious autobiographical connotations—by a solo female voice in movement five, "as a mother comforts her child." Brahms affords comfort a dualistic nature in op. 45: comfort is promised, and thus serves as a pivot between that which *is* and that which *will be*. By referring to the initial promise of *Trost* throughout the *Requiem*, Brahms is able to present a dichotomous viewpoint in the piece—that of the here and now and that of the hereafter. And as this theme recurs and develops across the work's seven movements, the separation between mundane and spiritual time realms emerges as a central idea in the piece.

Temporal divisions derive logically from the opening versicle, Christ's words (from the Sermon on the Mount in Matthew 5) on those who bear grief now but shall be comforted in the future. And this pattern continues further in verses 5 and 6 from Psalm 126, which make up the rest of the text to movement one:

	SORROW NOW (PRESENT)	COMFORT THEN (FUTURE)
Matthew 5:4	Blessed are they who bear grief	for they shall be comforted
Psalm 126:5, 6	They who sow tears	shall reap joy
	They go forth and weep, and carry noble seed	and come with joy and bring their sheaf

Some of this imagery is then picked up by the text of the second movement, where the farmer waits for the fruit of the earth before receiving rain, and where joy and gladness shall replace pain and suffering.

1 Peter 1:24	For all flesh is like grass / and all the glory of man like the blossoms of the grass. / The grass withers and the blossoms fall off.
James 5:7	Be patient now, dear brothers. / until the Lord's future. / See, the farmer waits / for the precious fruit of the earth, / and is patient for it, / until he receives the morning rain and the evening rain.

In a larger sense, the whole text of the second movement projects the minute oppositions of the previous one, as the transience of human flesh at the movement's outset is pitted against the eternal endurance of the Lord's word at its conclusion. Similar oppositions between worldly suffering and heavenly consolation across the work's seven movements help to carry the piece

through its various views of life and death, all deriving from the initial opposition of sorrow and promised comfort.

The possibility that the promise of comfort might be located simultaneously within human (worldly) time and beyond it in (divine) eternity is
central to the temporal framework of the *Requiem* and, by extension, to the
work's relevance to broader modes of thinking in nineteenth-century Germany. Although I pursue this idea more fully later in this chapter, it is worth
noting here how Brahms alludes to temporal ambiguity through a historical
confrontation of musical styles in his setting of the opening versicle from
Matthew (see ex. A.2 in the Appendix). When the chorus introduces the
opening text at bar 15 of movement one, the archaic quality of the sound
contrasts sharply with the murky and increasingly dissonant orchestral introduction that precedes it. The pure part writing, suspensions, syllabic
overlaps, and modal inflections of the choir evoke music of an earlier era
and specifically evoke the *stile antico* motet style of Heinrich Schütz and his
mid-seventeenth-century contemporaries. But that style is itself a fossilized
look back at the High Renaissance polyphonic style of the sixteenth century.
Brahms thus places the promise of comfort in a rich, telescoping musico-historical framework. We look back from the (nineteenth-century) present as
represented in Brahms's modern orchestral introduction (especially the sliding chromatic harmonies of bars 11–15) and the ensuing accompanied setting of the verse in bars 29–46, toward an earlier (seventeenth-century) style
that contains a backward glance of its own. At the end of the first large period of the movement (continuing beyond the musical example), the stylistic distinction between temporal realms disintegrates completely. Already in
bars 27–34 the orchestra's echo of the choir's cadence (bars 26–29) and the
trading of subphrases between choir and orchestra suggested a rejoining of
these previously isolated forces, before they merge completely in the long
pre-cadential passage of bars 37–42. Melding these two styles within the
setting of the opening verse helps project the promise and anticipation of
comfort across separate temporal realms.[3]

Within this opening to the piece one hears two melodic ideas that are often cited as ur-motives for the entire *Requiem*. The first, the violas' initial
gesture (B♭–C–D–C–B♭–A–G–A) has frequently been attributed to the chorale "Nun wer den lieben Gott läßt walten" (which Brahms is purported to
have mentioned as a chorale that "lay at the root of the entire work"); and
the opening three-note ascent in the sopranos at the words "Selig sind" (F–
A–B♭) has been cited as a central motive from which most of the themes in
the piece derive.[4] I am not comfortable with either nominee, and wonder if
both do not tell us more about how we like to think of Brahms than they do
about the music of the *Requiem* itself. For example, each plays into a separate favored truism about the composer, as I discussed in the introductory

chapter: one suggests that he was inspired by an ancient Protestant hymn (note Bach lurking in the background), while the other "proves" the economy and integral unity of his art.

What does seem to hold the first movement together, however, is the verbal gesture of the words "getröstet werden" and the musical phrases it generates. Several details argue for the verbal primacy of these motives: the text repetition at the word "getröstet" in bars 24–27 and again at 40–45; the orchestral echoes of the distinctive soprano figure (A–D–Bb–G–F) in bars 43–47; and finally the repetition of these events near the end of the movement. Although the last item may seem gratuitous, Brahms inserts a new, enigmatic orchestral interlude there (bar 136) that derives from the previously mentioned orchestral echo of the choir's "getröstet werden" clause (bars 28–29). That cadence was already reiterated at the end of the first large period in the movement, bars 45–47, where the echo cadenced deceptively to D-flat major exploiting the focus on D-flat from the opening phrase (a point I explicate later on). Now, at the end of the movement, D-flat is gone, but its enharmonic spelling, C-sharp, colors a new deceptive cadence to A major (bar 136; see ex. 3.1). Out of that distantly placed echo, Brahms develops a sequence of cadences that progress upward in real terms (from c'' in viola 1 at bar 137 to Bb'' in the flute at bar 139), but are held together by an underlying descending chain of thirds, one of Brahms's favorite architectonic devices. The effect is dazzling; out of the surprising A major in bar 136, the listener is drawn with accelerating musical speed toward a prolonged dominant cadence in bars 140–144. There the voices enter, and what had been a stretto of harmonic progressions in the preceding orchestral interlude becomes a cascade of voices on the text "getröstet werden," all driving home those words as the central meaning of the movement and F major as its home key. And the telescoping chronological framework that was created by the opening clash of musico-historical styles is reinterpreted more tangibly as an audibly perceptible headlong rush to the "present," that is, the strongest cadence to the tonic in the entire movement. Or, heard another way, the multiplicity implied by the shifting harmonic perspective of bars 136–139 and by the stretto of bars 140–144 could represent a variety of temporalities that are drawn together by the eternal promise of comfort.

The representation of juxtaposed temporalities through abrupt harmonic shifts is played out more vividly in the last movement. This is a special quality of the outer movements in the *Requiem*, which move independently of their inner counterparts—all of which will be discussed shortly. Movement five, by contrast, brings this interaction between the present need for, and the historical promise of, comfort into a more personal and visceral focus, largely through the quality of interaction between the soprano soloist and the choir. Brahms composed this movement while staying at his father's

Example 3.1   Ein deutsches Requiem, op. 45, movement one, bars 136–144: rising pitch and descending thirds.

home in Hamburg during the spring of 1868, following the two highly ac-
claimed Bremen performances of the (then) six-movement work. Possibly
fulfilling a preexisting seven-movement plan, he chose to add a second solo
with chorus to the piece.[5] It is by far the quietest, most uniformly slow, and
most intimate movement in the *Requiem* and thereby lends itself to biographical and subjective interpretation: as an elegy to Brahms's mother, for
example.[6]

Whereas the relationship of the baritone soloist and choir in movement
three (and later, on a smaller scale, in movement six) is fairly conventional
(i.e., the soloist introduces textual and musical material that is then expanded upon by the choir), in movement five the soloist and choir seem
to operate in closely related but clearly delineated spheres. One notices this
immediately in the disposition of texts: although the texts are similar in
content, the soloist and choir never sing the same text. As displayed below,
the soprano's words from John 16:22 resemble those of the choir from
Ecclesiasticus 51:35 when she sings "*Ich will euch* wieder sehen . . ." immediately before they sing "*Ich will euch* trösten . . .":

	Bars 4–16	Bars 16–23
Soprano solo (John 16:22)	Ihr habt nun Traurigkeit;	aber **Ich will euch wieder sehen** und euer Herz soll sich freuen, und euere Freude soll niemand von euch nehmen.
Choir (Isaiah 66:13)		Ich will euch trösten wie einen seine Mutter tröstet.

And later, when the soprano moves on to Ecclesiasticus 51:35, the key word
"Trost" in that text (from bar 34) prompts the choir to reiterate the relevant
passage ("Ich will euch trösten") from the Isaiah text:

	Bars 27–31	Bars 31–37; 38–49
Soprano solo (Ecclesiasticus 51:35)	Sehet mich an: ich habe eine kleine Zeit Mühe und Arbeit gehabt	und habe großen **Trost** funden;
Choir (Isaiah 66:13)		Ich will euch **trösten**

The relationship between soloist and choir here is far more than merely
syntactical, however: Brahms sets each of these text passages to melodic
lines that allude not only to each other but to other points in the movement
as well (see example A.3 in the Appendix). When the soprano sings "I will
see you again" at bar 16, she reiterates the opening eighth-note melody of
the movement, first heard (and now doubled by) the violins; as a return of

that material, then, her melody musically acts out the meaning of the text it-self. But refractions of the opening melody have been occurring constantly since the movement began. In the example I have highlighted significant melodic entrances through the first fourteen bars of the movement. Although they are certainly not identical, all are clearly related. In particular, the solo wind incipits that accompany the soprano soloist's initial melody seem at once like echoes of the strings at the beginning of the movement and like refractions of the soprano's slower melody. Likewise, the choir's material at bar 18 recalls the slower quarter-note motion of the cellos and basses from bars 1–3, while the choral sopranos echo the soloist in augmentation and transposed to D major. To add further depth to the swirl of thematic references beginning in bar 18, the flutes and clarinets simultaneously provide real-time (i.e., in eighth-note motion) and harmonically enriched recall of the violin's initial material, just as they had against the soprano soloist's first entrance (from bar 4).

What separates the winds' and the choir's material beginning in bar 16 most strongly from what had come before is the abrupt shift from the tonic G major to its dominant, D major.[7] Although Brahms frequently employs tonic-dominant formal polarities within the first section of three-part song form movements like this one, the lack of a modulatory transition is striking here.[8] A gradual change to D major would have been out of place, for it would imply a development from one temporality to another rather than illustrating the isolation of the soloist, and her promise to return, from the choir and its offer of comfort.

By suddenly placing the material at bar 18 in a related yet clearly delineated key area, Brahms intensifies the related but separate quality of the movement's texts. In fact, the tension between tonic and dominant is uncommonly strong in this movement. Brahms studiously avoids any strong closure to G major, opting for a delicate balancing act instead, in which D major, as often as not, serves to begin and end periods, either as a dominant harmony within G major or as a momentarily tonicized key area. Take, for example, the opening of the movement. Brahms begins off-balance rhythmically by displacing the bass line from where we might expect it to be, thereby landing on D for the first downbeat of the piece rather than the tonic G, which might be more conventional. (As I discuss shortly, this fits into an important pattern of off-balance entrances in the *Requiem*.) Then, when the strings finally have righted themselves rhythmically enough to produce a convincing half cadence to the dominant at bar 3, the soprano enters on D as the dominant continues unresolved through bar 5. Even when the tonic G major arrives in bar 6, it takes on a flat seventh, F natural, which pushes the harmony to C (bar 7), which then in turn is chromaticized to a C-sharp (viola, beat 4) en route back to D beginning in bar 8.

Having hovered delicately through this initial floating harmonic arrangement, the soprano seems to straddle the two key areas when she joins the choir in bars 19–23: although her melody fits easily within the prevailing key of D major there, nothing would preclude harmonizing her melody in G major. More significantly, her closing gesture, E–D, is only one in a series of such melodic cadences at transition points throughout the movement, beginning with the opening phrase in violin 1 upon which she alighted in bar 4. There the direction of the motive is upward (although the upbeat eighth notes in the cellos and bass offer a countereffect whereby E might be heard as the first note in the pair), but more often E–D cadences in this movement form falling gestures that are usually appoggiaturas. Brahms uses this motive at main transition points, and nearly all fall on full or half cadences to D major (such as the two that I have just mentioned).

Bars 46–49 are pivotal on this count; they bring the modulatory middle section of the movement to completion, shortly after the soprano and orchestra have ended a tortuous harmonic path away from and back to D major, through B-flat and B major on the way. Just as the choir had punctuated the arrival to B major in bar 34 with an oddly dissonant yet sweet cadential comma, they return at bar 43 with the same material, now transposed to D major to begin what should be a retransition to the tonic G. As the choir extends the cadence to D major in bar 46 for three additional bars, all but the basses close with suspensions and/or appoggiaturas. Brahms accentuates these figures by allowing each of the top three choral parts in bar 48 to move on a different beat. Against the choir, the orchestra reintroduces the first violins' undulating D–E figure from bar 4, now refracted throughout the ensemble and expanded to other pitches (and intervals) as well : F#–G in the viola and C#–E in violin 2 and flute 2. The direction of the dyad is yet more ambiguous here, alternating between D–E and E–D, but finally ending with the choral sopranos on E–D.

Again the E–D motive accompanies a vague transitional moment in the movement. For as the music crosses the double bar at 49, what initially sounds like a recapitulation proves instead to be more modulatory and developmental material (a typically Brahmsian "recapitulatory overlap").[9] D major is never more ambiguous than in these bars: initially thwarted by the C natural in the flutes, its resolution to G major brings no more stability as the added F's in bars 51–52 create a new dominant-seventh harmony to further propel the harmony toward C minor (bar 53) and E-flat minor before settling on D again in bar 59. From there the movement finally settles into G major, ending with a codetta in bars 72–82, where the soprano reemphasizes the E–D motive as she reiterates the words "ich will euch wider sehen" three times while the choir, for the first time, adds its syntactically matching verse, "ich will euch Trösten." The floating quality of that final D from the soloist is significant; the ambiguous opening G major chord of the ensuing sixth movement maintains D as its uppermost pitch, and the sopranos enter on D in bar 3. That, however, is a separate issue to which I return in greater detail near the end of the chapter.

Everything about the fifth movement of *Ein deutsches Requiem* conveys a delicate balance, epitomized perhaps by the E–D motive at its end. As a last breath of calm before the tumult of the sixth movement, this balance should not be mistaken for resolution. This is a balance born of tension, a cautious perch on a precipice. That musical quality reflects perfectly the anticipation of the text and the division between the soloist and the choir and the temporal duality captured by the present promise of future *Trost*.

The Word as Apocalypse

Within the tradition of interpreting the fifth movement as Brahms's elegy to his mother, Michael P. Steinberg hears the soprano solo as the very voice of Christiane Brahms. Steinberg takes the choir, by contrast, "to represent music itself, which claims the capacity to console *as* a mother would," thus empowering music with broad iconic meaning: "The consolation no longer available from the mother resides now in music alone, now in the inner self alone. Expressed in the *Requiem* in the reminiscent presence of a soprano voice uttering words of literal consolation, the consolation of music is then internalized, in the later works, into patterns of sound alone."[10] Steinberg's reading is a bold attempt to transfer a basic and deep meaning into the absolute musical canon (as represented by Brahms): an enduring quest in the tradition of music criticism of the past two centuries. If Steinberg is right, the *Requiem* is certainly the piece to which one ought to look for a source of meaning in Brahms.

Locating comfort in "patterns of sound" alone, however, privileges Brahms's role as a composer above all his other possible identities. By personally selecting sixteen separate passages from the Old and New Testaments as the text for the work, Brahms also strongly identified himself in the *Requiem* as a reader of Luther's Bible and—by extension—as a lover of the German language and the Protestant culture in which it developed. Steinberg may be correct in theorizing that Brahms retreated into a "North German tradition stretching back to Bach and Schütz,"[11] but the tradition is far broader than that. Music is only one component of the larger North German cultural tradition within which Brahms located himself and from which he derived "comfort." Lutheranism was surely a central aspect of that culture. And it is risky to consider a work such as op. 45 without paying some attention to its theological meaning, or at least to how religious thinking played into the work. As I argued in the preceding chapter, Brahms's religiosity is hard to pin down, but it is best described as cultural Protestantism; his deep interest in the words of Luther's Bible, even the faith therein, were more a matter of learned culture than of practiced religion.

It was inevitable that some of Brahms's contemporaries would seek a more definitive Christian statement than Brahms was willing to offer. Brahms was immediately confronted with this challenge by Reinthaler's suggestion to add a more proper Christian core to this work for its Bremen premiere. When Brahms distanced himself from the word "deutsch" in his response, he may have been reacting to the religious overtones of then-current politics in German-speaking lands. (See the Reinthaler-Brahms exchange in Chapter 2.) Brahms's ambivalence about his own chosen title for the piece had surfaced earlier in letters to Clara Schumann and Albert Dietrich where he referred to it as "a sort of *German Requiem*" and "my so-called German *Requiem*," respectively.[12] At least two possible explanations account for Brahms's misgivings about the title of op. 45. The first concerns the connections between the title's cultural meaning and political circumstances in Germany during 1866. Brahms seems to have worked most continuously on the *Requiem* during the winter and spring of that year; Hermann Levi asserted that most of the work was composed at Karlsruhe, where Brahms was living with Julius Allgeyer from February to April 1866.[13] It was during these same months that the war between Prussia and Austria broke out. Although brief, the war marked a decisive turning point in the political and social history of German-speaking lands in the nineteenth century. For decades, and especially since the revolutionary year of 1848, German political leaders had sought to establish a *großdeutsch* state, one that would encompass both Protestant and Catholic lands. The Austro-Prussian War dashed those hopes. At the same time, Prussia's military was propelled toward its preeminent position in central Europe, presaging the victory over France a few years later that completed the *kleindeutsch* solution of a unified *Kaiserreich* under Prussia's King Wilhelm and his chancellor, Bismarck. It was not long before Prussia's Protestant Church began to exert considerable influence in Wilhelm's government and Bismarck embarked on his *Kulturkampf* against Catholic influence in the empire.

In contrast to what would be his enthusiastic response to the events of 1870–71 (to which his *Triumphlied,* op. 55, stands as a monument), Brahms was apparently opposed to the Austro-Prussian War. In 1866 he wrote to Allgeyer, "Whether they fight for thirty or for seven years, it will be fought as little for humanity now as when they already fought for thirty and for seven years," a reference to the religious wars of the seventeenth century.[14] Brahms's friend and biographer Max Kalbeck averred that in the mid-1860s Brahms, like many other German liberals, had not yet been won over to the *kleindeutsch* Prussian cause and still had misgivings about Bismarck, despite the deep veneration he later developed for the "Iron Chancellor."[15] In this context, especially when one considers the strong religious overtones of the Austrian-Prussian conflict, it is quite possible to understand Brahms's disclaimer in October 1867 that he would "gladly omit the [word] German" in the work's title as a comment on political events of the day. In sum, Brahms might have been expressing a fear that with that title he would appear to be siding with Prussia, in that the German language to which the word "deutsch" in the work's title refers could be understood to represent northern Protestantism as opposed to Austrian Catholicism.

If this was the case, Brahms's sensitivity to the issue might also account for an acerbic remark he made to his friend Adolf Schubring, a prominent music critic, who in 1869 published the first substantial analytical commentary of the piece in the *Allgemeine musikalische Zeitung*. In his essay Schubring observed that the various themes of the third movement's eight sections all derive from three manifestations of a basic contrapuntal configuration. In a letter of 16 February 1869, Brahms thoroughly rejected Schubring's analysis, claiming the any resemblance among the themes was at best coincidental and at worst a sign of weak inspiration. More important, he added the sarcastic quip, "Have you then not yet discovered the political allusion in my *Requiem*? 'Gott erhalte' was begun precisely in the year 1866."[16] Brahms is alluding here to the similarly coincidental resemblance between the orchestra's introductory theme in movement one (see Appendix, ex. A.2) and Haydn's patriotic hymn "Gott erhalte unsern Kaiser" (perhaps better known by now as "Deutschland, Deutschland über alles"). Although Brahms's suggestion that his tune had a political source is surely not to be taken seriously, his comment does reveal his awareness—perhaps his anxiety—that his piece could be rightly or wrongly construed in political terms that had been associated with the Austro-Prussian War.

Brahms's religious convictions, murky though they may be, can more often than not be connected to secular concerns (philosophy, historicity, the veneration of folk culture, and so on). Religion also strongly infused politics in nineteenth-century Germany, and the *Requiem* belongs to a small group of Brahms's sacred works that access a major vein of religiously inspired political thinking of the day: the apocalyptic anticipation of the new German *Reich*. Along with two other biblically based works, the *Triumphlied*, op. 55 (1872), and the *Fest- und Gedenksprüche*, op. 109 (1889), the *Requiem* can be related to millennial concepts engaged by nationalistic fervor over the founding of the empire. Clearly, the latter two *opera* prompt more obvious and direct connections to apocalyptic thinking. Brahms based his *Triumphlied* on selections from Revelation 19, the most apocalyptic book in the Bible. He began composing the *Triumphlied* in the fall of 1870 in anticipatory celebration over the imminent Prussian victory in the war with France. In the *Fest- und Gedenksprüche,* three pieces for a cappella double chorus, Brahms uses the historical aura of the Bible and a massive vocal effect to depict the German nation directly and to comment on ominous divisions in the *Kaiserreich* near the end of the century.

The *Requiem,* as I outlined at the beginning of the chapter, was occasioned by more personal circumstances. But just as the German language of its text raises issues of cultural nationalism, certain features of the musical structure in op. 45 speak to the influence of biblical historical paradigms, and specifically to an apocalyptic worldview, on Brahms's compositional approach in the piece. Apocalypse is merely one aspect of biblical history, and only one of many that has affected Western art and culture. Given the Bible's centrality in the canon of Western religion, morality, and literature, it is hardly remarkable that its underlying structures and premises have left their mark on a variety of literary and artistic works. Several qualities distinguish biblical history from the historical views that characterized Greco-Roman thought. Cataloguing those differences, M. H. Abrams notes that "while the main line of change in the prominent classical patterns of history . . . is continuous and gradual, the line of change in Christian history (and this difference is pregnant with consequences) is right angled: the key events are abrupt, cataclysmic, and make a drastic, even an absolute, difference."[17] As Abrams goes on to list the great events of the Bible (Creation, the Fall, the birth of Jesus, and the Second Coming), he emphasizes the importance of separate ages in the biblical story. In this scheme the Apocalypse ushers in the final age, "the last act of the drama of history."[18] That age is, however, closely related to the origins of human history: the biblical end returns us to the beginning, to an age of felicity. The various ages, then, are related, even if they are separated by sharp and swift divisions. In distinction to our modern point of view, then (in which the word apocalypse is associated with "vague connotations of doom," according to Frank Kermode),[19] apocalypse can signify the arrival of redemption and renewal around sudden and violent events.

The French Revolution was seen as just such an event by nineteenth-century Europeans. Particularly in light of the Revolution's challenge to traditional theosophy, the familiar right-angle outlines of biblical history were adapted to mundane human history. Abrams writes, "The later eighteenth century was another age of apocalyptic expectation, when the glory and promise of the American Revolution and, much more, of the early years of the French Revolution, revived among a number of English Nonconformists . . . millenarian excitement," adding, "Major Romantic poets shared this hope in the French Revolution as the portent of universal felicity, as did Hölderlin and other young radicals in Germany."[20] When the promise of the Revolution faded, the paradigm of apocalypticism remained, channeled now through more secular goals. One realization of the apocalyptic was in the teleological paradigm that infuses much literature and other artistic endeavor throughout the nineteenth century. For Abrams, the case in point is Wordsworth's *Prelude;* for Kermode, it is a series of canonical literary works of the nineteenth and twentieth centuries. Although one hears less mention of apocalyptic paradigms in music (before the likes of Wagner and Mahler anyway), it is perhaps the same force that drives the shift in emphasis toward the ends of large-scale works, symphonies in particular. Anticipation and focus on a utopian end is familiar enough to music historians: the orientation toward endings in German music of the nineteenth century is a commonplace of our critical tradition. To be sure, *this* is the spiritual "Beyond" to which critics such as E. T. A. Hoffmann claim music has the ability to carry us.[21]

Recognizing the intersection of religious myth and historical paradigm as a type, Kermode writes of the "myth of Transition," the idea that "before the end there is a period which does not properly belong either to the End or to the saeculum preceding it. It has its own characteristics."[22] The myth involves believing that one lives at the critical turning point in human history, the final moment, in effect, before all moments cease. Imagining such a scenario allows one to see one's own death as equated with the end of time. Apocalypse, Kermode argues, is a fictive account that allows us to project ourselves beyond the age of transition, beyond our here and now, to imagine the end (and beginning, for that matter) that we cannot know. Kermode writes: "Men, like poets, rush 'into the middest,' *in medias res,* when they are born; they also die *in mediis rebus,* and to make sense of their span they need fictive concords with origins and ends, such as give meaning to lives and to poems. The End, they imagine, will reflect their irreducibly intermediary occupations. They fear it, and as far as we can see have always done so; the End is a figure of their own deaths."[23] Our life, then, is part of the transition, our death part of the greater finality.

An important component in the projection beyond the end is the idea of timelessness. Ironically, music—its temporal nature notwithstanding—may be the ideal medium for articulating timelessness. Just as the Romantics valued music above other arts for its nonreferential abstract qualities, music is best able to depict the "'dissociation' from earthly dependence—from purposes as well as from emotional imitation—to be raised to the depiction of the celestial."[24] Divisions between earthly and heavenly realms may be defined along several different axes, one of which is temporal: the presence of time in human existence, and the absence of time in divine existence. Within Brahms's *Requiem* itself, temporality is not so overtly messianic. Rather it arises through the dichotomous nature of the comfort promise—something offered in the present (and running throughout human time) that will come in a realm beyond human time, in eternity or the final age. Perhaps it is the distinction Brahms draws between these temporal realms that separates his from standard Requiem Mass settings of the Western tradition; whereas the typical Latin Requiem is apocalyptic in the more conventional sense (focusing on the Last Judgment), Brahms's *Deutsches Requiem* is apocalyptic in a deeper sense, referring as it does to the profound impact of the biblical-historical narrative on the modern paradigms of human history.

From its premiere down to the present, commentators have attempted to compare Brahms's *German Requiem* with the Latin Requiem Mass, noting—almost unanimously—that Brahms's work focuses on comfort for the living rather than salvation for the souls of the dead (à la MacDonald). Mediation between the common destiny of the dead and the living is epitomized by the transformation of the opening F major music and the words "Selig sind die da Leid tragen" (Blessed are those who mourn) at the return of that F major music in the final movement and its words, "Selig sind die Toten" (Blessed are the dead). The significance of that transformation for most listeners is borne out by the frequent attempts to demonstrate formal symmetry in the *Requiem*. Audibly, symmetry is suggested by the return to F major, the clear thematic links in the outer movements, and the syntactical parallelism around the "Selig" phrases that I just noted. A symmetrical interpretation of the *Requiem* depends on hearing the F major first and seventh movements as a connected part of the overall harmonic scheme (which I have outlined in fig. 3.1). In my own hearing of the work, however, I have always been struck at how little the final movement sounds like a progression from what preceded. Perhaps too much is invested in the lengthy and weighty C major fugue at the end of movement six. Although the opening gesture of movement seven, with its leap from F to E-flat and the gently descending line of the sopranos, clearly recalls movement one, it is not so much a logical return to that music as it is a sudden resumption of it. Heard in this way, the connected outer movements form a frame to movements two through six; they are a musically detached entity, operating in a separate sphere. Within this frame, the middle five movements of the *Requiem* form a peregrination, an essay in transience, indeed, in the earthly state of transition and anticipation, and it is in this sense that the work can be related to contemporaneous apocalypticism.

Various writers have attempted to demonstrate that the succession of keys in these middle five movements forms a logically directed harmonic progression from and to F major.[25] Indeed, there is some general connotation of direction in moving from the B-flat sphere of movement two toward the C major that emerges in a celebratory fugue at the end of movement six. It is, however, counterproductive to try and trace a direct line between the two. Rather, the primary keys of the inner movement can all be related individu-

Movement	1	2	3	4	5	6	7
Prim. keys	F	B♭min-maj	D min-maj	E♭	G	C min-maj	F
Sec. keys		G♭			E♭	F♯ min	A
Relation to F		iv IV	vi VI	IV/IV	V/V	V V	

Figure 3.1   Keys of the seven movements in *Ein deutsches Requiem*, op. 45. (Secondary keys listed here are only those marked by a change of key signature in the score. All keys are major unless otherwise noted.)

ally more or less closely to F major, as indicated in the bottom row of fig. 3.1. Movements two through six do not progress so much as they wander within the orbit of F major.

Wandering implies motion, and motion is presented as a musical topos from the work's outset (see Appendix, ex. 2), first by the F pedal in the bottom range and shortly thereafter by the overlapping chromatic descents and suspension-heavy voice leading in bars 3–15. The repeated quarter notes in the bass provide a temporal background against which the middle strings spin their dense contrapuntal web. And whereas it might be too facile simply to translate the steady passage of musical time that is articulated by the repeated quarter notes as a metaphor for real (i.e., human, historical) time, a variety of musical and textual details in the orchestral introduction to the first movement nevertheless point to a symbolic representation of time.[26] The second cellos' unprepared E-flat in bar 2, a dissonant seventh against the continuing low F, immediately evokes a sense of discontinuity since, technically, it should proceed from a missing consonant F.[27] Thus there is no clear tonal "beginning" but rather the emergence of something that began before the beginning of this piece or is in some other way inaudible to us.

As the E-flat descends chromatically in the second cello, overlapping thematic entries by the first cellos (bar 3) and violas (bars 5 and 7) begin to pile up, each spawning a chromatically descending line of its own. Although repeated thematic entries and descending chromatic lines have the potential strongly to define and measure a sense of time, the effect here is quite different. Rather than organizing his material in a rational manner, Brahms offsets the various melodic elements in these opening bars unpredictably: any given tone in the descending lines takes on a new harmonic role and is pitted against a different portion of the thematic statement upon its reappearance. For example, when the second cellos' initial thematic entry on B-flat is repeated an octave higher by the first violas in bar 7, it coincides with a dominant-seventh harmony (sub-posed by the tonic F pedal), not with the subdominant B-flat harmony over which it appeared in bar 3. Likewise, when the first violas cadence to A in bar 8, that note is reinterpreted as a suspension as the other parts continue their downward slide to a subdominant

harmony (major then minor) in bar 9. While the individual musical compo-
nents used in these bars are familiar, their constant reconfiguration against
one another confuses any sense of direction and progression the opening
passage may possess and the concomitant sense of time they convey.

In his analysis of op. 45, Adolf Schubring states that "already the first
bars leave no doubt that we have a thoroughly modern work before us."[28]
Our own late-twentieth-century interpretive stance might allow us to hear
in Brahms's quasi-imitative texture an air of the antique in these opening
bars, much as the similar-sounding contrapuntal texture among the strings
in the opening of Mendelssohn's Symphony no. 5 ("Reformation") are often taken to evoke Palestrinian counterpoint as a symbol of the Catholic
Church.[29] But Schubring was more concerned with vertical elements and
chromatic inflections that were peculiar to mid-nineteenth-century harmonic language. Especially characteristic is the use of the flatted sixth, D-
flat, which is briefly tonicized in bar 11 (forcing the bass pedal off F for the
first time) to highlight its function within the (German) augmented-sixth
harmony preceding the cadence of bar 12.

If the modernity of these opening bars is relative to the perspective of the
listener, their currency is thrown into stark relief by the choral statement
that follows. When the voices enter with the beatitude of Matthew 5:4, their
a cappella, highly consonant part writing marks them as archaic in contrast
to the preceding orchestral strains. What connects the two otherwise separate ideas is the presence of the flatted sixth degree, D-flat, as a constant dissonant element (enharmonically spelled as C-sharp in the choral bass at bars
37–39).[30] D-flat is more than local chromatic inflection in movement one,
however; it forms a secondary key area to the tonic F, allowing Brahms to
construct the movement upon a large-scale fluctuation between the keys of F
major and D-flat major (see fig. 3.2). The interplay of those keys provides
Brahms with a means for constructing a symmetrical three-part form, corresponding to the da capo disposition of the text, in which Matthew 5:4 begins and ends the movement. But cutting across such neat formal schemes is
a separate characteristic element, namely, the pulsating pedal figure and
overlapping quasi-imitative counterpoint of the orchestral introduction. As
indicated in fig. 3.2, that material intersects the tripartite, symmetrical structure of movement one at bars 65–79 and 96–104. In each instance, the resumption of the opening material suggests a new beginning and thus a formal division within the movement. But in both cases, the sense of beginning
merely blurs the formal divisions of the movement and thereby confuses the
listener's perception of time, that is, the perception of where we are within
the movement vis-à-vis the repetition of earlier material and the return to
the initial key, F major.

With that in mind, it is interesting to note how frequently Brahms begins

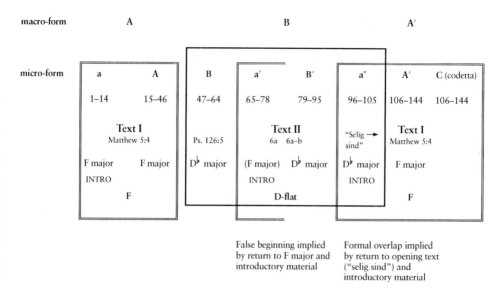

Figure 3.2   Overlapping formal divisions in *Ein deutsches Requiem*, op. 45, movement one.

movements off of the tonic or with an awkward rhythmic gesture in the *Requiem*. Although the beginning of movement two is fairly unremarkable in this regard, the use of the dominant-note pickup (F to B-flat) does provide continuity with the preceding (first) movement and thereby raises again the issue of time and motion. Movement three also begins on the dominant pitch, A, but fails to establish a clear tonic until the cellos' C-sharp in bar 7 prepares a cadence to D minor. More important, perhaps, is the vague rhythmic profile at the outset of this movement (ex. 3.2). Against the *piano* octave A's of the horns, the low strings are unable to provide a clear sense of meter as they melodically cough up an echo of the descending bass figure that began movement two, while rhythmically they weakly recall the martial rhythms that accompanied the initial statement of the fugue-like chorus at the end of that movement. In fact, there have been no completely satisfying cadences to a root-position tonic when the entire opening period closes in bars 102–104 on octave D's. Potential resting points at bars 16, 33, 48, and 93 are all undercut by some sort of deceptive cadence or dominant pedal.[31] Similarly, the off-balance rhythm with which Brahms begins movement five makes it difficult to hear the bar line in the initial five-beat phrase. Earlier I posited that the bass line of these bars is offset rhythmically: the initial G sounds more like a downbeat than the upbeat that is notated. Brahms presents us with a bass line here that could just as easily be in triple meter, and is only reined in to the stated common time by the force of the bar lines. In fact, he would later use this very bass line, in 3/8 meter, as the second

Example 3.2   Ein deutsches Requiem, movement three: unstable beginning.

theme of movement two from his Fourth Symphony (played by the cellos from bar 41).[32]

Movement Six and the Apocalyptic Moment

Independently, the introductions to these movements do not draw attention to themselves as unstable or problematic. But taken as a whole, they form a pattern of vague beginnings, another metaphor for wandering, like the undirected harmonic progression that their main keys form. Wandering also implies transience, and transience of various types dominates the text of these movements: the "withered grass" of movement two; the days of a life that are but a hand's breadth in movement three; and the soul that "longs" for the courts of the Lord in movement four. Of course, the most concrete manifestation of wandering in the text of the *Requiem* occurs at the beginning of movement six. (The text of that movement is presented as fig. 3.3; bars 1–37 are given as Appendix ex. 3). Following the harmonically unstable undulation between G major and D minor that begins the movement, Brahms avoids establishing C minor through the first period, implying F minor or a modally colored G major through bar 16, and he only establishes C minor through a half cadence to G in bar 32. The "walking" figure in the lower strings and the meandering harmonic progression paint a picture of searching and impermanence—perhaps the clearest tone painting in the piece.

After this brief epigrammatic passage from Hebrews 13, Brahms employs the most apocalyptic text in the *Requiem,* a passage from 1 Corinthians 15 that is heavily laden with revelatory symbolism and replete with mysteries—the last trumpet blast and the resurrection of the dead. Even the language with which the baritone soloist introduces this new text is revelatory: "Siehe, ich sage euch ein Geheimnis." Continuing on, both the mystery and transformation referred to in the text are musically depicted by the suddenness of the modulation that occurs in bars 28–34, where the soloist appropriates the alto's languorous G (at pitch) and effects a common-tone modulation when the high D-flat to which he leaps is tonicized in bar 30,

Hebrews 13:14

Denn wir haben hie keine bleibende Statt, sondern die zukünftige suchen wir.	For here we have no lasting city, but we are looking for the city that is to come.

1 Corinthians 15: 51–2

Siehe, ich sage euch ein Geheimnis: Wir werden nicht alle entschlafen, wir werden aber alle verwandelt werden; und dasselbige plötzlich, in einem Augenblick, zu der Zeit der letzten Posaune. Denn es wird die Posaune schallen, und die Toten werden auferstehen unverweslich, und wir werden verwandelt werden.	Listen, I will tell you a mystery! We will not all die, but we will all be changed, in a moment, in the twinkling of an eye, at the last trumpet. For the trumpet will sound, and the dead will be raised imperishable, and we will be changed.

1 Corinthians 15: 54–55

Dann wird erfüllet werden das Wort, das geschrieben steht: "Der Tod, ist verschlungen in den Sieg. Tod, wo ist dein Stachel? Hölle, wo ist dein Sieg?"	Then the saying that is written will be fulfilled "Death has been swallowed up in victory." "Where, O death, is your victory? Where, O death, is your sting?"

Revelation 4:11

Herr, du bist würdig zu nehmen Preis und Ehre und Kraft, denn du hast alle Dinge geschaffen, und durch deinen Willen haben sie das Wesen und sind geschaffen.	You are worthy, our Lord and God, to receive glory and honor and power, for you created all things, and by your will they existed and were created.

Figure 3.3   Text and translation of *Ein deutsches Requiem*, movement six.

only to be *re*interpreted as $\hat{5}$ in the new and distant key of F-sharp minor, in which the ensuing passage is set.

Figure 3.4 contains a schematic outline of movement six. As opposed to the lack of direction in the overall *Requiem*, there is a definite linear progression through this movement. The musical *Verwandlung* brought on by the baritone's vision produces a harmonic instability, F-sharp minor, that serves as a mere transitory station and provides kinetic impetus toward the establishment of the elusive tonic, C minor. Brahms reaches the remote intermediate key through the enharmonic modulation at bar 30, just mentioned. Enharmonicism here may be understood as a musical symbol of *Geheimnis*. Consequently, Brahms requires a similarly sudden musical transition to C minor in bars 67–76, which introduce the initial exposition of the chorus's *vivace* music. With the chorus answering in stark unison, the baritone now resolves C-sharp up to D, beginning a three-step sequential ascent to an E-flat-based harmony which resolves to C by bar 82 (ex. 3.3).[33] The shifting harmonies are carried by the trombones and tuba, which aurally evoke the apocalyptic moment by their first appearance since movement three. Brahms arrests the sequence in bar 75 by sub-posing a low G,

Bars	Andante			accel.	Vivace			
	1–28	28–33	33–67	68–81	82–107	108–127	128–207	208–349
Text incipit	Denn wir haben hie (Chorus)	Siehe, ich sage euch (Baritone)	Wir werden nicht alle (Baritone/chorus)	zu der Zeit (Baritone/chorus)	Denn es wird die Posaune (Chorus)	dann wird erfüllet werden	Der Tod ist verschlung-en	Herr du bist würdig (Fugue)
Key	(C minor)–V	(Db = C#) →	F# minor	mod.	C minor	(Db) →	C minor	C major
	UNSTABLE	→	→ stable (but distant)	// trans.	(ARRIVAL)	→	**ARRIVAL**	

Figure 3.4   Schematic outline of *Ein deutsches Requiem*, op. 45, movement six.

thereby returning to the very harmony, a first-inversion E-flat major chord, with which he began the *Geheimnis* music back in bar 29. Just as that earlier E-flat had resulted from an unexpected pivot over a timpani roll on G, the return to a G harmony in bar 76 does not grow logically out of the preceding sequence but rather dissolves that material and, by extension, all of the intervening F-sharp minor revelatory music. The net effect is to release a torrent of the pent-up dominant capacity of G, thereby strongly pushing the movement forward toward the long-awaited arrival of C minor with the choral entrance at bar 82. By the time the solo baritone returns in bar 109 to complete the prophecy, there is no looking back.

The baritone serves a prophetic function textually and a catalytic function musically; that is, the soloist heralds the mysteries of Scripture as he provides modulatory musical bridges between more stable choral episodes. Earlier, I posited that the sixth movement of the *Requiem* is progressive and harmonically directed toward its conclusion, unlike the piece as a whole. The same is true to a lesser degree in two other movements in the *Requiem*, the second and third, the other large movements that also begin relatively slowly in a minor key and end with a faster tempo, in the parallel major key, and with fugue-like material. Compared to these, the sixth movement seems to form an apex, an apotheosis of those progressively directed movements and of the general sense of wandering across all five of the inner movements in the piece. Indeed, its structure is tighter, more urgent than in the previous movements. Nowhere is that difference more tangible than in the soloist's final entrance, "dann wird erfüllet, das Wort das geschrieben steht," where the previously mysterious E-flat harmony and leap to D-flat sound breath-

Example 3.3 Ein deutsches Requiem, op. 45, movement six: three-step sequential ascent to C minor.

less. Now the mysterious D-flat is immediately "swallowed up" in a more logical (and hence directed) harmonic progression, in which D-flat descends to C and then B natural, preparing an immediate return of G as a dominant harmony in bars 118–122.

While the baritone's repeated motive (G–B♭–E♭–D♭) registers important structural moments throughout the movement, it also works along with his text to propel the musical material forward through an underlying rising pitch pattern. As noted earlier, the initial statement of this motive in bars 28–32 highlights the ambiguous role of D-flat/C-sharp. Brahms then "resolves" that pitch upward through the ascending sequence in bars 67–73. At first hearing it would sound as if D-flat resolves downward to C when

Example 3.4   Ein deutsches Requiem, op. 45, movement six, bars 122–133: chromatic octave ascent in choir from C-sharp to E.

the motive recurs, beginning in bar 108, specifically in bars 116–117. But Brahms has not finished with D-flat. An arresting and tonally perturbing passage intrudes at bars 122–133 (ex. 3.4) in which the choir moves upward chromatically in octaves on the word "Tod" (interspersed with part writing on the words "wo ist dein Stachel") from C-sharp to E-flat, before crowning its ascent by arriving on E natural at the word "Hölle" in bar 159. What we hear in this passage is a rough, more guttural rendition of the transitional sequence from bar 67. Even here, then, after the baritone has completed his solo, the motor of his repeated motive is still driving the music forward. Only now the chromatic ascent is carried as far as E natural, thus "transforming" the critical third-scale degree (E) in the process of moving from C minor to C major.

Fulfillment is the baritone's goal: fulfillment of "das Wort, das geschrieben steht." Only then ("*dann* wird erfüllet") will victory be achieved ("Der Tod ist verschlungen in den Sieg"). Fulfillment may be more than a localized concern, however. The baritone's motive here repeats the arpeggiated triad with which he entered in bar 28 ("Siehe ich sage euch ein Geheimnis; ex. 3.5A). It may thus also provide a connection to previous movements and cements the vague sense of progress from B-flat in movement two through C in movement six that I mentioned earlier. Similar instances of this motive occur in movement two as the theme of the fugal conclusion beginning in bar 206 (ex. 3.5B), and in movement five in bars 27–29, at a brief transition sung by the soprano soloist (ex. 3.5C). An arpeggiation of a major chord hardly constitutes a relationship among motives, but there are other striking similarities connecting these moments as well. Most noticeably, all three instances share a remarkably similar rhythmic profile and are accompanied by a relatively thin orchestral texture (especially in movements five and six). And all three instances of the motive occur at transitional junctures in their respective movements: its initial appearance in movement two completes a sudden transition from B-flat minor to B-flat major and initiates the lengthy choral section that concludes the movement; in movement five the motive ends on B-flat, but now effecting a common-tone modulation from D major; and, as we have just seen, it suddenly introduces the F-sharp minor episode in movement six, also by a common-tone modulation.

Donald Francis Tovey recognized the similarity of these motives in his analysis of op. 45 but dismissed them as coincidental. Their dissimilar texts, Tovey argued, provided no context in which to hear them as related, and therefore rendered any motivic congruity happenstance.[34] Yet there is, in fact, a textual connection across these instances; each sets or is somehow connected to a prophetic announcement. While this is readily apparent from the signal words "sehet" and "siehe" in movements five and six, it pertains to movement two as well (though less obviously). The passage from Isaiah 35 that Brahms uses there, announcing the coming of the Lord's ransomed, closes thirteen chapters (23–35) of the "Oracle concerning Sidon" which include the so-called "Isaiah Apocalypse." Like the later chapters of the book, which Brahms marked extensively in his own copy of the Bible, it shares an apocalyptic tone of Israel redeemed, Zion returned, and thus

Example 3.5   Baritone's "revelatory" motive in *Ein deutsches Requiem.* op. 45: (A) movement six, bars 28–32; (B) movement two, bars 206–208; (C) movement five, bars 27–29.

serves a prefiguratory function for Brahms, as an Old Testament signpost toward the final redemption, and the end of time signaled by the C minor music of the last trumpet call in movement six.[35]

A further and ultimately more telling connection lies in the relationship between that portion of Isaiah and the exact content of the baritone's second entrance in movement six. Paul speaks in 1 Corinthians 15 of "das Wort, das geschrieben steht," namely, the promise that death will be swallowed up in victory. Specifically, those words are written in the "Isaiah Apocalypse," 25:7, "He [The Lord] will swallow up death forever." Note also that Brahms introduces the fugal chorus at the end of movement two with these words from 1 Peter: "Aber das Herrn Wort bleibet in Ewigkeit" (But the Lord's Word remains in eternity). There are myriad ways to understood "the Lord's Word" in purely Christian or generally religious terms. But given the context in which Brahms is composing his *Requiem*, and given his comments to Reinthaler concerning its text, I believe "das Wort" connotes something else here. In a piece that articulates wandering and searching, and resolves these by extolling the permanence of the Word and, in the final movement, the permanence of our works, "the Word" carries at least some of the meaning that language held for the Romantics. And here we are speaking strongly of the German language.

Redemption is followed by rejoicing in the form of the mighty fugue that concludes movement six.[36] (And for what it is worth, Brahms chooses this

moment to introduce texts from the apocalyptic Revelation for the remainder of the piece.) Brahms imbues this fugue with a great sense of finality. On
the musical side, in moving from C minor to C major, he taps a by then familiar gambit from the symphonic canon. Beethoven's Fifth, with its famous
C major "breakthrough" at the end, had become a well-worn model for
ending a symphony (or other large-scale instrumental work), a tradition
that Brahms would later revisit in his First Symphony. Even more final
sounding here is the text. Unlike in the two earlier movements that ended
with large fugue-like sections (movements two and three), the text at the end
of the sixth movement has no direct connection to what precedes it but
rather provides an utterly generic hymn of praise to the Lord. Not only does
this textual disposition further distinguish the role of movement six from
that of the other "wandering" movements in the middle of the piece, but
also it offers a formula for comparing this movement with movements two
and three, one that does not founder on the dubious attempt to evince symmetry between one movement and a pair of movements, as most symmetrical interpretations of the piece must.

The choral fugue at the end of movement six is best heard as a synthesis
of those earlier concluding choruses. Textually, its generic character en-
compasses both of the earlier paeans: the "ransomed of the Lord" ("die
Erlöseten des Herrn") and the "souls of the righteous" ("die Gerechten
Seelen") fall now within the larger category of "all created things" ("alle
Dinge geschaffen") for which the Lord is to be praised. Musically, the bow
to baroque style is more pronounced here than in either of the earlier concluding choruses. Not only does the chorus begin as a legitimate fugue (as at
the end of movement three), but also the use of cut time and a running bass
line and countersubject (bars 213, 217, etc.) evoke an eighteenth-century
stile antico more clearly than at any point since the choir's initial entry in
movement one (though there is also much in the harmony and the orchestration here to remind us that this is a product of mid-nineteenth-century German musical style).

If this is a synthesis of the conclusions to the other two large-scale bifur-
cated movements in the piece, it is also a musical fulfillment to equal the
baritone's promise. One could draw that conclusion merely from the size
and grandeur of it all: 140 bars of nearly continuous four-voice counterpoint; a thick accompaniment from a large orchestra; swelling twice to *fortissimo* half cadences on the word "Kraft"; and so on. But the sense of
fulfillment here lies also in the array of fugal tonal relationships in which
Brahms places the subject entries. Only in the initial exposition are the four
voices disposed in the textbook manner, entering alternately on C and G.
The next set of entrances (bars 224–232) also begin on C and G (alto and
soprano) but pile up more quickly (first in two-bar then in one-bar intervals)

and soon shift to entries on D and G, beginning in bar 226, as part of a transition to G minor. Later in the fugue, Brahms explores all manner of pitch and durational intervals between entrances: thirds one bar apart in (271–275); fourths one bar apart (304–307), and seconds a half bar apart (333–334). Significantly, however, Brahms does not employ any technical devices (augmentation, inversion). He had certainly learned to execute those sorts of contrapuntal maneuvers in his counterpoint studies of the late 1850s, as a few short published choral works and fugues of the previous decade had borne out.[37] But the mood of this fugue is too bright, its praise too direct to allow for such artful distractions; these are the Last Days, the transition between an earthly time-bound existence and a divine eternity. The specificity of the preceding texts—their calls for comfort, their questioning of life's purpose, their promise of redemption—have been superseded by blanket exaltation and affirmation of the Lord.

We might also understand the lack of artificial compositional procedures here as directly related to the C major tonality of the fugue. Earlier I identified the shift from C minor to C major as a trope that can be traced back to Beethoven's Fifth Symphony. Certainly with the reception of that piece, if not earlier, that modal shift had been associated with the spiritual side of Romanticism. E. T. A Hoffmann put it most famously in his 1810 review of Beethoven's symphony: "It is like a radiant blinding sunlight which suddenly illuminates the dark night."[38] In movement six of *Ein deutsches Requiem,* this effect occurs in spectacular fashion a little before the notated key change, namely, at the drawn-out *fortissimo* statements on "wo (ist dein Sieg)" at bars 192–204. Brahms interprets the sopranos' A-flat three separate ways in those bars: as the third in an F minor harmony (iv in C minor); as the fifth in a D-flat, Neapolitan-sixth harmony; and, respelled as G-sharp, as the third of an E dominant harmony that leads to A natural in bar 201 over an A minor harmony. With this last chord, the relative minor of C major, we have shifted to C major, and the cadence before the double bar spreads that sonority throughout the entire performing ensemble.

When the altos emerge from this wall of sound at bar 208 (accompanied by the running quarter notes of the violins), the radiance they project is a matter not merely of the modal shift to C major but also of volume, texture, and harmonic clarity. Everything about this fugal entrance suggests purity and light, a cleansing of what preceded, and a glimpse into "the realm of the colossal and the immeasurable" (to quote yet another famous phrase from Hoffmann's Beethoven review).[39] All the fugal expositions and episodic material that follow are refractions of that pure light, reflections of the glimpse into the infinite that is afforded by the initial exposition. And whereas changing the time and pitch intervals of the entrances alters the later expositions enough to differentiate them from their pure model, it also preserves the model in a way that augmentations, inversions, and the like would not. Even the arresting *fortissimo* half cadences that threaten to pull the music strongly out of C major (D major at bars 289–290; E major at bars 215–216) are immediately assuaged by returns to C major.

Interwoven with those later expositions and pronounced half cadences are myriad developments of a rising motive from the fugal theme itself at the words "zu nehmen Preis (und Ehre und Kraft)" in bars 209–210, and of a secondary theme from the setting of the words "denn du hast alle Dinge erschaffen." Although the latter theme is slightly more pronounced in the choir's material, it is the "zu nehmen Preis" motive that provides the most climactic element in the chorus. Brahms approaches each of the *fortissimo* half cadences with a seemingly limitless extension of the ascending figure, beginning first in bar 282 (leading to the half cadence on D in bar 289) and then in bar 309 (leading to the half cadence on E in bar 315). He carefully worked out the second of these passages within a continuity draft of bars 290 to the end of the movement on a sketch sheet that also contains sketches for the middle of movement seven.[40] Although the main material of this draft would appear to be the basic two-part contrapuntal framework for the various sections at the end of the movement, Brahms devotes particular attention to the extended rising motive beginning in bar 309, where the counterpoint of the voices disappears and only the continuous rising instrumental line (which is eventually joined by the chorus in bars 311–313) is notated.

The C major fugue at the end of movement six marks the apocalyptic moment in *Ein deutsches Requiem*. It belongs neither to earthbound time nor to divine eternity; it is the pure state of transition between the two. The fugal texture here completes the suspension of time that the opening strains of the piece had implied. (And perhaps it was for this reason that Brahms abandoned the fugue of movement two so quickly and undercut the fugal texture at the end of movement three with the pounding quarter-note pedal of the timpani—it was too soon to evoke the full-fledged fugue at that point, too soon for the apocalyptic moment.) Now, at the end of movement six, it is not a sense of temporal dislocation as it was at the beginning of movement one, but rather a wiping away of time in a manner that only a fugue can achieve. Unlike most musical types, fugues are processes, not forms. Thus, unlike sonatas, binary dance movements, and the like, fugues have no designated arrival point, no telltale formal construct that signals the coming of the end. The larger tonic-dominant polarity that governs the whole of other instrumental types is encapsulated in the integral parts of a fugue, the pairings of voices against each other on tonic and dominant statements of the subject and answer. Perhaps it is not coincidental that Brahms chose to use a text from Revelation for this moment in the piece (he certainly could have found so generic an encomium at various other points in the Bible). Or perhaps it does not matter where the words come from; Brahms is, after all, expressing not the Christian apocalypse but rather a deep sense of arrival that was part of the German national spirit in the years leading up to 1871. The resplendent C major fugue at the end of movement six in *Ein deutsches Requiem* expresses that feeling of arrival better than any of the patriotic works written in the aftermath of the Franco-Prussian War would be able to—including Brahms's own *Triumphlied*.

An Apocalyptic Ending

What lies beyond time, in theological terms, is the Everlasting Gospel, the Age of Felicity, God's Kingdom on Earth; there lies rest from our labors, blessing, and comfort. It is not the business of *Ein deutsches Requiem* to achieve that state (and certainly not the business of its five inner movements), only to approach it. For that is all apocalypticism was capable of: anticipation. Thus, comfort is not the subject of movement six. Rather, the baritone promises to show us mysteries, and he prophesies that the Word *shall be* fulfilled. Comfort remains a plea and a promise, and so it is primarily the business of the two outer movements to articulate a vision of *how* the promise shall be fulfilled. By inference, then, it is the fulfillment of the Word that bestows comfort. A case could be made for a purely Christian, theological interpretation of fulfillment here ("Selig sind die Toten, die in dem Herrn sterben"), except that Brahms pointedly disavowed such meaning in his reply to Reinthaler. By his own account, he cited the quotation from Revelation as a mater of poetic necessity rather than Christian faith: "I have taken much liberty because I am a musician, because I had use for it, because I couldn't argue away or erase a 'henceforth' from my venerable poets." Language, then, is what endures *von nun an*. Luther's German language is transcendent and lifted to the status of *Ewigkeit*.

Brahms articulates these lofty sentiments through his transformation of the first movement into the seventh. The connection between these outer movements derives at least as strongly from their texts as it does through a series of explicit musical references. Syntactical parallels between the opening texts of the two movements create an overarching framework for the promise of comfort in op. 45:

Movement one
    Matthew 5:4

                Selig sind,
                die da Leid tragen,
                denn sie sollen getröstet werden

Movement seven
    Revelations 14:13

                        Selig sind die Toten,
                        die in dem Herrn sterben,
                        . . .
                        denn ihre Werken folgen ihnen nach.

Brahms draws particular attention to these syntactical similarities at either end of the *Requiem* by closely relating the musical setting of each passage. The seventh movement, the only one after the first movement in F major, commences with the same low F1 in the double basses that opened the piece and proceeds immediately up to a dissonant seventh (E♭3) in the cellos, thereby echoing a similar gesture in bars 1–2 of movement one. This orchestral reminiscence at the beginning of movement seven underpins the sopranos' simultaneous vocal recollection of the melodic material that ended the first movement. Brahms completes the reference by recapitulating the entire codetta from movement one (bars 144–158) at the end of the piece (movement seven, bars 151–166).

Notably, Brahms begins the last movement not with material from the opening of the first but rather with a transformation of the closing material from movement one, further enhancing the sense that this is a continuation of, rather than a return to, that movement. What remains of the *Requiem*'s opening at the beginning of the last movement is a radiant version of the orchestral introduction: the plodding quarter notes have been transformed into lilting eighth notes; the descending line from the flatted seventh, E-flat, has been rendered diatonic; violins have been added to the ensemble to brighten its timbre significantly: all in accordance with the designation "Feierlich," meaning "solemn, festive, or celebrative." The timeless realm that was merely alluded to in dark tones in the first movement is now depicted in brilliant tones at the end of the piece.

One manner in which the final movement builds on the first is in its dislocating sense of time and progress. Again, the similarities are clear, if somewhat less immediately noticeable. As he did the first movement, Brahms laid out the last in a broad tripartite scheme with a mediant relationship (now the parallel-major mediant, A major) as a central foil to F major at either end of the movement. And once again, most of the obvious juncture points in the movement's structure are marked by relatively sudden modulations or by no modulation at all. So, for example, the unexpected shift from F major to D-flat major in bar 47 of the first movement is matched by the sudden reappearance of F major from A major at bar 102 of the last. Absent in movement seven, however, are the thematic referents that turned up in unpredictable relationships among themselves to confuse the sense of time and formal

progress in movement one. There is disjuncture to be sure in the last movement, but of a different nature and quality, and one that could easily be labeled "apocalyptic." Long phrases, and in some cases large sections within
this movement, progress determinedly to nowhere: that is, they are abruptly
cut off by material from somewhere else in the movement (or from the first
movement) in a new and startling key, so that the juxtaposed bits of material stand in a practically random relationship to one another. By extension,
the sense of progression and order is nearly negated; this is as close as one
can come to a sense of simultaneity in musical form without actually super-
imposing disparate elements one atop the other.

The first strong instance of this effect comes with the aforementioned return of F major in bar 102. Brahms has just completed a well-rounded period in A major in bars 48–101 (replete with a modulation to the dominant,
E major, in bars 58–83), and suggests a large-scale structural cadence on A
when the opening material of the movement, in the home key of F major,
breaks in unexpectedly at bar 102. Unlike the sudden shifts of key that occurred in the opening movement (to D-flat in bar 47, and to F at bar 102),
the reprise of the opening is so nearly literal here as to practically negate the
material that came before; the path on which that musical material was
headed vanishes and the preceding material is there again as if we had never
left it. Brahms achieves a nearly identical effect with the two abrupt (one-
bar) crescendo modulations in bars 131–132 and 140–141, the first from F
to E-flat major, the second from E-flat to A-flat major, which in turn slips to
D-flat major by the next bar, 143. Both the keys of E-flat in bar 132 and D-
flat in bar 143 bring with them more (and more literal) echoes of the first
movement. E-flat draws the original rendition of the closing theme from
movement one (bars 106–110) with which the sopranos began the current
movement; and D-flat recalls the subsequent quote within movement one itself (bars 111–112) of the opening choral entrance in the piece.

Abrupt shifts like these are typical of biblical apocalyptic writing, as are
allusions to destruction and renewal. In the Bible, this type of imagery usually describes the sudden appearance of a new world from the destruction of
the old world.[41] To quote Abrams once again, "The line of change in Christian history is right-angled: the key events are abrupt, cataclysmic, and
make a drastic, even an absolute difference."[42] The concluding chorus of
movement six and all of the *Feierlich* movement seven could be heard as the
"appearance of a new world" out of the "cataclysm, or the "destruction of
the old world" in the middle of movement six. And the kaleidoscopic temporal effect of constantly breaking in with earlier material in movement
seven might be likened to the timelessness of that new world. Again, this resonates with the sensation of transition that was epitomized at the end of the
sixth movement, and which is so central to apocalyptic thinking in Western

history. This, according to Kermode, is "what Yeats called 'antithetical multiform influx'—the forms assumed by the inrushing gyre as the old one reaches its term. The dialectic of Yeats' gyres is simple enough in essence; they are a figure for the co-existence of the past and the future at the time of transition. The old narrows to its apex, the new broadens towards its base, and the old and the new interpenetrate."[43]

The apocalyptic character of *Ein deutsches Requiem* is largely a function of how Brahms treats temporality in the work and, narrowly, of how he separates the linear time(s) of the five inner movements from the timelessness of the outer ones, all the while creating references between these two separate realms, thus allowing the glimpses of the outer movements from within the inner ones to be seen as our worldly, human, and imperfect vision of a timeless world we cannot grasp. Brahms's apocalyptic impulse is nationalistic on several counts. First, through the disposition of biblical texts he grants language, *das Wort*, special eternal status, over and above the potential religious interpretation of eternity in the piece. And he willfully (and in some sense consciously) overturns the Latin language normally associated with a "Requiem," replacing it with passages from the ur-document of German literature, Luther's Bible. Second, he composed the *Requiem* during years (1866–1868) in which Prussia's military campaigns were viewed in Germany as events that were "abrupt, cataclysmic, and [made] a drastic, even an absolute, difference."[44] The tendency of Germans to foresee the coming of a new *Reich* in millennial, apocalyptic terms provides a useful framework for understanding the distinctive features of this *German Requiem*— of "ein" *deutsches Requiem*—a title that implies there are other types of German Requiems one might compose, but *this* one provides a particular, perhaps a singular, point of view, one that is true to the apocalyptic outlook of Brahms's Germany.

The *Triumphlied*, Op. 55, and the Apocalyptic Moment

Brahms's Anomalies

When Brahms completed the fifth movement of his *Requiem* in the summer of 1868, he was "home" at his father's house in Hamburg. Up until this time, he had been residing in Vienna during the winter, but he had not yet permanently settled in the Austrian capital. In the fall of 1869, several months after the first performance of the now seven-movement *Requiem* at Leipzig, Brahms rented an apartment in Vienna for the first time.[1] It would be over two years, however, before he would permanently settle into rooms at Karlgasse 4, which he called home for over twenty-five years, from December 1871 until his death. Thanks to two sets of photographs made by his friends, we have a relatively vivid record of how Brahms decorated his dwelling.[2] One of these is preserved near the end of Viktor von Miller zu Aichholz's *Brahms-Bilderbuch* (1905), which devotes twenty-two pages to images first of the exterior and then the interior of Brahms's apartment.[3]

Readers familiar with Brahms literature from the past hundred years know the two frequently reproduced photographs of these rooms. First and most familiar is the long wall in the music room, with its bust of Beethoven, bronze relief of Bismarck, Raphael's Sistine Madonna, and Ingres's portrait of Cherubini. It is easy to interpret each of the cultural symbols assembled here by Brahms with our modern understanding of who he was and what his music means to us: the Beethoven bust hardly requires comment; the Bismarck relief reminds us of Brahms's well-documented patriotism and admiration for the Iron Chancellor; the Sistine Madonna reflects his classicizing bent as well as his fondness for all forms of Renaissance art; and the portrait of Cherubini resonates with Brahms's own prediction (however mistaken) that his place in music history would be similar to that of Cherubini—a craftsman-like preserver of the style he inherited from his immediate predecessors. Not visible in this photograph are the prints of other famous works of art on the other walls of the room, including Leonardo da Vinci's Mona Lisa. Aichholz also presents images from Brahms's bedroom, where more artworks were found on the walls, most notably the print of the Rohrbach Bach portrait, reemphasizing Brahms's penchant for surrounding himself with images of ancient masters or their products.

All the images in these two rooms depict individuals, and they speak to Brahms's personal identification with either the historical figures represented (Bismarck, Beethoven, Bach) or an artist of historical import (Leonardo, Raphael). Only Barthel von der Helst's *Friedensschluss zu Münster*, in the middle of his bedroom wall, moves beyond the realm of the personal through its depiction of the accord that ended the Thirty Years' War in 1648. But even here, Helst's realism conveys an intimacy that is in keeping with the individualistic bent of the other objects hanging on the walls in Brahms's living quarters (while recalling the most momentous German war to precede the events of 1871).

A separate set of circumstances govern Aichholz's photographs of the last room in the apartment, a private library whose space was made available when Brahms took over a third room in 1877.[4] Perhaps as familiar as the image of the long living room wall is a picture of this library, complete with Brahms's standing desk and sitting area. The collection of books and scores seen here speaks to Brahms's love of literature, both verbal and musical. He is reported to have been extremely well read in historical literature, both German and foreign (though always in German translation) and in books on more recent political history.

This is the end of the tour. Yet Aichholz provides one last picture of Brahms's dwelling, this of the outside wall of the library. Unlike all of the other photographs of the apartment, this final picture seems relatively barren. There are no musical references, none of the mass-produced copies of famous portraiture (the Mona Lisa, Rohrbach's Bach), none of the coffee and tobacco paraphernalia (of which Brahms was so fond) that occupy all of the other interior photographs: merely a static picture between two windows and some piled-up suitcases. This, then, would appear to be an incongruous end to the tour.[5] The particular picture in question also might seem inappropriate as a conclusion; it is an inexpensive reproduction of a popular image of the time, Peter Cornelius's "Apokalyptischen Reiter" (The Riders of the Apocalypse; fig. 4.1). Cornelius's chalk drawing is, as the title suggests, a detailed depiction of a violent scene from chapter 6 of Revelation, namely, the unleashing of the Four Horsemen upon the earth.

Figure 4.1   Peter Cornelius, "Die Apokalyptischen Reiter."

Revelation 6:
[1]Now I saw when the Lamb opened one of the seven seals, and I heard one of the four living creatures say, as with a voice of thunder, "Come!"

[2]And I saw, and behold, a white horse, and its rider had a bow; and a crown was given to him, and he went out conquering and to conquer.

[3]When he opened the second seal, I heard the second living creature say, "Come!"

[4]And out came another horse, bright red; its rider was permitted to take peace from the earth, so that men should slay one another; and he was given a great sword.

[5]When he opened the third seal, I heard the third living creature say, "Come!" And I saw, and behold, a black horse, and its rider had a balance in his hand;

[6]and I heard what seemed to be a voice in the midst of the four living creatures saying, "A quart of wheat for a denarius, and three quarts of barley for a denarius; but do not harm oil and wine!"

[7]When he opened the fourth seal, I heard the voice of the fourth living creature say, "Come!"

[8]And I saw, and behold, a pale horse, and its rider's name was Death, and Hades followed him; and they were given power over a fourth of the earth, to kill with sword and with famine and with pestilence and by wild beasts of the earth.

Such bellicose, apocalyptic imagery seems a strange place to end the pictorial review of Johannes Brahms's life that occupies Aichholz's book. Yet this picture clearly had significance for Brahms. After all, he granted it a place of honor: apparently the only artwork on the walls of his beloved *Bibliothek*.[6] It is not known when Brahms acquired his print of the "Riders of the Apocalypse." Julius Thäter's popular engraving was produced in 1849 and the same artist's "considerably improved" version became available in 1863.[7] In any event, it seems likely that Brahms would have waited until he moved into his more permanent lodgings in 1871 before acquiring wall art such as the Cornelius print or other, larger pieces in the other rooms.

Cornelius's image resonates with one of Brahms's most problematic works, the *Triumphlied,* op. 55 of 1871. This is one of Brahms's largest musical conceptions, based on selected texts from Revelation 19, and scored for double chorus, orchestra, and baritone soloist. Brahms wrote the piece in celebration of the Prussian military victory over France in 1870 that ushered in the new German Empire of Wilhelm I the following year. And although it is nowadays labeled an "occasional" work, its popularity continued beyond the war's immediate aftermath, lasting until the end of Brahms's life.[8] Just as Cornelius's "Riders of the Apocalypse" may seem out of place in Brahms's library, the *Triumphlied* similarly seems to be an anomaly amid his output according to the attributes we normally assign to Brahms's music. It has been described as loud, bombastic, and relatively lacking in the sort of refinement and contrapuntal detail we usually expect from Brahms.

Brahms's contemporaries recognized a "monumental" character in op. 55, as evidenced by the frequent use of the words "Gewalt," "Kraft," "Macht," and, indeed, "Monumental" in reviews of the first performances. The widely reported powerful effect of the *Triumphlied* derives from a directness and simplicity of expression. As Herman Kretzschmar, who published the only contemporaneous critique of the score, asserts, "In this work the most grandiose effects are achieved through the simplest means."[9] Some early reviewers observed that these were unusual qualities in Brahms's music up to that time. Already Brahms was noted for the subtlety and contrapuntal intricacies of works such as the *Requiem,* the F Minor Piano Quintet, op. 34, and the *Handel Variations,* op. 24. Most of these writers were able to accommodate the *Triumphlied* as a logical means of expressing the exuberance of the national moment. To them, this was a Handelian style in a composer who up until that time had displayed more of a Bachian bent. That was a significant distinction for nineteenth-century German music critics, who tended to regard the music of Bach and Handel in a complementary sociological relationship: Handel as a populist composer for the masses and Bach as an elite composer for the connoisseur. Although modern commentators often adduce Handel's *Dettingen Te Deum* (which Brahms had conducted in Vienna in 1871) as an inspiration for the *Triumphlied,* contemporaneous critics were referring more generally to the frequent homorhythmic writing within each chorus and the clarity such vocal writing grants the text.

To his contemporaries, then, the *Triumphlied* was singular among Brahms's works for its forceful clarity and populist tone. To modern audiences, however, the *Triumphlied* stands out among his many works for chorus and orchestra merely for its lack of familiarity. (Friedhelm Krummacher rightly remarks that the negative reception of the *Triumphlied* has received more attention than the piece itself.)[10] This work has not simply been overlooked during the past half century or more; it has been actively avoided, even disdained. Reasons for its fall from grace are not mysterious. Already by the First World War, any massive work, such as this one, that celebrated the German Empire found little sympathy outside Germany. And even there the euphoric tone of the work rang hollow after Germany's defeat in 1918. With the rise in the 1930s of Adolf Hitler, and with the National Socialists' preference for Wagner and Bruckner over Brahms, the *Triumphlied* was both musically and ideologically unwelcome just about everywhere for the remainder of the twentieth century.[11]

Accordingly, the work received no serious scholarship during the twentieth century until a lengthy essay by Friedhelm Krummacher appeared in 1995.[12] But Krummacher raised the specter of the *Triumphlied* only to deny the militaristic patriotic bent that other writers ascribed to Brahms on account of the piece. In other words, he sought to strip op. 55 of its real historical value, as an anomaly within our perception of Brahms as a liberal and our reception of his music as politically neutral. Instead, Krummacher finds in the work, and in Brahms's attitude toward it, an ironic, distanced, and ambivalent stance vis-à-vis the events of 1871 and even the new *Reich.* He thereby reinforces the idea that the militaristic, patriotic side of Brahms never truly existed in the first place, and that earlier readings of the work as a genuine patriotic expression (especially Max Kalbeck's in his Brahms biography) are colored by the nationalist enthusiasms of those writers, not Brahms's own.[13]

To bolster his revisionist stance, Krummacher takes aim at one of the most characteristic anecdotes in the reception of the *Triumphlied:* Brahms's supposed musical allusion in the first movement to the second half-verse of Revelation 19:2, "He has judged the great whore who corrupted the

Example 4.1   Triumphlied, op. 55, movement one: possible allusion to Revelation 19:2. Text that Brahms entered in pencil into his *Handexemplar* ("daß er die große Hure verurtheilet hat") in parentheses.

earth with her fornication" ("deß er die große Hure verurtheilet hat"). Kalbeck had claimed in his biography that the wind theme in bars 70–74 fit the unsung (German) text "note for note," an intentional "Witz," according to Brahms's friend Bernhard Scholz (ex. 4.1).[14] We need not rely only on Scholz's word, however; Brahms copied the questionable verse into his *Handexemplar* beneath this theme in the score. Whether or not he had these words in mind when he conceived the piece, Brahms verifies Kalbeck's claim that these words should figure into a complete understanding of the work despite their absence from the printed score. And Kalbeck makes it clear to whom he thinks the "great whore" would refer in Brahms's allusion. Reflecting on the apocalyptic presage of Revelation 19, he writes, "What the angels in heaven would one day sing over the fall of Babylon as a '*Triumphlied* of the elect,' that can also be sung after so many thousands of years by the elect who have witnessed the fall of the modern 'Babylon on the Seine.'"[15]

Much as nineteenth-century Germans longed for national unification on its own merits, to achieve that goal at the expense of France carried special mythical meaning. As countless historians have suggested, the German nationalist movement might never have gained its sustaining momentum without France as a hated foil against which to strive. German Romantics had been roused to political awareness by the Napoleonic domination of German-speaking lands and their sense that the laudable principles of the French Revolution had been betrayed. France was seen not only as a decadent nation but also as an aggressive roadblock to German nationhood. At stake was nothing less than a resurrection of the medieval Germanic Empire under Frederick Barbarossa, and this could be achieved only by vanquishing the Latin demon: then Rome, now France. From the beginning, the battle against French influence (cultural, political, and otherwise) was pitched in implicitly or explicitly religious terms. France was portrayed as "Babylon" in opposition to Germany's role as God's chosen nation. Thus, awaiting the rise of a new German state took on distinctly messianic, apocalyptic overtones. These expectations were not limited to the political realm. Paul J. Alexander, chronicling the "Legend of the Last Roman Emperor," observes that "also the philosophy, literature, and historiography of nineteenth-century Germany were permeated by the hope for a united effort of the German principalities and peoples against foreign domination and influence."[16]

Krummacher goes to great pains to de-fang Kalbeck's story and, after a painstaking critique of the evidence, ultimately deems Kalbeck's interpretation "not only forced, but simply impossible."[17] He adds, "Thus Kalbeck's representation—as momentous as it is—belongs not merely to the realm of fable, but rather presents a falsification that serves the express purpose of claiming a pointedly national character for the work."[18] I cannot agree with Krummacher's conclusion; if nothing else, it seems to fly in the face of the evidence left by Brahms. Along with other recent writers on the *Triumphlied* (Peter Petersen and Sabine Giesbrecht-Schutte), I still hear the work as an undeniable expression of anti-French, pro-Hohenzollern patriotism.[19]

But it is not an uncomplicated patriotism, and I agree with Krummacher's perception of ambivalence in this piece and his doubts about Brahms's inner convictions in writing it. This has less to do with the composer's political outlook, however, and more to do with the overall insecurities many Germans felt toward their new empire during the founding years and their consequent tendency to overcompensate in expressing their enthusiasm for the new nation. Despite the euphoria of the moment (outwardly expressed in Brahms's *Triumphlied*), the arrival of the *Kaiserreich* in 1871 engendered inward misgivings about the role of the new government in relation to the increasingly spiritual and irrational quest for a German nation. The historian Reinhard Alings writes that "the *Reich* was characterized externally and internally by a feeling of uncertainty," which led at the time to a deluge of national monuments. "Just like a confession of faith repeated again and again," he adds, these moments "conjured up something which, obviously, did not exist to a sufficient degree: a single national identity of the Germans."[20] The *Triumphlied* may bear traces of such misgivings, not as a conscious political statement on Brahms's part but rather against the composer's conscious intentions, as a typical overcompensation that glorifies the new nation too unambiguously to be taken at face value.

Krummacher, citing the authority of Brahms's friend Philipp Spitta, warns against reading the *Triumphlied* as a purely political tract at the expense of its "mystical sacred meaning."[21] In other words, a complete interpretation of op. 55 must take into account not only its occasional subject (the Prussian military victory of 1871 and the German state it produced) but also the ways in which that subject interacts with the *Triumphlied*'s status as a biblical setting. At the intersection of these political and religious meanings stands the apocalyptic core of the piece. But the *Triumphlied*'s particular expression of the apocalyptic paradigm differs substantially from that of *Ein deutsches Requiem*. Brahms's apocalyptic stance in this work is blatant and relatively uncomplicated. By selecting verses from Revelation 19 for a work that explicitly celebrates the Prussian victory over France and the founding of the *Kaiserreich*, Brahms claims this as an apocalyptic moment in history. He makes this apocalyptic meaning manifest in op. 55 by adding the biblical citation "Offenb. Joh. Cap. 19" (Revelation 19) directly beneath the title *Triumphlied* on the symbol-laden title page of the original score.[22]

Whereas the *Requiem* provides an apocalyptic time frame against which the individual can measure his or her existence, in the *Triumphlied*, Brahms abandons any sense of individuality and opts instead for an emphasis on communal expression. Specifically, he adopts a monumental stance in the *Triumphlied* to celebrate the deeply rooted authority of the new German state in the figure of the Kaiser; he dedicated the piece to the living Kaiser, Wilhelm I, but it is the crown itself which is immortalized in the *Triumphlied*. That distinction is highly significant for understanding the apocalyptic character of the piece and for the changing nature of monumentality between the *Gründerjahre* and the fin de siècle, separate threads that I gather as this chapter progresses.

Brahms's correspondence from the years 1870 and 1871 clearly maps out the origins of the *Triumphlied* as a direct response to the Prussian military victory over France and the founding of the *Kaiserreich* in those years. In 1870 Brahms was enjoying a newly won reputation as one of Germany's leading composers. Only the previous year his first great success, *Ein deutsches Requiem*, had received its first complete performance (18 February in the Leipzig Gewandhaus). The ensuing success of his *Alto Rhapsody*, op. 53, which premiered in 1870, not only cemented Brahms's status as a composer of the first rank but also established the choral-orchestral medium as the outlet through which, for the time being, Brahms could best reach German concert audiences. With the outbreak of war between Prussia and France in August 1870, he quickly set to work on yet another such composition, which he first labeled his "Lied auf Paris," in a letter to P. J. Simrock.[23] By 12 December Brahms wrote to Karl Reinthaler, "Were I able, and had I the courage, I would write a good Te Deum, and then I would travel to Germany. The better one has tried to write, the better one feels—with a normal fellow, it is not even a question of trying," to which Reinthaler replied: "Indeed!! What a time! My wife always says, you should have gone secretly onto the battlefield; I think you should still preserve the world!— Dear Brahms! Do it! In your God there will be light. Write the Te Deum that you must write. It is my rock-solid conviction that it is to be the second great act of your life. . . . You can do it and you must do it. Let it be the twin brother to your 'Requiem'!!"[24]

Brahms sent Reinthaler the completed first movement in February, which served (at Brahms's suggestion) as a conclusion to a performance of the *German Requiem* at Bremen in memory of victims of the war. Brahms put off completing the planned second and third movements until the fall of 1871, turning instead to complete the *Schicksalslied,* op. 54, which he had at least begun (and probably drafted in full) the previous year. By the fall of 1871, he had composed the remaining two movements of his *Triumphlied,* which he sent to Hermann Levi in Karlsruhe in November. Levi conducted the premiere of the completed work in the Karlsruhe court theater on 5 June 1872, and within two years the *Triumphlied* had been performed to great acclaim in all the major German-speaking cities—Vienna, Berlin, Munich, Leipzig, and Zurich.

Music critics at these first concerts immediately recognized the distinctly different sound of the *Triumphlied* by comparison with the by then premiered *Requiem, Alto Rhapsody,* and *Schicksalslied.* In particular, they noted the frequent combining of the two four-part choirs in passages of homorhythmic declamation, producing a massive effect akin to that found in Handel's several Te Deums and, in the case of the "Hallelujah"-dominated first movement of the *Triumphlied,* the *Messiah's* "Hallelujah" Chorus. Although many critics complimented the various moments of contrapuntal interest throughout the work, nearly all were in agreement that Brahms's greatest accomplishment in this piece was its overwhelming and powerful effect on the listener.[25]

Fig. 4.2 provides a brief schema of the three-movement work. As in so many celebratory works of the eighteenth and early nineteenth centuries, Brahms chose D major as the tonality, and he does not stray far from the home key throughout the piece. This is no mere obligatory observation. Rather it indicates the consistency of affect that dominates the *Triumphlied:* there is little relief from the ebullience expressed at the work's outset. I do not mean by this to disparage the piece. In fact, I think it is crucial for un-

Movement 1

Orchestral intro.	*Lebhaft, feierlich*						*Tranquillo / Animato*
	Choral entrance:	A	B	A'	trans.		C
	"Halleluja"	Choral theme 1: "Heil und Preis"	Choral Theme 2: "Denn wahrhaftig und gerecht"	"Heil und Preis"	"Halleluja"		"Heil und Preis" "Halleluja"
D major			D minor	D major			
1–18	18–35	36–66	66–116	116–157	157–182		183–206

Movement 2

Mäßig belebt	*Lebhaft*		*Ziemlich langsam, doch nicht schleppend*
Orchestral intro	A aba'	B	C
	Choral theme 1 "Lobet unsern Gott" "Und die ihn fürchtet . . ."	"Halleluja. Denn der allmächtige Gott . . ."	"Lasset uns freuen und frölich sein"
	G major	D major	G major
1–8	8–110	110–143	143–185

Movement 3

Lebhaft	*Un poco animato*	*Etwas lebhafter*			*Feierlich*
Orchestral intro	A	B	C	Baritone interlude	D
	Baritone solo "Und ich sahe den Himmel"	"Treu und Wahrhaftig"	"Und er tritt die Kelter"	"Und hat einen Namen geschrieben"	"Ein König aller Könige"
D minor →		D major	F♯ minor	→	D major

Figure 4.2   Formal schema of *Triumphlied*, op. 55.

derstanding the meaning of the *Triumphlied* to acknowledge its relative monochromaticism—a point to which I return shortly. The third movement, also in D major, does introduce a baritone soloist for contrast. But he is allotted only two brief interjections, one at the outset, one midway through the movement. And, by and large, the tone of movement three is similar to that of the first.

Real contrast in the *Triumphlied* comes only with the shift to triple meter,

G major, and the relatively gentler tone of the second movement. But the change in tone is, indeed, only "relative." Like the outer movements, this one begins with *forte* martial dotted rhythms, often across octave leaps. Moreover, a D major "Hallelujah" returns, along with the marking "Lebhaft" from the beginning of the piece, to introduce the substantial middle portion of the movement. The return to G major at the close of the second movement (containing a quote of "Nun danket alle Gott," discussed later in this chapter), however, does truly provide a lyrical and quiet pause. Yet, perhaps ironically, it is precisely in these quiet strains that the truly monumental function of the piece surfaces. To understand how this is so, it is useful to examine the general role of the chorale in the expression of monumentality in German music of the nineteenth century.

Of Monuments and Chorales

Cornelius's "Riders of the Apocalypse" and Brahms's *Triumphlied* were created at different times and under different social and political circumstances. Yet each was directly inspired by Prussia's drive toward German unification. Cornelius was one of the so-called Nazarenes, German painters working in Rome during the first half of the nineteenth century. Like Böcklein and Runge, Cornelius sought to revive German painting by recapturing the neoclassical techniques of the sixteenth century, thereby drawing an equation between modern Germany and Greco-Roman antiquity as cultural paragons. The Nazarenes' underlying impulse to connect Germany to a lineage backwards through Renaissance Italy to Greece and Rome is not far removed from the similar historical gesture of Jakob Burkhardt in history or Karl Friedrich Schinkel in Prussian official architecture. "The Hellenic ideal belonged," writes Tony Davies in his penetrating study of humanism, "for Hegel and Humboldt as for Goethe and Schiller, not to the remote past and the post-mortem formalities of an ancient language, but to the future. For them, the modern Germany they were engaged in building, cultured, orderly, and modern, would be the fruition of what the ancient Greeks had dreamed."[26] In much of Cornelius's work the classical impulse led to static representations of allegorical figures. But the intimations of circular design in "Riders of the Apocalypse" convey real drama and panic as befits the work's subject matter.[27]

Cornelius conceived his "Riders of the Apocalypse" as part of a series of frescoes for the proposed Campo Santo in Berlin. He came to Berlin in 1840 at the invitation of the newly crowned King Friedrich Wilhelm IV, who sought a reorganized German Christian Church as the cornerstone of the Prussian state. The new king envisioned a vast rebuilding of the state cathedral to match the neoclassical museum that stood opposite it. Friedrich Wilhelm never realized the bulk of his reforms, yet in the process or pursuing them, he assembled some of the greatest artists and thinkers in the German-speaking world. Cornelius was only one of many luminaries drawn to Berlin by the king and his emissary Wilhelm von Humboldt. Others included the brothers Grimm, Friedrich Schelling, Ludwig Tieck, Friedrich Rückert, and Karl von Savigny. Cornelius had spent the previous twenty-one years in Munich working on large civic frescoes for King Ludwig of Bavaria, most famously for the Glyphotek Museum and the Ludwigskirche.

When Cornelius fell out of favor with the king in the late 1830s, he was only too happy to accept an invitation to come to Berlin to work on a proposed rebuilding of the Hohenzollern Cathedral. Friedrich Wilhelm charged Cornelius with designing a series of frescoes for the open colonnades that were to connect the cathedral with the royal family tomb. Although plans for the new cathedral were halted after the revolutions of 1848, Cornelius continued to sketch the designs. First and foremost among these was the "Riders of the Apocalypse," which Cornelius began while in Rome in 1845. For this and a few of the other planned frescoes, he made vast cartoons, which were exhibited in museums during the late 1850s, long after plans for the cathedral had been scrapped. In addition to these exhibits, mass-produced engravings and enthusiastic critical reactions to the cartoons helped popularize the "Riders of the Apocalypse" in Germany long before the public could have imagined Prussia's precipitous rise to power at the end of the 1860s. Yet the work is not without its own nationalist significance, recognized by several contemporary critics. The Berlin art critic Hermann Grimm (son of Wilhelm Grimm and an indirect acquaintance of Brahms through Joseph Joachim) recognized in Cornelius's cartoons for the Berlin Campo Santo an expression of the modern national character, in distinction to the more Italianate qualities of similar subjects among Cornelius's earlier works in Munich. Grimm called the frescoes "monuments to the German spirit."[28] And in a separate essay on the 1859 exhibit of Cornelius's cartoons at the Prussian Academy of Art, a pamphlet that Brahms owned, Grimm again singles out the Berlin frescoes as untouched by the Italian ideas (and Catholic co-workers) that aided in realizing Cornelius's frescoes of Greek mythological imagery for the Glyphotek in Munich. "Here he sketched like a German whose imagination [*Phantasie*] is stimulated to the highest individual activity by the content of the Bible."[29] Similarly, Cornelius's first biographer, Herman Riegel, compares the painter in 1867 to his fellow Nazarenes Asmus Jacob Carstens, who "took refuge in antiquity," and Johann Friedrich Overbeck, who similarly escaped to the religiosity of the Middle Ages. "Cornelius," writes Riegel, "permeated with the same insight, driven by the same power as were they, chose neither antiquity nor Christianity; he reached for the full life, and stood on the side where the spiritual center of the masses resided. He chose the national side."[30]

Grimm's and Riegel's choice of words reminds us that this "national side" was expressed in monumental terms. Here some clarity on the term "monumentality" is in order. Too often in music and art criticism the word is used merely to convey physical scale or is substituted for the sublime. This is certainly the case for Carl Dahlhaus, whose brief essay on the monumental falls within his discussion of Beethoven's symphonic style and flows immediately out of his exposition "The Sublime and the 'Noble Ode.'" Within this context, Dahlhaus provides a useful beginning toward an understanding of monumentality in music, and he identifies three specific and closely interrelated attributes of the style as it appears in Beethoven's symphonies. First, he asserts that "one of the essential ingredients of the monumental style is a simplicity that stands up to being stated emphatically without collapsing into empty rhetoric." He then identifies "a slow regular harmonic rhythm" as a building block of that emphatic simplicity, and the ability to be seen as a balanced whole as the style's aesthetic goal.[31] These observations are valuable for defining monumentality within the symphonic tradition and (particularly) within the aesthetic of the sublime.

But Dahlhaus makes little attempt to look beyond the musical implications of his definition. In fact, he begins his explication of the monumental by purposefully moving the discussion of Beethoven's symphonies out of the realm of the sociological, where Paul Bekker had placed it at the beginning of the twentieth century.[32] Nevertheless, Dahlhaus does touch on a spatial metaphor that begins to point toward a broader definition of musical monumentality, one that might include how this style functions like monumental forms in other arts, particularly in architecture and sculpture. While attempting to explain how the first movement of the Ninth Symphony can be simultaneously monumental and dramatic (which "would seem to be mutually exclusive"), Dahlhaus avers that the apparent existence of two opposing impulses (the stasis of monumentality and the forward push of drama) are "characteristic of the monumental style in music, which may be comparable to architecture, but differs from it by reason of a temporal element which always contains a trace—however diffident—of the dramatic."[33] Dahlhaus nearly concedes here that music, on account of its temporality, cannot be monumental in the same manner as a *Denkmal*. Such a definition is of no value for any musical work that, like the *Triumphlied*, does not claim to be autonomous. But by raising the aura of architecture, Dahlhaus acknowledges that some connection should exist between the two. If it can, that definition has to explain how music can achieve the same *effect* as a plastic monument.

As public structures, be they statues, buildings, or some combination thereof, monuments must transcend the individual and personal; they must convey ideas that are shared by the larger community and, in fact, help that community to define itself. (Here, Bekker's approach to Beethoven's symphonies as "society forming" would serve us well.) Thus, even when commemorating an individual, monuments must refer to more general principles and ideas for which that individual stands. Additionally, public monuments must allow the individual viewer to recognize his or her place in relation to the larger community by providing both a spatial and a temporal dimension to the act of remembering: spatial by orienting the individual toward symbolic representations of the community (and/or nation); temporal by concretizing a specific hero, act, or event from the past and making it present to the viewer.

Perhaps the only systematic approach to defining musical monumentality that takes this spatial metaphor into account is Arnold Schering's 1934 essay "Über den Begriff des Monumentalen in der Musik" (On the Idea of Monumentality in Music).[34] Most relevant for Schering's metaphorical comparison between music and architecture is the feeling of spaciousness that a structural monument provides and to which music may aspire. He places particular emphasis on music of the baroque period, with its characteristic separation of the performing forces (i.e., the concerto principle) as inherently monumental and as a model for achieving spatial effects akin to those of physical monuments.[35] Schering's baroque ideal may be applied to the most often cited moment in the *Triumphlied*: the quotation of the chorale "Nun danket alle Gott" near the end of the second movement. Most notable in this passage is the spatial separation of performing forces, particularly when considered against the material in the preceding two thirds of the movement. As outlined in fig. 4.2, the movement divides into three distinct parts, according to the separate verses of Revelation 19 that Brahms sets here. In sections A and B, Brahms constantly interweaves the various sections of the orchestra and the two choirs to fill the sound space. Even when the instruments are not literally doubling the voices in those sections of the movement, their figures accent vocal entrances and complement the choirs' melodic lines. So, for example, in the apparent diversity of material at the choral statement of "alle seine Knechte, lobet unsern Gott" in bars 12–23, the busier string lines merely add eighth-note motion to the choral material, while the accented hammer-stroke quarter-note figures in the winds (bars 12, 14, and 16) announce the alternating entrances of choirs 1 and 2.

By contrast, the roles of the various sounding bodies in the last section of movement two ("Ziemlich langsam, doch nicht schleppend," bars 143–185) are mostly differentiated and complement, rather than intertwine with, one another. Brahms makes this immediately apparent through the notated metrical contrast (4/4 against 12/8) between the two choirs (ex. 4.2). Only when

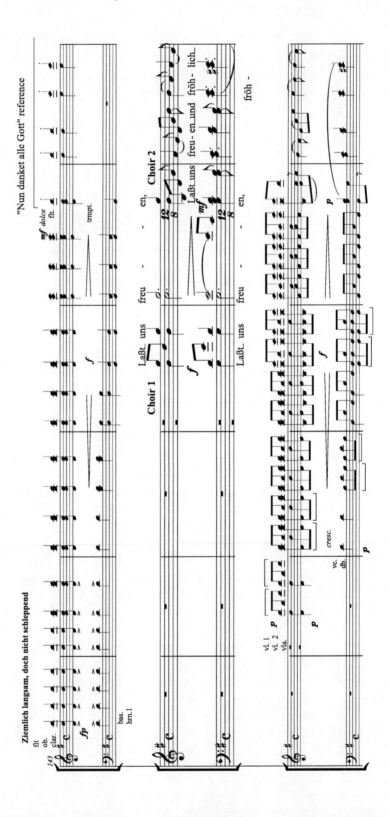

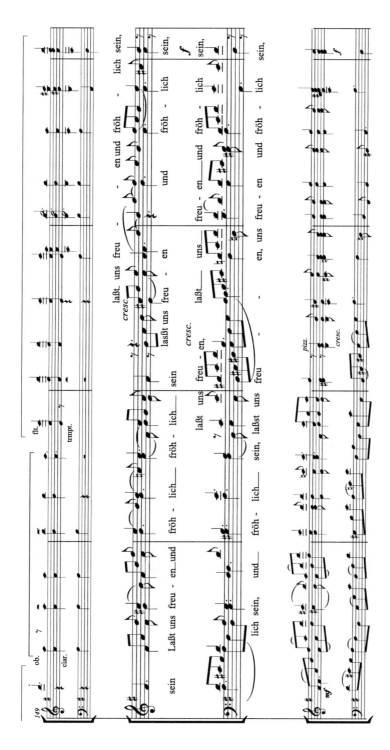

Example 4.2   Triumphlied, op. 55, movement two, bars 143–153.

the second choir enters in 12/8 do the strings double: choir 1 always stands alone with its duple material. Additionally, the unwavering quarter-note motion of the winds stands apart as a rhythmic "continuo," from which emerges a reference to the first six notes from the chorale "Nun danket alle Gott." This tersest of quotations is played in unison first by the trumpets and flutes (on D–E–D, bars 147–149) and then by the oboes, clarinets, bassoons, and first horn (A–B–A, bars 149–150). Unlike the enmeshed figures of the preceding sections, the unison wind writing here stands out as a distinct line that hovers above the lilting, 12/8 roulades of choir 2. By sharply distinguishing content and timbre, Brahms creates a sonic allusion to spaciousness akin to the large spaces one associates with a monument. The chorale, referred to here only by its incipit, is memorialized in the manner that an inscription on a monument might quote a hero or other historical figure and thereby encapsulate that figure's meaning. In both cases, the object of veneration is set apart and made as broad and easily perceptible as possible. We are not asked to contend with the subject's true complexity, potential contradictions, or blemishes, only with simplified abstraction. Thus, the hushed tones of this passage notwithstanding, Brahms's allusion is a model of how musical monumentalism may approach the effect of a plastic monument.[36]

This chorale already had symbolic status, however, as did the entire genre by this point in the nineteenth century. Sabine Giesbrecht-Schutte claims that this was one of those chorales "whose exclusively Christian tradition became overlaid with a militant nationalism in the course of the late eighteenth and nineteenth centuries," adding, "after 1848 one can practically consider it a motto of Prussian *Expansionspolitik*."[37] Giesbrecht-Schutte makes her point while comparing Brahms's chorale quotation in the *Triumphlied* with Karl Reintaler's use of the equally well known "Ein feste Burg ist unser Gott" within his own commemorative piece for the new *Reich*, the *Bismarckhymne*, op. 29 (1874). Reintaler adhered to a familiar pattern of employing chorales in large-scale compositions: he placed it near the end, as an apotheosis. In the most concrete terms, this practice dates back to the Leipzig chorale cantatas of J. S. Bach, whose closing four-part chorale harmonizations brought the modern tendencies of the preceding arias, recitatives, and choruses into a religious tradition that led directly back to Luther and the origins of the German Protestant Church. Something of this function was brought over into the symphony by Beethoven with the hymn of his Ninth, and then more directly still by those nineteenth-century symphonists who used actual chorales in their symphonic finales. A familiar example is the Symphony no. 5 ("Reformation") by Mendelssohn, in which he fashions an entire finale out of a fantasia-like development of "Ein feste Burg."

Brahms did not hesitate to treat the chorale iconically within his own First Symphony (C Minor, op. 68), but to very different effect. Like the opening movement of that work, the finale is initiated by a slow introduction that contains kernel motives of the ensuing allegro. Brahms differentiates the latter introduction, however, by moving beyond the abstract jagged and dissonant motives of bars 1–29 to concrete themes. Specifically, two symbol-laden episodes alternate at the end of the introduction to the finale: one, an alphorn melody set against shimmering string tremolos; the other a four-voice "imaginary" chorale whose setting in the brass and low winds unmistakably alludes to a Lutheran chorale in the most religious guise possible. Brahms initially moves beyond these two evocative melodies in the allegro of movement four to an elegiac main theme, whose resemblance to the "Freude" theme of Beethoven's Ninth Symphony has been the fodder of much debate since the premiere of Brahms's First Symphony. But both the alphorn and the chorale themes "replace" the allegro's main theme in turn: first, the alphorn theme serves as a point of arrival in bar 285 to usher in the "recapitulation" of this quasi–sonata form movement; and later, at bars 407–415 of the coda, it is the chorale that marks the most emphatic arrival of the entire symphony. Whether one hears this substitution for the "Ode to Joy"–like main allegro theme as affirming or effacing the Beethovenian tradition, there can be no doubting the power of the chorale to suggest a spiritually tinged shared cultural memory. It is not merely the volume and rhythmic breadth of these bars that create the effect of arrival here, it is the symbolic sound of the chorale itself that evokes monumentality.

But Brahms's imaginary chorale could hardly sound more different from Mendelssohn's chorale fantasy in the finale of the "Reformation" Symphony. Mendelssohn composed that work in anticipation of a performance in Berlin during 1830, the three-hundredth anniversary of Luther's Augsburg Confession.[38] Though edifying, Mendelssohn's commemoration merely affirms Luther's centrality for the German cultural traditions that by 1830 included the symphony. This is too direct a celebration and too much a reflection of the audience's own image of itself to provoke listeners to reconsider their identity; it does not carry the active character of Brahms's dramatic triumph of the chorale. Brahms, by contrast, forces his audience to grapple with the unconventional use of an unsung four-voice chorale (with all of its attendant historical connotations) at the height of a symphony. Myriad symbolic associations are set in play (religion, Luther, Bach, Beethoven, the symphonic tradition), all of which demand to be interpreted.

This difference between Mendelssohn's chorale finale in 1830 and Brahms's chorale "apotheosis" in 1876—specifically Brahms's apparent need to offer his listeners an edifying lesson—speaks to the changing nature of German identity in the *Kaiserreich* and how the German public defined itself in relation to the new regime of Bismarck and Kaiser Wilhelm I. At issue was how and whether the German public would come to recognize itself in the state. Art would come to play an increasingly active role in forming that image of the nation. Brahms's First Symphony, with its triumphant chorale, laid strong claims to speak for the traditional and learned side of German culture, as opposed to the more progressive and less rational art of Richard Wagner. Reinhold Brinkmann has argued that by supplanting a Beethovenesque theme with the alphorn theme and the chorale, Brahms was "taking back" the hopeful, humanistic message of Beethoven's Ninth (à la the fictional composer Adrian Leverkühn of Thomas Mann's *Doktor Faustus*), presenting instead a more resigned and regressive faith in nature and religion.[39] Brinkmann's is a challenging view of Brahms that fits into a broader picture of the composer as a latecomer and melancholic, looking back pessimistically from the later nineteenth century on the promise of Beethoven's "Ode to Joy." In this light it is not surprising that one year after composing his First Symphony, Brahms penned the motet "Warum ist das Licht gegeben?" which also reaches its apotheosis (and conclusion) in a chorale—a move that might be considered pessimistic in its own right.[40]

These somewhat later (1876–77) and more problematic treatments of chorales aside, in 1871 Brahms uses "Nun danket alle Gott" in his *Triumphlied* to deliver a purely affirmative message to the public and one that is clearly monumental in conception. The message is concretized closer to the end of movement two, when the complementing second half of the chorale's opening phrase is supplied by choir 1 in bars 172–176 (ex. 4.3) and 180–182. Krummacher observes that Brahms has cleverly alluded to the text of the chorale through the biblical passage at that moment, as the biblical phrase "und ihm die Ehre geben" is sung to the same melodic half phrase that sets "und edlen Frieden geben" in the second stanza of the chorale.[41] The connection to the chorale text is stronger still if we consider the entire half stanza from which that half phrase is drawn:

> Der ewig reiche Gott
> Woll uns bei unsrem Leben
> Ein immer fröhlich Herz
> Und edlen Frieden geben

In the *Triumphlied* both choirs sing "Laßt uns freuen und fröhlich sein" immediately preceding "und ihm die Ehre geben," alluding to the same granting of an "ever joyous heart" in the relevant chorale verses. Amid the tumult of the *Triumphlied,* the end of the second movement is indeed a moment of "noble peace." One cannot be so certain, however, whether Brahms expected listeners to make such a specific association to that text in "Nun danket alle Gott." Equally notable (though less verbally immediate) is the

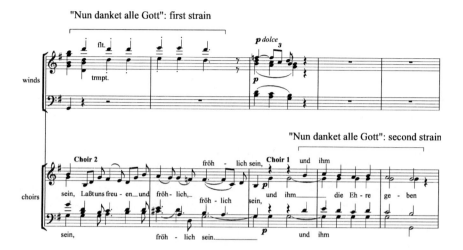

Example 4.3   Triumphlied, op. 55, movement two, bars 172–176.

allusion to a kingdom from that melodic half phrase in stanza three of the chorale, "Im höchsten Himmelsthrone," or the mention of the "great things" God does for us in stanza one ("Der große Dinge tut / An uns und allen Enden"). Among God's great deeds is the founding of the *Reich*, as stated in the preceding portion (section B) of the *Triumphlied*: "Denn der allmächtige Gott hat das Reich eingenommen." Since all three stanzas contain text at the half phrase in question that might relate to the biblical passage used by Brahms, it is fair to conclude along with Kalbeck (and several later commentators) that Brahms is indeed pointing to the newly revived figure of the emperor as the underlying object of veneration in the *Triumphlied*.

At every functional level the music and text are working toward a monumentalizing effect at this juncture in the piece.

1. Brahms evokes a chorale that already connotes both ancient (Luther) and recent (nationalist) history, thereby bringing the past(s) into the present.
2. By tying those temporal realms to the Bible, Brahms not only extends the time line of the chorale back into biblical antiquity but also adds a sacred meaning to recent political events: God is directly responsible for the Prussian military victory of the previous year.
3. The layering effect of the orchestration that separates and elevates "Nun danket alle Gott" creates a sonic "space" in which the listener can place himself or herself in relation to the larger community.
4. The object of veneration (a chorale) is communal rather than individual.

The last point has special significance when one considers that Brahms did, in fact, dedicate the *Triumphlied* to an individual, the newly crowned Wilhelm I. Not only does the Kaiser's name appear as dedicatee on the title page, but also the dedication page that follows in the score is unusually ornate, featuring the Hohenzollern crown and radiant beams streaming toward the inscription "To his Majesty Kaiser Wilhelm I. reverently dedicated by the composer."[42] Many commentators from 1872 to the present have even seen Wilhelm I in the person of the rider on the white horse in the last movement of the *Triumphlied*. Yet the object of veneration in this piece is not Wilhelm the individual but rather the crown itself. And this was typical for monuments of the *Grunderjahre*. In the thoroughgoing study of national monuments in Germany, Thomas Nipperdey distinguishes the highly personal commemorations of Wilhelm II from the generalized veneration of his grandfather, which "are always less individual monuments of the represented monarch[;] they are much more monuments to the princely office, monuments to monarchy as a form of rule, and then also monuments to the nation."[43] A good example of this principle in action is the refusal of Wilhelm I to be realistically represented in the narrative circular fresco at the base of the *Siegessäule* in Berlin, at the time the largest and most expensive monument to German unification in the Prussian capital.[44] According to the fresco's painter, Anton von Werner, Wilhelm did not want to particularize the identity of the new *Reich* as "Prussian" at a time when political stability dictated that all parts of the newly united Germany feel that they too had a place in the state.[45] Brahms's monumentalization of the chorale "Nun danket alle Gott" is entirely in keeping with that tenor of the times and is an appropriate glorification not merely of the Kaiser as monarch but of the monarchy itself. And this in turn is in keeping with Brahms's strong support of the new state under Wilhelm I and Bismarck as the embodiment of Germany, a position that Brahms was to maintain until his death and that clearly distinguishes his modernist patriotism from the *völkisch* nationalism that grew in opposition to the *Reich* through the last quarter of the nineteenth century. The events of 1870–71 briefly suppressed the conflict between these two sides of German nationalism. But they gradually resurfaced over the next two decades, as Brahms addressed in his *Fest- und Gedenkspruche*, op. 109 of 1889. I return to that part of the story in the next chapter.

Apocalypse Now

Brahms's *Triumphlied* also shares an aesthetic quality with Werner's fresco; both works present a tremendous sensation of motion that nevertheless seems already to have reached its conclusion. Whereas Werner's oil canvases in celebration of the new *Reich* exercised realism, most famously *The Proclamation of the Empire at Versailles,* his fresco on the *Siegessäule* attempts to convey the story of the Reich's arrival since the Napoleonic Wars in historicist terms reminiscent of Cornelius's "Riders of the Apocalypse" (and recalls that work's similar deviation from its artist's more typically classicizing style). Allegorical figures abound in Werner's fresco amid the motion-filled scenes of battles, suggesting that the meaning of the events depicted are eternal, that the story of German unification narrated here is more than a current event but rather part of an ageless drama of cosmic import. Because Werner's images circumscribe a column, and are therefore inherently circular, the viewer literally concludes where he or she originated; there is no real beginning or ending to this fresco, or, rather, they are one and the same. Clearly, there is a beginning and an end to the *Triumphlied*—such are the practical limitations of music in the European common practice tradition. But lacking in this piece is the usual sense of directed forward motion that we would expect from Brahms. Even in *Ein deutsches Requiem,* which wanders between the pillars of its outer movements (as I argued in the preceding chapter), the plodding bass F's that begin the first and last movement suggest a forward-moving continuum which reaches its conclusion in the fading strains that end each of those movements. And the climactic fugue at the end of the sixth movement suggests an arrival, even if the path toward it is unclear.

In the *Triumphlied* there is, instead, a sense of constantly beginning in mid-stream. Hence, the dotted-rhythm motives that begin all three movements seem more to pick up a continuing thread than to start anew. In the work's opening bars (as highlighted in ex. 4.4), the convergence of a tonic statement of the introductory orchestral theme in the winds (bars 1–3) and a dominant statement of the same in the strings (bars 2–3) blurs the notion of a "beginning," as does the awkward metrical displacement of the strings' entrance to the fifth eighth note of the bar. That syncopation spawns a sequence of weak-beat entrances on diminished chords in bars 6–9, from which the music does not right itself rhythmically and harmonically until the eight-bar dominant "pedal" of bars 11–18. Thus, more than half of the orchestral prelude is delivered in an imbalanced developmental fashion, something we might expect near the middle or end of a movement, not at the outset.

Although the dotted rhythms at the beginning of the other two movements are not accompanied by quite so drastic a dislocation, the very gesture of returning to this martial motive with every new movement suggests an ongoing thread throughout the entire piece, as if it were all cut from the same cloth. And these two movements' openings are not without their own rhythmic digressions, each of which undermines a sense of a clear begin-

Example 4.4   Triumphlied, op. 55, movement one, opening: tonic dominant statement of theme and metrical displacements on diminished-seventh chords.

ning. So, for example, at the outset of movement two the competing accents in ¾ meter among the dotted figures of the high, middle, and low strings (with contrabassoon) in bars 1–6 (ex. 4.5A) fail to provide any convincing sense of downbeat, an effect that is exacerbated by the initial entrance on beat two by the violins and viola.[46] Just six bars later (ex. 4.5B), the initial choral entrance in G major is promptly interrupted, not only by a harmonic shift first to E major (choir 1, bars 12–14), then to E minor (choir 2, bars 14–16), but also by an awkward seven-beat phrase that takes its rhythmic cue from the second-beat entrance at the beginning of the movement. As in the previous movement, the rhythmic peculiarities that accompany the dotted motive at the movement's outset foster rhythmic irregularities that confuse the listener's sense of meter and thereby diminish a clear sense of a beginning. Finally, there is a hint of the *Schrekensfanfare* (à la Beethoven's Ninth Symphony) in the dissonant clash between the strings' melodic descent B♭–A–G–F against the winds' sustained-interval A–C♯ which initiates the final movement. And again the dissonance is not merely a harmonic effect; once more the strings enter on an odd beat (the pickup to beat three), forcing the introductory phrase of paired two-bar phrases to come to a gear-grinding halt that requires an "extra" two-bar unit to reach the closing *fortissimo* figure on the second beat of bar 4.

Nowhere, then, in the three-movement work does Brahms offer a clear commencing point. Rather, we are constantly plunged into the fray. Adding to this effect are the recurrent references to the opening "Heil und Preis" motive throughout the piece.[47] In the second movement, a direct statement on D major (within a prevailing key of G major) surfaces in bars 36–38 to the words "unsern Gott." Less direct, but nevertheless significant, is the first complete choral statement in the third movement beginning at bar 22 at the text "Treu und Wahrhaftig." The motivic connection here is far more general but maintains enough of the rhythmic and intervallic profile to recall the "Heil und Preis" motive of the first movement. I point out these relationships not to make a claim of thematic unity in the *Triumphlied*, but rather to suggest that it would be a meaningless quality to seek in a work that never progresses from where it started, that is frozen in one ecstatic and jubilant moment. Appropriate though this aesthetic may be to the occasion for which the piece was conceived, the potential stasis in this design is fraught with aesthetic difficulties. The issue lies not in a dearth of contrapuntal details or colorful effects, of which there are many in this work, but rather in the way they are placed in relation to one another. A more detailed analysis of one distinct theme and its treatment within a movement serves to illustrate. Brahms's setting of the words "und die ihn fürchten, Kleine und Große" in the second movement counts as one of the most delicate passages in the entire piece. This idea appears as a secondary theme beginning in bar

Example 4.5   Triumphlied, op. 55, movement two, opening: (A) metrical displacement of theme; (B) seven-beat interjections, bars 12–16.

22, after which it alternates for the rest of the large opening period with the initial choral theme and its text, "Lobet unsern Gott, alle seine Knechte" (ex. 4.6). Were this passage to appear in any of Brahms's other works for chorus and orchestra, it likely would be praised for the canonic inversion between the bass and soprano of choir 2 (bars 22–25) and again between the alto and soprano of choir 1 in bars 26–30. Equally laudable would be the gradual crescendo and transformation in bars 30–38 of the descending eighth notes at "beide Kleine und Große" into the cascading set of entries on

Example 4.5   (continued)

"lobet unsern Gott," all concluding in an echo of the "Heil und Preis" motive from the first movement (in D major, no less).

   There is, however, something about this passage (and many other admira-
ble places in the *Triumphlied*) that is utterly un-Brahmsian, and this has
more to do with what is *not* here than with what Brahms *has* composed. In
the *Triumphlied*, passages like this one lack the needed musical space to set
them off from their surroundings; there are no unaccompanied passages for
the choirs, nor prolonged statements by either the wind or the string choirs
alone or as a unified counterpart to the choirs. Instead, here, and in the entire piece, all available forces—winds, choirs, and stings—are continuously
present.[48] One consequence of such full-throttle writing is that there are
none of the long-breathed, elegiac lines with which Brahms frequently begins a large-scale piece or movement. In the *Triumphlied*, Brahms does not
provide enough of the continuity in either choir or any section of the orchestra that is necessary to form a fully developed melodic sentence. Therefore,
what ideas do emerge have little in the way of a formal frame of the kind we
are so accustomed to hearing in Brahms's music. Things happen too immediately in this piece for those sorts of moments to form. It would be easy to
assign the sense of immediacy I have just described in the *Triumphlied* to the
sudden and dramatic impact of the event that occasioned the piece, the

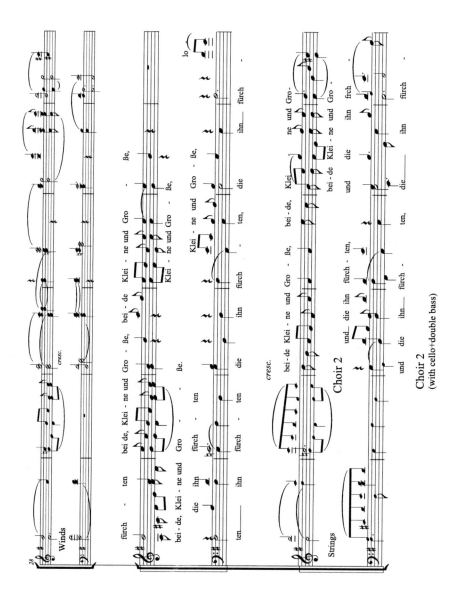

Example 4.6   *Triumphlied*, op. 55, movement two: bars 22–33.

Franco-Prussian War of 1870. Yet, as I have already discussed in the preceding chapter, that sense of millennial anticipation in nineteenth-century Germany was bound up with long-standing apocalyptic historical paradigms. And it is in this context—that is, when measured against an apocalyptic paradigm—that the *Triumphlied* (ironically) fails. Its failure lies not in its ability to satisfy pure musical expectations or in its stylistic qualities per se. Rather, its failure is directly tied to the inherently problematic political identity of the *Kaiserreich* as an apocalyptic arrival point in modern German national history.

For a piece that assertively announces its apocalyptic purpose—recall Brahms's insistence that the biblical source of the text be stated on the title page of the published score—op. 55 does not match the sense of anticipation and yearning that characterized so much of the apocalyptic tenor of German national striving before 1870. Like the *Kaiserreich* itself, the *Triumphlied* is completely upon us; the problem, apocalyptically speaking, was the very real attainability of this goal. In comparison to the cultural manifestations of apocalyptic thinking that the drive toward German nationhood occasioned before 1870, the feeling of living in a transition before the end (Kermode's idea discussed in the preceding chapter) was directly politicized for citizens of the *Gründerjahre*. If one could relate one's own death to the unknowable ends of time before the founding of the *Reich*, one could, conversely, project one's *life* onto the idea of the new nation, striving toward its own lofty "End." But the end here is distinctly an arrival rather than an extinction. Ironically, when the *Kaiserreich* became a reality in 1871, the idea of a restored kingdom immediately began to lose its apocalyptic power. Despite the biblical (and indeed apocalyptic) language with which many writers described the events of 1870 and 1871, the experience of witnessing the arrival of the restored kingdom on earth (i.e., the crowning of King Wilhelm of Prussia as Kaiser of the new *Reich*) overshoots the framework of Western apocalypticism by knowing, in fact, how it all ends. The *Triumphlied* is a work that reflects this dilemma. As I noted earlier, this is the only one of Brahms's works for chorus and orchestra that does not end quietly. Here Brahms provides no reflective frame, and precious few moments of repose amidst the tumult, and he eschews the apocalyptic gesture (as witnessed in its sister work, the *Requiem*) of stepping outside the scope of time to imagine the apocalypse. Instead the idea of the "End" comes rushing at us at every turn. Perhaps the same is true of any artwork that self-consciously attaches itself to the earthly realization of this political apocalyptic arrival, such as Cornelius's "Riders of the Apocalypse" or Werner's fresco on the *Siegessäule*. Like those works, then, the *Triumphlied* could be described as one great ending. Brahms himself labeled the first movement as such when he announced to Hermann Levi in a letter of April

1871 that he had recently performed his *Requiem* again in Bremen and added, "This time we have added a *fortissimo* conclusion." Unlike the formal frame that separates the arrival of an ending in movement six of *Ein deutsches Requiem* from the quasi-timelessness implied by the sameness of the outer (first and seventh) movements in that work, the end in the *Triumphlied* is ever present and immediate.

This lack of a classicizing frame also affects the larger formal scheme of the *Triumphlied*. In part this is a function of the work's unusual (for Brahms) episodic character. None of the three movements follows a cyclical (A B A etc.) or otherwise overtly rational form. My own labeling in fig. 4.2 bears out this episodic quality in op. 55. Both the first and second movements contain internal restatements of their respective opening themes. But in neither case does this return amount to a reprise per se. Rather, those themes are developed anew, their constituent motives are reorganized, and new developments of the themes are pursued. Formally, the scheme of each of these movements has more of the rambling character of baroque style to it than the classical attention to proportions one associates with Brahms. In both movements one and two, the thematic return gives way to transitional material that brings the movement to a close with new material. The close of the first movement has a particular formal peculiarity, in that it displays many of the clichés of a finale, most notably that of a symphony. After rounding off the main portion of the first movement with a highly altered return to the opening theme in bars 116–157, Brahms gradually works his way to a *piano* dominant pedal (beginning in bar 170) that builds through a gradual crescendo and an increasing level of harmonic tension (it arrives at a viio7/V over the 5 [A] pedal) to an *animato* conclusion at bar 183.[49] Now the "Heil und Preis" motive is taken up in block chords by all eight voices across the two choirs, who are eventually joined by the entire orchestra for a brief *fortissimo* diversion to the parallel (D) minor (bars 191–192). Although Brahms does not set this interjection off with a new tempo, it bears all the marks of a brief pulling back before a final acceleration, one of the most typical devices in Beethovenian finales. Indeed, when the choir splits off from the instruments again, its unison octave-leap articulations of "Heil und Preis" against the upsurging torrents of sixteenth notes in the strings and lower winds strongly recall the concluding choral exclamations from Beethoven's Ninth Symphony.

Everything here signals the end—not just of a movement but, specifically, a finale. In a piece in which the end is everywhere, it matters not that we are only at the end of the first of three movements. Even in a one-movement work, however, this sort of drive to the final bar is out of character for Brahms. A quick comparison with his other large-scale choral-orchestral works demonstrates how unusual this formal approach is for him. The

Schicksalslied is the most explicitly tripartite among these other works. Indeed, it is specifically the return to the opening material that makes Brahms's setting of Hölderlin's text so compelling. As discussed earlier, Brahms completed this work in the spring and summer of 1871, taking time off from composing the last two movements of the *Triumphlied* to do so. Most of the compositional questions that absorbed Brahms in his final work on the *Schicksalslied* concerned its ending. In Hölderlin's text the graces of the gods in the first passage (set in E-flat major) are sharply juxtaposed with the miserable lot of humanity in the second passage (set in the relative C minor). Brahms, however, did not feel comfortable leaving the piece with such a pessimistic conclusion and brought back the elegiac strains from the opening of the work at its close as an orchestral *Nachspiel* in the parallel C major rather than the expected key of E-flat in which that material was first heard. Here, then, Brahms chose to manipulate the rational A B A form and thereby displays his typical need to reconcile thematic material (if not key) at the end of a large-scale work, even when that need trumps the composer's instinct to reflect the spirit of the poem accurately, as Brahms does not do in setting Hölderlin here.[50]

In the later *Gesang der Parzen* (1882), Brahms eschews any strong reprise. Instead, the turn to a narrative voice ("So sangen die Parzen") prompts an eerie echo of the opening motive that dissolves into *pianissimo* unison choral gasps and a chilling concluding fifth in the orchestra as the exiled old man "shakes his head." Here (by comparison with the through-composed forms of the *Triumphlied*) the nature of the text dictates the quiet conclusion of the music. The *Alt-Rhapsodie*, op. 53 (1869), is built on a progression from a C minor solo to a C major "hymn" for alto and men's chorus, although its constituent parts are both cyclical. Following a stormy introduction, a distinct three-part aria in C minor and triple meter ("Ach, wer heilet die Schmerzen . . ."; bars 48–115) grounds the piece, before the change to C major, duple meter, and the entrance of the men's chorus initiates yet another closed three-part song form ("Ist auf deinem Psalter").

As he had in the *Requiem*, Brahms balances his formal impulse to recapitulate against a dramatic progression in the three single-movement works for chorus and orchestra. The *Triumphlied* lacks either character. Neither in its overall conception nor in the forms of the individual movements is there any strong sense of return. And none of the movements progress toward their conclusion with the same feeling of a logical process one finds in the concluding C major transformation of the *Schicksalslied* or the dying echoes of early turmoil at the end of the *Gesang der Parzen*. If any part of the *Triumphlied* approaches the linear conception of these other works it is the third movement, where the alternation between the baritone soloist and chorus offers a greater sense of formal progression than in the purely choral preceding movements. As the soloist enters in bar 7 with the revelation "And I saw the heavens opened," his prophetic tone reminds one immediately of movement six in *Ein deutsches Requiem,* where the baritone serves a similarly oracular function. Also reminiscent of that moment in op. 45 is the fluctuating harmonic ground on which the baritone stands in bars 8–21 of the *Triumphlied*'s third movement before a re-transitional passage ushers in D major. The choral theme that begins thereafter ("Hieß Treu und Wahrhaftig") similarly matches the vivid and vigorous C minor *vivace* from the middle of the *Requiem*'s sixth movement. At this point in the *Triumphlied,* an "apocalyptic Rider" appears: not one of the horrific horsemen portrayed in Cornelius's painting, but rather one who "makes war and judges in righteousness (Revelation 19:11), from whose "mouth comes a sharp sword with which to strike down the nations, and he will rule them with a rod of iron," and whose name is inscribed "King of kings and Lord of lords." At the moment when the rider's first appellation, "Treu und Wahrhaftig," is announced (he receives many between verses 11 and 17), Brahms unleashes a torrent of militaristic writing that is heard nowhere else in his music.

A comparison of this passage's function with that of the aforementioned C minor choral episode from movement six of the *Requiem* gets to the heart of the *Triumphlied*'s hard sell to modern audiences. As I discussed in the previous chapter, the text in the C minor episode from the sixth movement of the *Requiem* (bars 82–104 and again at 127–204) conveys the transformation of the dead and the living into the immortal inhabitants of God's everlasting Kingdom. Appropriately, Brahms executes a striking set of modulations there to transform C minor to C major through the choir's upward chromatic octaves from C-sharp to E-flat on the word "Tod," and on to E natural at the word "Hölle" in bar 159. Significantly for a comparison with the third movement of the *Triumphlied,* that striking passage from the sixth movement of the *Requiem* is integrally connected with an earlier arresting event, namely, the three-step sequential ascent to an E-flat harmony at bars 67–76, the original entrance into the C-minor choral episode (see exs. 3.3 and 3.4 in the preceding chapter). As those events in the *Requiem* drive the music forward to its resplendent goal, the C major fugue, they provide everything we expect of Brahms and everything we value in him as a composer. This is music that is strongly linear and goal oriented, and moves confidently and logically through a complex set of harmonic and motivic relationships to reach a satisfying conclusion.

On the surface, there are several similarities between this material and the "Treu und Wahrhaftig" material beginning in bar 22 of the third movement of op. 55; both present a mixture of *forte* unison and part writing for the chorus, frequently doubled by winds, along with driving arpeggio figures in the strings. But whereas the former passage serves a long-range function within its movement and within the *Requiem* generally, this passage in the *Triumphlied* is formally static. Having attained the tonic (D) major to resolve the dissonance of the movement's opening in D minor and F major, this passage veers off constantly toward F-sharp minor, the loosely expressed key of the ensuing section on the text "Und er tritt die Kelter des Weins" (bars 71–93). If anything, the "Treu und Wahrhaftig" music regresses when it veers to the key of the mediant, losing whatever tonic tonal ground it had gained from the tonally unstable opening of the movement (bars 1–21).

In its own right, however, this "Treu und Wahrhaftig" music is every bit as effective as the C minor material in the *Requiem*. Nowhere is the martial theme of the piece made so musically explicit as here with the motoric galloping rhythm of the strings, the sixteenth-note string flourishes (bars 40, 42, etc.), and the ubiquitous trumpet fanfares (bars 23, 25, etc.). Even the dotted figures that dominate the rest of the piece are highlighted here in the setting of the words "mit Gerechtigkeit," which are—more often than not—set to hemiolas as in bars 27–29, or in the extended sequence of bars 32–40 that bring the first sentence of this section to a half cadence. Brahms extends this material for another thirty bars, constantly veering toward the sharp side: once to V (A major, bar 40) and twice to V of iii (C-sharp major from bar 56 on and bars 68–71). The eventual half cadence in bar 71 to a C-sharp dominant chord sounds less like an arrival than a detour. In other words, this material does not develop musically so much as it redirects its fury.

What truly develops in this music is its jingoistic intensity, and it is here that *Triumphlied* becomes dangerous, even threatening. What had appeared as militaristic enthusiasm at the beginning of this section deteriorates into wild-eyed fanaticism when the various martial motives (fanfares, homorhythmic unison choral statements, and string flourishes) cease to occur in a predictable, rational order but pile up instead. Originally, these three elements worked together in a balanced presentation of phrases. First, at bars 22–25, the trumpet fanfares serve a clear punctuating role in the second bar of the men's, then the women's, statement of "Treu und Wahrhaftig." When that material returns in bars 40–46, those statements (now by the combined choirs) are introduced by string flourishes and are extended for an extra bar (44–45) against an elongated trumpet fanfare. After a further development of the "mit Gerechtigkeit" hemiolas (bars 49–56), now leading to the first half cadence on C-sharp, Brahms leads back to D major and the constituent martial elements beginning in bar 59. Here, however, they pile up atop one another (with the timpani added anew) out of sequence and, perhaps, out of control. Harmonically as well, the "Treu und Wahrhaftig" motive has taken on a more ominous tone; it now ends on an F-sharp minor chord as opposed to the more decisive-sounding tonic or dominant (D or A major) to which it had cadenced in the earlier statements. The tendency toward C-sharp, then, is foreshadowed in the reconfiguration of the theme itself, which never turns back toward D major, sliding instead toward another cadence to C-sharp major on the way to the key of F-sharp minor in the ensuing period of the movement. To reiterate, this sounds less like an arrival at a goal than it does a diversion to dwell on something darker and more problematic than the ebullient D major in which the "Treu und Wahrhaftig" began. Appropriately, the text in this segment of movement three accentuates the violence of the rider on the white horse: "He will tread the winepress of the fury of the wrath of God the Almighty."

If the prospect of Brahms composing music that lacked a classical framework or clear sense of direction causes discomfort by going against the grain of our stylistic expectations, to hear his music threatening to lose control as it does in these bars is downright frightening. It is not merely the violence of the musical material that disturbs here, for Brahms certainly matched the sheer volume and driving force of this figuration in other works: in addition to the C minor material from the sixth movement of the *Requiem*, one could count the dirge opening of movement two in that work, the allegro middle portion of the *Schicksalslied* (also in C minor), countless moments in the *Gesang der Parzen* (such as the orchestral introduction), and a host of passages in the symphonies. In each of those instances, however, musical violence might be heard as a means to some nobler end, be it the edifying point of the texts in op. 54 and 89, or the eventual breakthrough to the relative major keys in the two examples from op. 45. In the *Triumphlied*, however, our prejudices necessarily prevent us from hearing the violence in the same way. Already in Brahms's day, the specter of a militarily and industrially powerful German state in central Europe was a threat to its neighbors. Since 1945 our associations with such militant strains in the name of the *Reich* are all the more problematic. It may be impossible to hear the violence in these bars as a musical posture or an imaginative response to a text, as we might hear it in the other works just listed. More upsetting still is to hear these strains coming from Brahms, the antipode to Wagner and the rational purveyor of the detached, classicizing style in late-nineteenth-century German music. If even *he* could descend into the roar of the rabble, what is safe in German art? One might also fear how this reflects on Brahms's other seemingly rhetorical outbursts. How innocent are they after all? To what extent are they also manifestations of the German imperial tone? This is not our Brahms. And so the *Triumphlied* must be branded an aberration, and we can ascribe the powerful effects of the piece on listeners reported by contemporaneous critics as a mere side effect of the audiences' patriotic euphoria, not a genuine aesthetic response to the music. Going further in his seminal

1959 study of Brahms's choral music, Siegfried Kross projects that attitude onto the composer himself, asserting that it derives less from an artistic than from a patriotic impulse.[51]

To be sure, the patriotic impetus behind the work influenced its compositional style, and our post-1945 discomfort is largely based on the very notion of a nationalistic German work celebrating a Prussian military victory. But there is a larger issue at stake here than one occasional work by a canonical composer. Brahms's sober, goal-oriented, and complex musical language is celebrated not only for aesthetic reasons but for political ones as well. For these are the things that separate him from composers whose style more neatly accommodated German nationalist ideologies, namely, Wagner and Bruckner. I would in no way suggest that the *Triumphlied* sounds anything like a piece by one of those composers. (And for what it is worth, Wagner is known to have despised the work.) On the contrary, it sounds very much like Brahms—just without the surrounding context. But the lack of complex motivic relationships, the lack of a classicizing frame, the broad brush with which Brahms casts his ideas in the *Triumphlied* threaten our modern concept of Brahms's cultural meaning. In coming to terms with how the *Triumphlied* fails musically to meet our expectations (not simply why we are repelled by its politics), we become ever more aware of the political significance of Brahms's music, beyond the political context of one anomalous piece.

Gebet Einer König: National Prayers in the *Fest- und Gedenksprüche,* Op. 109

Community and Polychorality

Brahms never wavered from the patriotism he displayed in the *Triumphlied*. Over the last quarter century of his life he continued to revel in the events of 1870–71, acquiring numerous books on the war, collections of Bismarck's speeches and letters, and various other works related to the *Reich*. Writing of Brahms's last days, Kalbeck claims that Brahms "could never get enough of newly published books about the war and victory of 1870–71," and writes of the Bismarck calendar that Clara Simrock had sent Brahms for Christmas 1896. Brahms wrote her husband, Karl Simrock, that "my own [Bismarck calendar] was horrible and every page made me angry at the year; it was a Hamburg product, and every day it gave a daily menu and lousy verses, [only] a pair of Bismarck quotes per month—but this calendar is solid Berlin and pure Bismarck. Every morning it revives me to be greeted by a word from him."[1]

But for all of his veneration of Bismarck and the *Reich*, Brahms never again expressed his national pride so overtly in his music as he had in op. 55. Instead, he publicly displayed his connection to the German culture of which the *Kaiserreich* was a political culmination and manifestation by overcoming his long silence in the field of the symphony. Brahms had already mastered large-scale instrumental forms by composing a variety of chamber works—the String Sextets, opp. 18 and 36; the Piano Quartets, opp. 24 and 25; the Piano Quintet, op. 34; and the Horn Trio, op. 40—all composed between 1859 and 1865. The *Triumphlied* itself may be seen as one in a series of pieces by which Brahms worked his way in measured steps toward symphonic composition. Along with *Ein deutsches Requiem*, the *Alto Rhapsody, Rinaldo* (op. 50 of 1869), and the *Schicksalslied*, the *Triumphlied* gave Brahms valuable experience in writing for the orchestra.

Last in this lineage was the orchestral version of the *Variations for Orchestra on a Theme of Haydn,* op. 56a, 1874 (simultaneously published in a two-piano version as op. 56b). Only two years later, Brahms finally completed the symphony his followers had anticipated since Schumann's "Neue Bahnen" essay of 1853 spoke of "veiled symphonies" in the piano pieces and called for Brahms to write for "the power and masses of the choir and orchestra." And by 1877 a second symphony (D major, op. 73) followed quickly on the heels of the first.

Brahms's arrival on the symphonic scene in the 1870s was timely; it was during this decade that the genre made a comeback, as new German symphonies were being composed in large numbers for the first time since the 1840s. The reasons for this resurgence are debatable, but nearly all commentators agree that the symphonies that Brahms and Bruckner composed during the 1870s eclipsed the efforts of their immediate predecessors in the genre: Hiller, Raff, Reinecke, and others. (The resurgence was also fueled by non-Germans writing in the Austro-Germanic symphonic tradition, most notably Tchaikovsky, who had composed his first four symphonies by 1878 and popularized them on his many successful conducting tours of Europe during that decade.) Reinhold Brinkmann suggests that the drop and subsequent rise in the numbers of German symphonies may be partly a consequence of political events in Germany from 1848 to 1871, a fallow period between the failed revolutions of the former date and the latter year of unification.[2] Although it is difficult to find a direct cause and effect, this thesis has much merit, for only after the German concert-going public had a sense of itself as a national community could the symphony regain its Beethovenian "society-forming" function—to use Paul Bekker's famous formulation.[3]

Beethoven wrote his symphonies during the initial decades of the German drive toward national unity, and thus they were directed more to a perceived humanistic community than a distinct nation (however much German nationalism was tied up in a neo-humanist revival in the early nineteenth century).[4] Theodor Adorno labels those works "orations to mankind, designed by a demonstration of the law of their life, to bring men to an unconscious consciousness of the unity otherwise hidden in the individual's diffuse existence."[5] Adorno's slight change in nomenclature—he speaks of the symphony's "*community*-forming" *(Gemeinschaftbildend)* effect—may reflect the slightly later vantage point than Bekker's from which he viewed the social history of the symphony. In the second half of the twentieth century, Adorno was all too aware of "how deeply the humanity and universality of music entwine with the national element they are transcending" in the Austro-German tradition.[6] Thus to him, as opposed to Bekker, writing half a century earlier, the symphony creates not only a sense of society but also

one of community—and (at one level) a community that is specifically national. Brahms entered the symphonic stage at the moment when this distinction became not simply meaningful but imperative. Just as the construction of monuments in the *Kaiserreich* was "like a confession of faith
repeated again and again" to "conjure up something which, obviously, did
not exist to a sufficient degree" (to revisit Reinhard Alings's statement,
quoted in the previous chapter), the community-forming role of the symphony in post-1871 Germany served a national-confirming purpose for its
audience. Having built a national consciousness on the strengths of their
cultural traditions in the first half of the nineteenth century, German
concertgoers saw the political achievement of the nation newly reflected in
the "second age" of the symphony after 1871.[7]

Walter Frisch traces the social function of Brahms's symphonies back to
Ein deutsches Requiem. Although he argues that "for the composer the language and culture were less important than the larger message of comfort
and faith" that bespeaks a secular humanism, Frisch nevertheless recognizes
that Brahms reached across religious boundaries to an "intended audience
that was the broader society that shared his native tongue and culture."[8]
That Brahms would choose to achieve this effect through a choral work, no
less one based on sacred texts (whatever their humanistic cachet), points to
the important linking of the Lutheran religious liturgy with mass music
making in the formation of a national communal identity. Even the secular
works that fall between the *Requiem* and the *Triumphlied* play into this paradigm by evoking the historic religious aura of choral singing. Compared,
however, with the symphonies and the large-scale choral-orchestral works
of the early 1870s (op. 54 and 55) and early 1880s (op. 83 and 89), the
works Brahms produced during this period included little in the way of a
cappella choral music, less still in the sacred area. Even the two impressive
motets of op. 74, "Warum ist das Licht gegeben den Mühseligen" and "O
Heiland, reiß die Himmel auf," were constructed largely from preexisting
material.[9] And whereas one can make a case for the national import of
works such as these that so strongly refer to the legacy of Bach, there is
nothing overtly political about them.

Not until the late 1880s would Brahms once again use large choral forces
to express his political outlook. In 1889 he produced two separate collections of sacred a cappella works: the *Fest- und Gedenksprüche*, op. 109, and
Drei Motteten, op. 110. The former set comprised three ceremonial settings
of biblical texts; the latter included one on biblical texts (no. 1, "Ich aber bin
elend") and two on *Kirchenlieder* (no. 2, "Ach, arme Welt," and no. 3,
"Wenn wir in höchsten Nöten sein"). A clear link between these two collections is the normative use of a cappella eight-voice polychoral writing, a
new format for Brahms. (Only op. 110, no. 2, is set for a single, four-voice

choir.) In opp. 109 and 110, polychoral writing is one compositional means by which he reflects the plural voice or references to a community that occur in most of the texts through phrases such as "*Unsere* Väter," "ein *Haus*," "ein jeglich' *Reich*," "*unser* Gott," and "Wenn *wir* in höchsten Nöten sein."[10] Brahms's choice of communally oriented texts indicates his concern around that time for the "community" that was the German *Reich*, as events in German politics colored his previously chauvinistic attitude toward Germany with a feeling of urgency bordering on despair.

From the start, Brahms seems to have conceived of and referred to opp. 109 and 110 as a pair. That assertion runs contrary to the widely held notion that the *Fest- und Gedenksprüche* were written first, probably during 1888–89, and that only then did Brahms compose op. 110. He gave a manuscript score of op. 109 to Theodor Billroth in April 1889 and sent another to Hans von Bülow in Hamburg a month later for performance in a music festival there the following September. The first explicit mention of the op. 110 motets comes slightly later, when Brahms offers them to Simrock in a letter of 13 June 1889 as a companion set to op. 109. But an earlier reference to some of the late motets casts this accepted chronology into doubt. In a letter of 11 May 1889, Franz Wüllner asks Brahms whether he would be interested in contributing "one or the other of the new eight-voice works" to a collection of works for five to sixteen voices which Wüllner planned to publish as the next installment of his *Chorübungen*.[11] We do not know when or how Wüllner came to know of these works before writing this letter, but this earliest reference suggests that Brahms had begun, or perhaps even completed, the op. 110 motets before sending the score of the *Fest- und Gedenksprüche* to Billroth a few weeks later in May. Brahms continues to mention the two collections as a pair in a number of subsequent letters to Simrock, and in February 1890, opp. 109 and 110 were published together according to the composer's wishes.[12]

Taken together, opp. 109 and 110 have generally been understood as a *heiter und dunkel* pair, like so many *opera* in Brahms's middle and later periods. The op. 110 motets paint a consistent picture of gloom, marked as they are by their minor-mode chromatic lines and generally dense textures, and by a seemingly unending litany of distress through words such as "elend," "Wehe," "Leiden," "Not," "eitel," "sorgen," "Rettung," "Angst," and "Trübsal." Most of these occur in the context of calling for God's help. Indeed, the first two motets end with prayers ("Gott deine Hilfe schütze mich" in no. 1, and "Hilf mir Herr zum Frieden" in no. 2), as does the end of the first verse in no. 3 ("Wir . . . dich rufen an, o treuer Gott, um Rettung aus der Angst und Not"). On the other side of the coin are the *Fest- und Gedenksprüche*, which are musically characterized by their predominantly bright major-mode and diatonic writing, leading most writers to describe them as celebratory, radiant, and "festive," as their name would suggest. And although their texts are hardly as effusive or full of praise to God as the patriotic *Triumphlied*, they are often cited as a similarly positive statement of Brahms's patriotic zeal.

What many commentators fail to observe in the texts of op. 109, however, are the oblique calls for God's help, not unlike those in op. 110: "Unsere Väter hofften auf dich"; "schrien sie" (no. 1); "zu dem Götter also nahe sich tun als der Herr, unser Gott, so oft wir ihn anrufen." (no. 3). If we consider the *Fest- und Gedenksprüche* in this light, we become more aware of words such as "hoffen," "schrien," "erretten," "bewahren," "rufen," and "hüten," words that convey a feeling of danger and need which is not so far removed from the distress of the op. 110 motets. Our present prayers are not yet answered in op. 109: we know only that God answered the prayers of "Unsere Väter," not that He will come to *our* aid. Therefore, despite the apparent contrasts between these two *opera*, they share an underlying similarity in outlook (if not in musical character) which speaks directly to the generally communal and religious imagery of their texts. More than any other works by Brahms, these pieces convey a national community that is bound by its Lutheran heritage.

Ironically, the event that is usually cited as the impetus for Brahms's expression of positive patriotic feelings in the *Fest- und Gedenksprüche*, namely, the so-called *Drei-Kaiser-Jahr* of 1888, probably prompted Brahms to select texts that expressed prayers for help in all of the late motets. I have already cited, in Chapter 2, Max Kalbeck's account of how Brahms was troubled by the deaths of Kaisers Wilhelm I and Friedrich in 1888, and by the strife between Bismarck and the young new successor, Wilhelm II, in that year. As I posited there, Brahms apparently selected a group of six biblical passages at that time as a response to the crisis that the difficult transfer of power posed to the German Republic. He copied those texts onto folios 15v–19r in his pocket notebook of biblical texts (see Chapter 2). The most poignant of these texts is Wisdom of Solomon 9:1–12 (18v–19r), in which "Solomon" delivers a formal and formulaic prayer to God for the strength and wisdom he will need to lead his "Volk." Verse 7, "You have chosen me to be king of your people and to be judge over your sons and daughters," strongly supports Kalbeck's contention that with this text, Brahms was referring to the newly crowned Kaiser Wilhelm II.

When Brahms composed opp. 109 and 110, however, he used none of the newly selected texts on folios 15v–19r. Instead, he turned back to others that he had copied onto folios 13r–15v of his notebook sometime earlier. That pool of texts is listed in fig. 2.4. Significantly, he seems to have rejected some of the more positive endings he had originally considered for these previously compiled texts, opting instead to bring out a sense of praying to

God for help in both *opera*. "Ich aber bin elend" (op. 110, no. 1), for example, contains two texts that seem originally to have been conceived in conjunction with some of the texts that were used for the "Warum" motet,
op. 74, no. 1, of 1877 (James 5:11 and Lamentations 3:41), based on the
proximity of all the texts on folio 13r in the notebook. When he eventually
composed "Ich aber bin elend" with texts from that page, Brahms envel-
oped the longer passage from Exodus 34:6–7 ("Herr, Herr Gott, barmherzig
und gnädig") with the two lines from Psalm 69:30 ("Ich aber bin elend und
mir ist weh, Gott deine Hilfe schütze mich"). In his notebook of biblical
texts, however, the more faith-affirming lines from Exodus originally followed the darker thoughts of Psalm 69, and thus the call for God's help
would not necessarily have ended the motet. And whereas the eventual textual configuration of op. 110, no. 1, mitigates the despair of the Psalm 69
text by setting a view of God as "barmherzig, geduldig und gnädig" in its
midst, it nevertheless focuses attention on prayer by placing the words
"Gott deine Hilfe schütze mich" at the end of the motet, where they are musically extended for eighteen bars. Furthermore, Brahms had originally considered a more positive passage with which to conclude this work (or some
prototype made up of texts on folio 13r), Hebrews 4:16, which is copied
at the top of folio 13v. That passage suggests a more hopeful stance than
any to be found in op. 110 or 109: "Let us therefore approach the throne
of grace with boldness, so that we may receive mercy and find grace to
help in time of need." The optimism supplied by God's "Gnade" and
"Barmherzigkeit" in Exodus 34 is joined in this passage with the call for
his "Hülfe" from Psalm 69. The text that Brahms fashioned by 1889 for
op. 110, no. 1, however, lacks such an explicit synthesis, leaving us less con-
fident about the effectiveness of its concluding prayer. That text displays a
considerably greater sense of *Elend* and urgency than at least one possibility
he had considered earlier.

A similar situation pertains to the texts of op. 109, which are all found—
among other texts—on the next opening of the notebook (13v–14r).
Whether these were copied into the notebook around the same time as the
texts of op. 74, no. 1 (as Siegfried Kross has suggested), or sometime later,
they were almost certainly selected before Brahms set them to music in the
aftermath of the *Drei-Kaiser-Jahr* (1888).[13] Like the text of op. 110, no. 1,
the larger group to which the op. 109 texts belong seems to continue onto
the top of the following page (14v), where the group is concluded by a passage from Genesis 28:16–17. Just as the Hebrews 4 text on folio 13v could
have provided a more positive ending to op. 110, no. 1, than the call for
God's help in Psalm 69, likewise the tone of Isaac's revelation from Genesis
28 is decidedly more upbeat than Moses' admonition to the "Volk" of Israel
in the Deuteronomy 4 text with which Brahms actually concluded op. 109:

Deuteronomy 4:9 folio 14v (actual conclusion of op. 109, no. 3)	But take care and watch yourselves closely, so as neither to forget the things your eyes have seen nor to let them slip from your mind all the days of your life; make them known to your children and your children's children.
Genesis 28:17, 22 folio 14r (not set)	"Surely the Lord is in this place—and I did not know it!" / "How awesome is this place! This is none other than the house of God, and this is the gate of heaven. / And this stone, which I have set up for a pillar, shall be God's house."

As in the text of op. 110, no. 1, Brahms ended the *Fest- und Gedenksprüche* with a far less optimistic *Spruch* than the evidence in his biblical notebook suggests he might have, one which cannot fully reassure those who were "hoping," "crying," and "calling out" for God's help in the texts of op. 109.

Brahms's reasons for focusing on prayers of deliverance in the late motets could perhaps be attributed to the general melancholy that most modern Brahms scholars understand to cast a shadow over the entire later period of his life.[14] But we have already seen firm evidence in the prayerful address to God contained in Wisdom of Solomon 9:1–12 (which Brahms himself labeled "*Gebet* eines Königs" in the biblical notebook), that repeatedly calling for God's help in prayer was a more specific response to the national "tragedy" of 1888. When Brahms composed the *Fest- und Gedenksprüche* around 1889, he could not look past his doubts and concerns about the future of the *Kaiserreich*, even though he employed a group of texts that had been copied when the German Republic's political fortunes seemed clearer and brighter. Thus his need for prayer found its way into his selection of specific texts from that group and, as we shall see, into the musical style of the *Fest- und Gedenksprüche* as well. The net result in op. 109 (and op. 110) is an ambivalent mixture of faith and hope on the one hand, and uncertainty and urgency on the other.

Why did Brahms turn from such a distinctly individualistic response to the political events of 1888 as the "Gebet eines Königs" to the primarily pluralistic texts that he ultimately used in op. 109? One impetus for the switch may have been musical, namely, Brahms's documented interest in polychoral music during the late 1880s.[15] Brahms copied numerous passages from Heinrich Schütz's settings of the Passions and Psalms into the manuscript collection Gesellschaft der Musikfreunde A 130 after those pieces were published by Philipp Spitta as volumes one and two of Schütz's complete works in 1885 and 1886, respectively.[16] Virginia Hancock has ably demonstrated the many ways in which the three *Fest- und Gedenksprüche,* along with "Ich aber bin elend," borrow techniques from the Schütz *Abschriften* of the late 1880s. She concludes that the apparent "elemental grandeur" of op. 109 masks Brahms's use of sophisticated compositional techniques in those pieces as compared with the explicit contrapuntal intricacies of the op. 110 motets.[17]

Another reason why the complexities in the *Fest- und Gedenksprüche* are not so evident as they are in the op. 110 motets is that the handling of the polychoral texture is more sophisticated in op. 109. In op. 110 Brahms treats the choral texture differently in each motet, and he even changes the relationship of the two choirs from section to section within a single piece like "Ich aber bin elend." Finding so much variety in choral technique among these motets is no surprise, since they form a decidedly varied set to begin with; a four-voice motet ("Ach, arme Welt") appears between a through-composed double-choir motet on biblical texts ("Ich aber bin elend") and a strophic double-choir motet on a *Kirchenlied* ("Wenn wir in höchsten Nöten sein"). Only in the latter piece does Brahms display the same sophistication in the handling of polychoral texture that distinguish the *Fest- und Gedenkspruche*. Although "Wenn wir in höchsten Nöten sein," like the other two numbers in op. 110, conjures up the sound of the German seventeenth century, it is perhaps closer in spirit to the *Fest- und Gedenkspruche* than its opus mates. The similarity has less to do with melodic, rhythmic, or harmonic language than with the equally sure handling of polychoral textures in each. From the outset of op. 110, no. 3, Brahms handles the two choirs with great subtlety (see ex. 5.1). After the two choirs delineate themselves through an "echo" phrase to the textual incipit (bars 1–3), individual voices from each choir introduce the next line of text ("und wissen nicht, wo aus und ein") to the same head motive in staggered entrances (bars 3–6). Before these fragmented melodies conclude in bars 6–7, the second choir has recommenced with the initial phrase, but now continues along with the first choir's echo (bars 8–9).

Brahms's use of the two choirs in op. 110, no. 1, is far less suave. The opening period of the piece creates the effect of one five-voice choir (or perhaps two successive five-voice choirs), first blending both soprano 1 lines with all the men's voices, then both second bass lines with all the women's voices (see ex. 5.2). When Brahms suddenly introduces two distinct choirs in bars 17–34 of op. 110, no. 1, he does so in order to articulate two separate communal identities. As nearly every commentator on this motet has noted, these bars evoke responsorial psalm singing, a context that implicitly requires two separate groups.[18] The effectiveness of polychoral texture to express a communal voice is all the more pronounced in op. 110, no. 1, for at no point does the text of that motet mention a plural voice. The only protagonist that is made clear in the text is the *Ich* at the beginning and the end of the work ("Ich aber bin elend . . . schütze mich"). We are left, perhaps, to

Example 5.1   Op. 110, no. 3, "Wenn wir in höchsten Nöten sein," bars 1–11.

Example 5.2 Op. 110, no. 1, "Ich aber bin elend," bars 1–11. (Sopranos, then basses, of respective choirs separated off for illustrative purposes.)

wonder why Brahms chose to evoke communality in op. 110, no. 1, at all. The answer likely lies in Brahms's twofold preoccupation in the late 1880s with polychoral music and with the troubled community of the German nation. There is not a clear "cause-and-effect" relationship between the two factors, but they seem to have become closely related for Brahms and led to a distinct mode of presentation in the late sacred choral works. What is clear is that Brahms's employment of polychorality to evoke a communal voice formed a continuous thread in his later choral music.

Brahms and the Drei-Kaiser-Jahr

"They are three short hymn-like sayings for eight-voice choir a cappella, which are specifically intended for national Festival and Commemorative days, and which would be especially well suited and expressive for Leipzig, Sedan, and Kaiser Coronation festivals. (Then again better not [*Doch besser nicht*]!)"[19] With these words, Brahms offered the *Fest- und Gedenksprüche* to Hans von Bülow and made the nationalistic impulse of the works quite clear. The publication by Kalbeck of Brahms's letter and Kalbeck's own commentary on the *Gedenksprüche* in 1914 in his Brahms biography began a long reception history in which op. 109 has been interpreted as a patriotic companion piece to the earlier *Triumphlied*, op. 55 (1872). For works that are so uniformly perceived as patriotic, the *Fest- und Gedenksprüche* contain relatively few words that would connote either a nation or a political state. Some potential referents to things national or political were abandoned when Brahms turned away from the newly selected biblical passages on folios 15v–19r of his notebook for op. 109 and returned to texts from folios 13v–14r instead. Wisdom of Solomon 9 (18v–19r), for example, speaks repeatedly of "laws" and "ruling": the word "Thron" occurs three times. And 1 Kings 6:11–12 (15v) focuses on the building of "Gottes Haus" and following His "rules." The only text that Brahms ultimately used in op. 109 which presents anything political or national is Jesus' metaphor from Luke 11:17 in the middle section of no. 2 (bars 31–51). There a "Reich" is mentioned, but it is associated with something distinctly negative: a kingdom that is brought down and laid waste when it is divided against itself. Brahms figuratively surrounds this *Reich* with a "starker Gewappneter" (strongly armed man) by setting Luke 11:21 with nearly identical music to begin and end no. 2. Despite being flanked by a more positive image, however, the troubled image of the *Reich* falls in the absolute center of the three works— the middle section of the middle piece—and thus forms a dark core to the entire opus

A more positive—though less direct—idea of patriotism is derived from the national imagery of *Volk* and ancestry in the first and last of the *Fest-*

und Gedenksprüche. Brahms begins the set with the basically reassuring observation that when our fathers prayed to God, their prayers were answered (a signal of faith), and ends with a charge to the present *Volk* to pass on their history to their children and grandchildren (a signal of hope). The juxtaposition of "Reich" and "Volk" creates a critical tension in op. 109, since these two concepts represent opposing strands of German patriotism in the late nineteenth century, pitting a *Volk*-centered and religious view of nationalism in contradistinction to a state-centered and legalistic one. That difference became a major dividing line between conservatives and liberals in the *Kaiserreich*.[20] It is very difficult to distinguish the meaning of words such as *Staat, Reich, Volk,* and *Nation* in the nineteenth century. Around 1800, the idea of a new German state was closely bound to the legacy of the medieval Heiliges Römischer Reich deutscher Nation. That concept of *Staat* contained, ironically, many characteristics that would come by mid-century to be associated with the German *Volk:* a powerful spiritual force whose divine authority could be traced back through the history of Christianity. While *Nation* and *Volk* gradually took on this meaning during the first half of the nineteenth century, the idealized reestablishment of a powerful German political state continued to occupy the patriotic movement. Indeed, it is nearly impossible to separate nineteenth-century Germans' longing for such a "kingdom" from the purely Christian notion of a godly *inner Reich* that unites all of God's chosen people.[21]

One explanation for this mixture of religious and patriotic aspirations is the active role played by the Protestant Church in the burgeoning nationalist movement at the turn of the century. Friedrich Schleiermacher, the leading Protestant theologian of the early nineteenth century, openly equated the German patriotic cause with a "new religion," thereby building on a long-standing Pietistic tradition in which the Prussian state was "sanctified" and "increasingly viewed as the embodiment of the true Church" and as the earthly forerunner of God's Kingdom.[22] For the Romantics, religion and nationalism were inextricably linked. Brahms's choice of an apocalyptic biblical text for the *Triumphlied* was related directly to this "Pieto-Romantic" outlook and reflects his own position within the nineteenth century. He was born in 1833, midway between the dissolution of the German Kingdom by Franz II in 1806 and the revival of the German state in 1871, and he grew up in Hamburg, a city that had suffered severe economic and physical consequences of the wars of liberation from France in 1815. Brahms's personal circumstances practically dictated a deep-seated patriotism and a particular dislike for modern France; it is not surprising that he reacted with a mixture of pride and glee to the victory over France at the Sedan and chose such a celebratory text as Revelations 19 to mark the occasion.

By comparison, Brahms's selection of texts for the *Fest- und*

Gedenksprüche signals a change in his attitude toward the modern *Reich* by the late 1880s. It is significant that Brahms did not choose the sort of contemporary patriotic texts for op. 109 that were so commonly set for national festivals around that time. His use of the Bible to express a less optimistic view of Germany's political situation has to be read as a (mostly negative) comment on the more positive role that Scripture had played in the formation of the Romantic nationalism that set the stage for the attainment of the *Kaiserreich*.

Toward the end of the century, German patriotism's spiritual legacy belonged to the *Volk*, while the state became a largely bureaucratic and legalistic entity. The establishment of the Prussian *Reich* had largely satisfied the liberal agenda for national unity. Conservatives, however, sought a more organic realization of German unity, one in which the state was subservient to the mystical will of the *Volk*. They did not feel that this could come about under the present regime, and hoped instead for a nationalism that was less legalistic and more moralistic, less concerned with politics and more concerned with spirit, less bureaucratic and more ritualistic. A typical expression of this attitude is found in the writings of Paul de Lagarde, who desired the establishment of a "national German religion" that would recapture the true essence of Christianity, stripped of the Jewish and Roman elements that had corrupted German Protestantism.[23] In particular, Lagarde objected to the legalisms of Old Testament religion, including the idea of a "covenant," which he found demeaning to the spiritual relationship between God and humanity.

Such disdain for laws and covenants is a separate issue from Brahms's own aversion to religious dogma and orthodoxy. A survey of the biblical texts Brahms copied into his notebook reveals that he did not reject the concept of laws and the legalistic, political character of the Bible. On the contrary, he dwelled on them.[24] Many of the texts there speak directly or indirectly of God's laws, and frequently of the Ten Commandments, which symbolized the Jewish covenant from which Lagarde felt Christianity had to be freed. In the "Gebet eines Königs" from Wisdom of Solomon 9, Solomon prays for the wisdom to follow God's "judgment" and "laws." Similarly, in Kings 6:11–12, God commands Solomon to maintain his "laws" and "commandments." Jacob's revelation from Genesis 28 (14v) also represents the passing on of God's covenant from Abraham to Jacob through Isaac. Thus, all three of these biblical passages emphasize the constancy and perpetuation of God's laws and commandments.[25]

Less explicit on this subject, but no less meaningful, is the text of op. 109, no. 3, from Deuteronomy 4:7 and 9. These verses are spoken by Moses in the midst of his appeal to the Israelites—his *Volk*—to follow God's "statutes," "ordinances," and "commandments." The text that begins no. 3,

"For what other nation has a God so near to it as the Lord our God is when-ever we call to him?" (Deuteronomy 4:7), is followed in the Bible by a direct reference to God's laws: "And what other great nation has statutes and ordi-nances as just as this entire law that I am setting before you today?" (Deu-teronomy 4:8). Brahms, as I have argued, had already limited his selection to verses 7 and 9 before the crisis of 1888, probably several years before. We can imagine that, had he copied this text into his biblical text notebook later, he might have included verse 8 and thus made the reference to laws more clear, as he did in 1 Kings 6 and Wisdom of Solomon 9, texts that *were* copied into the pocket notebook as a reaction to the *Drei-Kaiser-Jahr*. The various mentions of laws and statutes in these texts are not meant to stand for the legal code of the German Empire. Rather, by dwelling on the trans-mission of laws and commandments from generation to generation, Brahms suggests that the Bible could stand for tradition and social continuity in a historical context.

Insofar as that use of the Bible is a positive reception of Old Testament laws, Brahms opposes reactionary rhetoric like Lagarde's. At the same time, statutes and laws evoke the legal aspects of a state, or *Reich*, and by combin-ing the idea of the state, on the one hand, with the idea of social continuity (or history), on the other, Brahms's approach to the Bible resonates with the late-nineteenth-century "national-liberal" school of history, in which the Prussian state was accepted and even championed as the proper means by which the aspirations of the German *Volk* could be realized. Two histori-ans whose books Brahms owned were counted among the national liberals: Heinrich von Treitschke and Heinrich von Sybel. Although they condemned Bismarck's strong-arm political tactics within the German Parliament, Treitschke and Sybel nevertheless accepted the Bismarckian "power state" as the proper vehicle for German unity and as a logical outcome of historical development. Moreover, they saw the apparatus and processes of the state as a necessary mechanism of political and social stability and "shied away from the romantic probing of the obscure origins of custom and community in the *Volksgeist*."[26] Treitschke, the more influential and widely read of the two authors, is represented in Brahms's library by two books: *Historische und Politische Aufsätze* (1870) and *Zwei Kaiser* (1888).[27] Whereas we have no record of Brahms's reaction to Treitschke's writings, the publication dates of these books suggest a connection between Brahms's reading of Treitschke's national-liberal ideas and the two significant events in German history that prompted the composer to write pieces on patriotic themes—the founding of the *Kaiserreich* and the *Drei-Kaiser-Jahr*.

More direct information is available about what Brahms thought of Sybel. Brahms's friend Laura von Beckerath sent him the first volume of Sybel's *Kleine historische Schriften* as a Christmas gift in 1883, and sent a new volume of Sybel's *Begründung des deutschen Reichs durch Wilhelm I* every Christmas from 1889 through 1894. The latter volumes would have arrived too late to have any impact on the *Fest- und Gedenksprüche*, but Brahms's reaction to them is nevertheless telling. In a letter to Beckerath in 1892 he writes: "It is especially nice that the volumes of our *Kaisergeschichte* always arrive from the Niederwald. And this time I must, with the greatest pleasure, think of the great festival day, which I spent so happily with you in your house. But I am not the least bit impatient for the seventieth volume! In volumes 66–70 Sybel can hardly recite [*erzählen*] to me long enough."[28] The "great festival day" to which Brahms refers in this letter was 28 September 1883, which marked the completion and official unveiling of the *Niederwald Denkmal* by Johannes Schilling at Rüdesheim. Schilling's statue of the goddess "Germania" was one of the many monuments erected in the late nineteenth century that drew connections between the modern state and Germany's mythical past. Kalbeck waxes eloquent on Brahms's deep emotions upon seeing the newly finished *Denkmal* while visiting the Beckeraths. And although Kalbeck may go too far in estimating how profound this experience was for the composer, Brahms himself draws the connection between the monument and Sybel's *Kaisergeschichte* when he says that the arrival of the new volume by Sybel reminded him of the *Denkmal*'s commemoration, a day he remembered as "herzlich" and "schön." We can infer from this connection that Brahms agreed with Sybel's historical interpretation of German politics and shared his state-centered patriotism.

Brahms's selected biblical quotations indicate his agreement with the state-dominated historical nationalism of Treitschke and Sybel, and thereby his opposition to the *Volk*-dominated religious nationalism of the right. Orthodox or not, Brahms saw no need to supplant the Lutheran Church with a national German religion. He expressed that sentiment by selecting a whole series of biblical texts that deal with the very laws and covenants that Lagarde sought to overcome with a new religion. Through this subtle act of cultural criticism, we see Brahms clinging to the Lutheran Bible as the transmitter of German culture.

Opus 109, Brahms told Bülow, "would be especially well suited and expressive for Leipzig, Sedan, and Kaiser Coronation festivals," the three most important national holidays of the German state. Modeled on the large public celebrations of the French Revolution, festivals had arisen in Germany during the first half of the nineteenth century to promote the idea of national unity.[29] Initially, they incorporated a mixture of religious ritual and folk symbolism to create what George L. Mosse has described as a "nationalist cult."[30] After 1871, the new empire attempted to use these festivals to celebrate the *Reich*'s founding, and eventually settled on a commemoration of the final military victory of the war with France, the *Sedantag* on 2 September. Along with the Kaiser's birthday and other state-sponsored festivals, however, the *Sedantag* met opposition from many of the groups that had led the initial festival movement: gymnasts and sharpshooters to name two of the most important. These groups began to hold their own festivals, in which they fostered a separate form of nationalism from the one promoted by the Wilhelmine government.[31] Ultimately, because of this opposition, the state's festivals failed to inspire much patriotism or enthusiasm of any sort, and became mere parades of military pomp and imperial aggrandizement.

Brahms's closing aside "Doch besser nicht!" in the letter to Bülow probably alludes to the dubious position national festivals occupied by 1889. In fact, op. 109 would have made perfectly appropriate music for such occasions.[32] For despite their secular pomp and regalia, most festivals around this time included a church service, which would easily accommodate a cappella settings of biblical texts. For example, a program for the *Sedantag* celebration at Stuttgart in 1875 indicates that the main festival day began with the chorale "Nun danket alle Gott" performed from the church tower (probably by brass), followed by a large procession to the church, where the Society for Classical Church Music and members of the *Hofkapelle* sang "Hoch thut euch auf" from Handel's *Messiah*.[33]

Since there was no formal or functional reason why the *Fest- und Gedenksprüche* should "better not" be performed at national festivals, Brahms's retraction must display some ambivalence toward, or uneasiness about, the festivals themselves. In contrast to his frequent attendance at— and even participation in—*music* festivals all over Germany, there is no evidence that he similarly attended *national* festivals. In lieu of such information, Brahms's reaction to the dedication of the *Niederwald Denkmal* in 1883 in the letter to Laura von Beckerath nine years later may give some indication of his mixed emotions about celebrations of this type. Brahms was inspired (says Kalbeck) by the sight of the "Germania" monument and was probably equally moved by the spectacle that accompanied its unveiling. From the Beckeraths' vineyard overlooking the Rhine, Brahms watched as "the Kaiser and his brilliant procession, the heroes of 1870, the princes and representatives of the German *Volk* processed toward the Niederwald to attend the dedication of the national monument."[34] Admiring though Brahms may have been, he only looked on *from a distance*. There may well have been compelling reasons for him not to actually attend the ceremonies himself, but the image that Kalbeck presents to us suggests a degree of separation, of distance, and perhaps of an underlying ambivalence or uneasiness about the whole affair. Any latent negative feelings Brahms had harbored toward national festivals in 1883 would have become that much more pronounced five to six years later, when the *Fest- und Gedenksprüche* were written in response to the crisis of the *Drei-Kaiser-Jahr*.

Another indication that Brahms did not want to associate himself too strongly with patriotic festivals is the meager amount of music he wrote for men's chorus. The *Männerchor* played an important role in nineteenth-century public festivals, and the development of these partly musical, partly social organizations was closely tied to the nationalist movement in Germany. Outside of the oratorio-style works *Rinaldo*, op. 50, and the *Alto Rhapsody*, op. 53, in which men's choruses (and orchestra) accompany a soloist, Brahms produced only the modest five unaccompanied lieder for four-voice men's chorus, op. 41.[35] Whereas most of the other small-scale choral works he wrote in the late 1850s through the 1860s were intended for the various choirs Brahms directed in these years—a women's chorus in his native Hamburg and mixed choruses in the nearby court of Detmold and later in Vienna—there is little evidence concerning when or for what possible occasion these *Männerchor* lieder may have been composed. Most likely, Brahms was merely tapping into the rich tradition of patriotic men's choral music that dated back to the *Liedertafeln* from the first decades of the century, in which men could gather to sing, as an extension of bourgeois domesticity, as well as to instill a sense of community and, by extension, patriotism in German lands. Along with other social institutions such as gymnastics clubs and sharpshooting societies, the men's choirs became closely associated with the German nationalist drive in the first half of the nineteenth century.[36]

German *Männerchor* music in the early nineteenth century tended toward military and/or patriotic texts with musical devices (march rhythms, for example) to match. Those qualities are very much what distinguish Brahms's writing for men in op. 41 from his contemporaneous works for women's or mixed choirs. An exception must be made for the first number in op. 41, a faux-Renaissance setting of the old folk song "Ich schwing mein Horn in Jammertal." With its block-chord texture and modal melodic style it sounds more in the style of "Ach lieber Herre Jesu Christ" (discussed in Chapter 1) and less like a member of this generally modern, militaristic set of men's choruses. Brahms arranged the same setting for his women's chorus in Hamburg, and a still earlier version for men's voices may have existed.[37]

The other four more modern-sounding choruses in op. 41 all set texts from Carl Lemcke's *Lieder und Gedichte* (1861), a book Brahms acquired in 1862. Unlike the triple-meter dance rhythms that run through much of his contemporaneous music for women's chorus, such as the *Twelve Lieder and Romances*, op. 44 (published one year earlier in 1866), songs 2–5 of op. 41 are dominated by duple march rhythms, frequent unison writing, and energetic melodies that either directly state or outline triads. These characteristics are evident even in the less forceful middle songs of the set, nos. 3 and 4. Both of these songs, for example, are designated with march tempos (*tempo di marcia moderato* and *im Marschtempo*). Moreover, no. 3,

Example 5.3   Op. 41, no. "Geleit," bars 1–7: alternations of unisons and block chords.

"Geleit," borrows heavily from clichés of the *Männerchor* style, like the unison E-flats across all four voices on the pickup and initial downbeat that gradually give way to harmony by the middle of the first bar and subsequent alternations of unisons and block chords in the first seven bars (see ex. 5.3). Yet one cannot easily dismiss this piece as a product typical of its genre, for Brahms supplies many subtleties that go well beyond the normal textural and harmonic simplicity one encounters in most of the mid-nineteenth-century German repertoire for men's choruses. Right away, for example, Brahms departs from the home key of E-flat major, as subtle shifts of harmony around the pitch D-flat provide coloristic effects and an aura of melancholy befitting the text: an homage to fallen comrades. This is achieved harmonically in bars 7–8, where the move from an A-flat minor harmony (iv) at the end of bar 7 to the major tonic in bar 8—with only the briefest intervention of the dominant harmony (a sixteenth note)—conveys an odd modal mixture. As I discuss momentarily, such subtle handling of unison phrase incipits plays heavily into the cultural-political meaning of the *Fest- und Gedenksprüche*, op. 109.

Both op. 41, no. 3, and the ensuing no. 4, "Marschieren," are texts (and settings) that depict the soldier away from the battle. By contrast, the second and fifth pieces in the set ("Freiwillige her!" and "Gebt Acht!") are aggressively chauvinistic and leave no doubt as to how far toward military enthusiasm Brahms's youthful patriotism could lean. That is especially true of the fifth and final song, where Lemcke's four strophes depict a world where "enemies" *(Feinde)* encroach on every side and will use trickery to defeat the "Vaterland." The battle to which these texts summon the German "Volk" and "Brüdern" is the pre-1848 liberal-democratic unity movement, as the strongly accented "Schwarz, Rot, Gold" (the *Trikolore* of the liberal movement) in bars 8–9 of op. 41, no. 2, makes clear. Their patriotism, therefore, is directly tied to a Romantic conception of nationhood, and hence resonated with Brahms's youthful Romantic roots—not with the later festivals of the *Kaiserreich*. Brahms composed no more works for men's chorus after op. 41, but that is not to say that he lost his chauvinism over the years: there are many recorded comments by him surrounding the Franco-Prussian War that bear witness to his continued pride in Prussia's military successes.[38] Moreover, Brahms continued to support the major military-political figures in the *Reich*—Bismarck, Wilhelm I, Wilhelm II—avidly enough to cause a serious rift in his close friendship with Joseph Widmann in 1888, after the Swiss playwright penned a disparaging article about the new Kaiser's first speech to the army. When the time came to select texts for the *Fest- und Gedenksprüche*, Brahms apparently found his sympathies split between the *Reich* and the *Volk*; mediation and reconciliation are the main impressions that one gains from the music of op. 109.

Prayer and Reconciliation

Brahms turned to a prayer (Wisdom of Solomon 9) within his notebook of biblical texts in reaction to a national crisis, and his inclination to pray eventually found its way into the *Fest- und Gedenksprüche* through other texts that had been collected sometime earlier. In the previously cited letter to Bülow, Brahms called these pieces "hymnartig," a term that by the late nineteenth century had come to mean a large-scale work for chorus.[39] The style of op. 109 is not so grandiose that we would expect such a label, but the element of prayer in these works might account for Brahms's characterization. Prayer is most strongly and directly evoked in op. 109 by the opening text of no. 1: "Unsere Väter *hofften* auf dich . . . zu dir *schrien* sie." At the same time, the fear of disunity that prompted these compositions is most clearly depicted in the music of this first piece as well. Right from the opening, Brahms employs polychoral textures that depict separate groups in the most vivid musical terms possible. Choir 2 begins the piece with a unison arpeggio (F–C–A–C) that is immediately embellished by choir 1 in bars 2–4 with highly figured four-voice counterpoint. Out of this opening gesture, a pattern emerges in which starkly simple statements by choir 2 are juxtaposed with and elaborated by a more sophisticated and learned tone in choir 1. And while simplicity and sophistication would hardly account for all of the potential divisions in German society, they nevertheless imply low and high

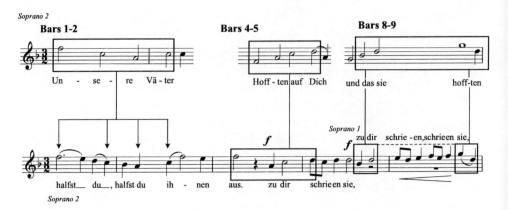

Example 5.4   Op. 109, no. 1: motivic relationships between bars 1–9 and 13–17.

art, a distinction that could be understood to represent the division between the *Volk* and the educated middle-class bourgeoisie.

In this opening section of op. 109, no. 1 (bars 1–15), the two choirs present the same idea (i.e., musical material) in their own very distinct manners, suggesting that despite their outward differences, the two groups basically share a common identity. Thus, there is an underlying unity, or at least a basis for reconciliation between them. The concept of a straightforward statement followed by a more elaborate one also holds true for the overall structure of the opening piece. For just as choir 1 expands and embellishes the immediately preceding statement of choir 2 in the opening bars, the second and third sections of op. 109, no. 1 (bars 15–29 and 29–51, respectively), vary and elaborate the material of the first fifteen bars. Bars 15–29 divide into two halves: 15–21 and 21–29. Although a large degree of ornamentation and figuration obscures the resemblance, each half is derived from the same kernel motives as bars 1–15 and highlights the significant harmonic outlines of those bars. Each section (bars 1–15 and 15–29) can be traced back to the succession of unison statements by choir 2 in bars 1–2, 4–5, and 8–9, followed by a return through D minor to F major (see ex. 5.4).

The final section of op. 109, no. 1 (bars 29–51), forms a clearer variation of bars 1–15 and has been more widely recognized as such.[40] Like the second section, the third divides into two similar halves. Perhaps the most striking feature here is the appearance of a "men's chorus" in the first half, bars 29–36. Whereas Brahms may very well have intended the male voices to symbolize the "Kraft" that God grants to His *Volk*, the use of that timbre for an entire half section also amounts to a textural variation on the opening gesture of the piece, a unison arpeggio of the sort that is heard at the beginning of many *Männerchor* pieces. By collecting the *Männerchor* textural references of bars 1–15 into a continuous phrase in bars 29–36, and following that phrase with an extended and contrapuntally more elaborate variation in bars 37–47, Brahms expresses in *consecutive* terms a variation structure that had been stated *simultaneously* in the opening section. In essence, bars 29–47 form a "structural variation" of bars 1–15—and so, for that matter, do bars 15–29.

From a number of perspectives, the structure and choral textures in the first of the *Fest- und Gedenksprüche* demonstrate the unity in the face of diversity that Brahms hoped would hold the *Reich* together. Two dissimilar groups (i.e., choirs 1 and 2) are pitted against each other, sometimes in stark relief, yet they display undeniable common roots and ultimately flow together at the ends of sections in prayerful plagal cadences.

In op. 109, no. 2, the element of prayer disappears while a direct reference to the "Reich" surfaces. In accordance with the unity and stability for which the modern *Kaiserreich* stood (in the national-liberal view), this piece displays the most balanced and stable form of the three, with a clearly contrasting middle section in the tonic minor between two nearly identical outer sections in C major. Key words such as "starker" and "bewahret" match the decisiveness of musical form in the piece. But underlying an edifice of strength and stability are musical clues that all is not well in the "Reich"; the instability expressed in the middle section is actually foreshadowed—and then echoed—in the C major portions of the piece, which therefore are not as self-assured as their opening bars might suggest.

The first twelve bars of no. 2 remain solidly in C major with martial-like rhythms and short, clearly defined motives that project confidence, decisiveness, and uniformity. Unlike most of the previous piece, the choirs here present exactly the same material (except at the ends of phrases where cadences must be articulated: bars 4–6 and 11–12), enhancing the image of agreement and precision. Without any harmonic preparation, however, Brahms suddenly introduces a prolonged passage in F major at the words "so bleibet das Seine mit Frieden" in bars 12–25. While the martial rhythms persist through bar 17, nearly every other parameter changes here. Bars 12–25 are as clearly in F as the opening twelve bars were in C, but they are much less solidly anchored on the tonic and dominant harmonies, especially the first phrase of that passage (bars 12–21), which moves in descending thirds from F to D minor, B-flat, and G minor before cadencing on D major (V of ii). Moreover, the second half of the passage dwells on the relative minor (D) of F, before C major is reestablished as the tonic when all eight voices articulate the same phrase together for the first time in the piece at the words "mit Frieden" in bar 25.

Like the relatively less stable harmony in this subdominant episode, the disposition of the choirs here is also less cohesive than it was in bars 1–12. Choirs 1 and 2 continue to share the same motives in bars 12–25, but vary them as in the chain of thirds just described. That variety leads to clashes like the overlapping hemiolas between the choirs in bars 15–17 (see ex. 5.5) and a new level of harmonic dissonance, best demonstrated by the series of major-second suspensions between the two soprano parts in bars 16–21. Whereas the rhythmic character of this material may not be overtly different from the opening period of the piece, devices such as overlapping hemiolas and suspensions suggest a style that is decidedly more ecclesiastic than military. In this sense, the F major episode resonates with the pervasive "hymnartig" plagal cadences throughout op. 109, and the whole first part of no. 2 can be heard as a large articulation of the harmonic progression I–V (F–C) in bars 1–12, and IV–I (B♭–F) in bars 12–25, which is realized locally in the three-bar "codetta" to the section at bars 26–28. The reversion to a prayerful and religious musical style in bars 12–25 of no. 2 corresponds directly with the sudden return there to F major, the tonality of no. 1. Likewise, the end of the textual phrase in bars 25–28, "mit Frieden," recalls the closing text of the previous piece, "der Herr wird sein Volk segnen *mit Frieden*," replete with a plagal cadence. Amidst the martial confidence in the outer sections of no. 2, therefore, Brahms offers a subtle reminder that the unity and cohesion of the *Reich* cannot be taken for granted: one must pray for it.

The point of those prayers is the feared disunity of the *Reich*, which is portrayed both textually and musically in the middle portion of no. 2 (bars 31–57). Two of the most powerful examples of tone painting in Brahms's entire choral oeuvre occur here: the depiction of the "wasteland" that a divided house becomes, through the hollow and dissonant tones of bars 36–41; and the implication of "one house falling upon another," through a rushing sequence of cascading keys all the way from C minor in bar 46 to D-flat major in bar 48. While these devices serve an immediate text-painting function, the falling tonalities in bars 46–48 grow out of the earlier F major episode in bars 12–25 (see ex. 5.6A–C). First, one must recognize that although the falling keys in bars 46–49 progress tonally by *fourths* (G–c–f–B♭–E♭–A♭–D♭), the melodic motion of that progression is produced by a chain of descending *thirds*, beginning on the second sopranos' G in bar 46 (ex. 5.6C). Looking back to the head-motive of the middle section, we see that this chain of thirds develops out of a descending arpeggio G–E♭–C that is introduced by tenor 1 in bar 31 (ex. 5.6B). And in turn, we can trace this arpeggio to the end of the earlier chain of thirds in bars 12–15 (i.e., F–D–B♭–G: ex. 5.6A), of which it is an extension. It will be recalled that the thirds in bars 12–15 marked the first loosening of harmonic precision and control in the opening section of the piece. If, as I have argued, the F major

Example 5.5   Op. 109, no. 2: overlapping hemiolas between the choirs in bars 15–17. (Sopranos separated off from respective choirs for illustrative purposes.)

Example 5.6   Op. 109, no. 2: "falling" tonalities in op. 109, no. 2: (A) bars 12–15; (B) bars 31–35; (C) bars 46–49.

episode in bars 12–25 symbolizes the general prayerfulness of the *Fest- und Gedenksprüche* amidst the martial depiction of the *Reich* in no. 2, then the continuation of that third chain by the head-motive of the middle section (G–E♭–C) links the prayer with the dissolution of the *Reich*. Ultimately, those thirds continue in the falling keys that propel the musical depiction of the *Reich*'s collapse.

Both Michael Beuerle and Virginia Hancock have referred to various parts of the middle portion of op. 109, no. 2, as "chaotic." That effect is mostly achieved by dividing each choir against itself. Like the motivic foreshadowing of falling thirds in bars 12–15, the rhythmic disagreement be-

Example 5.6   (continued)

tween choirs 1 and 2 that ensues in the cross-hemiolas of bars 15–17 prepares the listener for a more intense rhythmic fragmentation that occurs
within each choir throughout the middle section of no. 2. A climax of
disjunction arrives at the eight-bar retransition into the reprise of the opening section (bars 51–58). Here a five-beat asymmetrical motive is tossed
among the voices of both choirs on nearly every conceivable beat, as the
middle section's 4/4 meter dissolves back into the 3/4 meter of the opening
material. In bar 54, for instance, a textual phrase begins on every beat
("wenn ein starker"), while an accented syllable falls on every beat: "*Starker*" and "*Ge-wapp-neter*" on beat 1 (soprano 1, alto 1, alto 2, tenor 2);
"*Stark-*er" on beat 2 (bass 2); "*Stark-*er" and "*Ge-wapp-*neter" on beat 3
(bass 1, tenor 2); and "*Stark-*er" on beat 4 (tenor 1). When the uniform and
precise phrasing of the opening section returns beginning in bar 57, it is as if
the "starker Gewappneter" has forcefully restored order and precision to
the chaotic *Reich*.

Whereas op. 109, no. 2, focuses on division, the music of no. 3 depicts
union. Unlike the separate groups portrayed at the beginning of no. 1, from
which an underlying unity was merely suggested, various combinations of
voices at the beginning of no. 3 vividly portray the coming together of separate strands into one integrated whole. Immediately, the men's voices of
both choirs begin together in bar 1, after which the addition of all four
women's voices in bar 2 expands the timbre and masks a transition into a

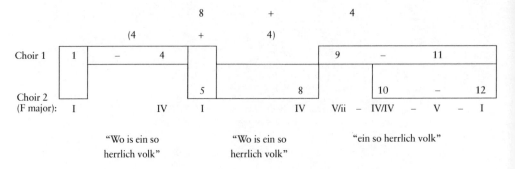

Figure 5.1   Phrase structure and divisions of four-voice units in op. 109, no. 3, bars 1–12.

single S A T B unit, choir 1, in bars 2–5. Brahms similarly smooths over the emergence of choir 2 as a second four-voice unit in bars 5–8 by extending tenor 1 and bass 1 past the first choir's cadence in bar 5. The wavelike repetition of the ascending arpeggio, A–C–F, in these opening bars adds to the fluid effect that draws the listener's attention away from the division between the separate choirs (outlined in fig. 5.1), which is actually quite distinct and articulates an 8 + 4 bar period.

Throughout the opening section of the piece (bars 1–42), Brahms employs a variety of voice combinations and timbral mixtures that join one or more voices from one choir with voices from the other, thereby helping to blur the distinction of separate groups. The interrelation of the two choirs here serves as a musical metaphor for integration and unification. From bar 13 on, Brahms doubles at least one voice part at all times to bring out a specific line against a blended choral texture: sopranos in bars 13–15 (against altos 1 and 2 and tenor 1) and basses in bars 17–22. When the basses begin moving in octaves at bar 24, the remaining six voices act as a "responsorial choir" to the basses' *forte* upward leaps (bars 24–29). But thereafter (bars 29–33), choirs 1 and 2 divide into a passage of conflicting hemiolas, against which only the basses provide an anchor in the prevailing 3/4 meter.[41] At the same time that the music is threatening to become rhythmically unglued, the harmony drifts away from the tonic F major through a series of fourths: C–F–Bb–(g)–Eb–(c)–Ab–(Eb–Bb)–Db, not unlike the "falling houses" motif of op. 109, no. 2.

As in that earlier instance of "chaos" which had to be forced back into order by the "starker Gewappneter" in no. 2, a sudden C-major harmony in bar 33 of no. 3 wrests the spiraling harmonies of the preceding passage back toward F major. Brahms accents the effect of that dominant chord through a syncopation (bar 33, beat 3) that introduces a new hemiola sequence. Choirs 1 and 2 enter separately with the words "als der Herr unser

Gott" in bars 33–36, but their rhythms begin to merge here, and they join completely in a new set of hemiolas beginning at bar 37. Now, as the upper voices of the two choirs articulate their text in perfect alignment, a completely diatonicized variation of the earlier hemiola material (bars 29–33) proceeds to an extended four-bar authentic cadence in F major. What has been won by the wrenching return to F major, therefore, is a completion of the uniformity and agreement between the two choirs that had been only partially realized throughout the first thirty-six bars of the piece. If we recall how suddenly Brahms introduced the F major interjection in bars 13–25 (and 68–81) of no. 2 to conjure up the prayerfulness of no. 1, it is well worth noticing the text that is set in no. 3 at bars 24–42: "als der Herr unser Gott *so oft wir ihn anrufen.*" By making an equally sudden return to F major in this piece around the word "anrufen" (pray), Brahms draws the listener's attention to the congruity of choral texture in bars 37–42 and once again emphasizes prayer within the *Fest- und Gedenksprüche*. Here, prayer can be specifically understood as an agent of unification.

Other musical symbols of unification appear within bars 1–12. Earlier I referred to the repetitions of the ascending F major arpeggio (A–C–F), which is passed from voice to voice in wavelike fashion and which stands out as a head-motive for this movement. That figure is generally set against the descending melodic figure F–E–D as part of a motivic pair: alto 1–bass 2 (bar 1); soprano 1–alto 2 (bar 2); tenor 2–bass 1 (bar 5); and so on. Locally, this motivic pair binds the two choirs together, in that every occurrence involves one voice from each choir. Both motives form a unifying function within the larger context of the three-piece opus as well, in that each is closely related to motives from nos. 1 and 2. The ascending F major arpeggio can be easily traced to the beginning of no. 1, where the opposite figure (F–C–A) is intoned in unison by choir 2. There, at the beginning of the entire opus, the two choirs shared that motive in a way that offered the hope of agreement and unity. Here, in the last piece, that hope is realized at one level by the integration of two choirs through the inverted (rising) form of the same motive.

The other melodic motive at the beginning of no. 3, F–E–D, presents itself less obviously throughout the *Fest- und Gedenksprüche* but proves to be a consistent and significant motive in all three pieces. Examples 5.7A–C trace this motive's transformation throughout op. 109. The motive first appears in no. 1 at the "elision" of bars 11–15, where the opening arpeggio gradually reemerges from the descending unison F–E–D–(A)–C of choir 2 in bar 11 (ex. 5.7A). At the end of no. 1 the final variation of the opening section concludes in bars 46–48 with an extended treatment of the motive from bar 11 to the words "segnen mit," now truncated to just three pitches, F–E–D (ex. 5.7B). In no. 2 the F–E–D motive is used more subtly, but its various

Example 5.7   Op. 109: transformation of F–E–D motive: (A) no. 1, bars 11–15; (B) no. 1, bars 46–48; (C) no. 2 bars 21–25.

manifestations occur at particularly important junctures. Most prominent is the twofold F–E–D statement to the words "das Seine" by soprano 2 in bars 21–23 and by soprano 1 in bars 23–25 (ex. 5.7C). The F that begins the first statement on beat three of bar 21 causes a cross-relation with the first alto's F-sharp on the previous beat.[42] The cross-relation defines beat three as the beginning of a new phrase and thereby focuses on the F–E–D motive in soprano 2, which is immediately repeated by soprano 1. Brahms also distinguished the end of this twofold motivic statement by bringing all eight voices together for the first time in the piece on the word "mit" at bar 25, beat three. Along with the plagal cadence and ecclesiastical tone of bars 13–28, the F–E–D motive at the words "das Seine mit Frieden" forms a link to the words "segnen mit Frieden" at the end of no. 1.

When Brahms combines the ascending F major arpeggio with the descending melodic motive (F–E–D) in no. 3, he saturates the harmony of the opening bars with an effect that Virginia Hancock has described as "diatonic dissonance."[43] In fact, much of the "dissonance" in the present case is caused by the sustained F's against which the F–E–D motive descends to produce frequent passing minor seconds, as in bass 1 and 2 (bars 1 and 5) and altos 1 and 2 (bars 2 and 6). Even when the descending melodic motive reaches the higher register of soprano 1 and is broadened slightly in bars 3–4, Brahms sets the rising A–C–F arpeggio below it in tenor 1 so that the final F of the arpeggio creates a minor ninth with the passing E of the soprano (bar 3, beat three). Hancock rightly ascribes to these diatonic dissonances a "characteristic warmth" that one senses throughout the first twenty-four bars, especially in 12–24, where every bar contains a suspension or an unresolved dissonance on the downbeat. It is this characteristic warmth that, along with the ascending arpeggio, supplies the opening section of no. 3 with an affirmative tone and renders the prayers hopeful rather than urgent, a quality that complements the musical unity of the two choirs in these same bars.

Having overcome the urgency of nos. 1 and 2, Brahms steps back in the middle of op. 109, no. 3, to offer a basis for the preceding prayers, a reason to believe in their effectiveness. This middle portion, therefore, forms a core of meaning not just to no. 3 but to the whole of the *Fest- und Gedenksprüche,* forming a contemplative center to the work. Only in this section are the *Volk* themselves addressed, "Hüte dich nur," indicating a point of self-reflection within the *Fest- und Gedenksprüche.* Brahms appropriately singles out this material within all of op. 109 through its fine dynamic gradations. Elsewhere in the three pieces, he almost exclusively employs *forte* dynamic markings, which are intended more to demarcate where entries of individual voice parts should stand out than to indicate actual changes in volume.[44] Bars 43–82, however, are replete with *pianos,* as well as *crescendo, diminuendo, espressivo,* and *dolce* markings, rendering this music more contemplative and less festive than that which surrounds it.

Another defining feature of this section is its archaic style. Although there are many instances of older techniques throughout the *Fest- und Gedenksprüche,* it is only in the middle portion of no. 3 that Brahms maintains a discernibly baroque style, which is signaled right away by the double canon in choir 1 during bars 43–52 at the words "Hüte dich nur und bewahre deine Seele wohl." Thereafter, the interplay of the two choirs is closely modeled on baroque polychoral techniques such as the overlapping entries of bars 57–66, and the consecutive statements of the same material in bars 66–77. The allusion to the music of composers such as Schütz and Giovanni Gabrieli is basic and generalized but unmistakable. Brahms uses a canon and historical style here to depict musically two aspects of the text from Deuteronomy 4:9—the overt mention of the "history" that we have seen with our own eyes, and the submerged allusion to "laws" in this passage, which is spoken by Moses to the Israelites as he reminds them of their covenant with God in the Ten Commandments. Within the Pentateuch of the Bible, the opening chapters of Deuteronomy act as a summation and culmination; Moses has led his people to the verge of the Promised Land and is reviewing with them their history and their obligation to the Lord. But, as one writer states, "Here the legal tradition of the book of Exodus . . . is not just repeated; it is interpreted in contemporary terms."[45] Brahms's setting of this passage also serves a "contemporizing" function. The musical reversion to historical style and technique (canon) at this point in the *Fest- und Gedenksprüche* corresponds to the rhetorical stance of the text; these historical foundations of German music (i.e., canon and polychorality) are invoked as symbols of the past within a larger musical context (the entire opus) that is contemporary. After the prayers of nos. 1 and 3, and the depiction of their subject (the troubled *Reich*) in no. 2, the middle section of no. 3 supplies a completely new perspective within op. 109. It is here that Brahms, by treating Moses' text with a musically historical perspective, preaches to *his* people much in the same way that Moses did to the Israelites. Significantly, Brahms turns to the words of Moses, the lawgiver, to preach the necessity of maintaining historical tradition and legalism as the means by which the community's prayers can be answered. In this way he elevates the very characteristics of the Old Testament, and of the modern state, that were opposed by Lagarde and the reactionary champions of the *Volk,* and offers these as a basis from which to maintain hopefulness in a time of national crisis.

By returning to the opening material of no. 3 in bar 82, as the "Kindern und Kindeskindern" are evoked, Brahms provides a musical symmetry within this one piece while a textual symmetry across the entire cycle is be-

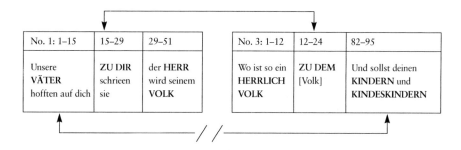

Figure 5.2   Textual symmetry across op. 109, nos. 1–3.

ing broken. Multiple generations of children signify the future and look ahead here at the end of the cycle, whereas our fathers signified the past and looked back at the outset of no. 1. All of this occurs within an otherwise (generally) symmetrical text pattern, as diagrammed in fig. 5.2. At the last instant, Brahms breaks the symmetrical pattern by opposing "Unsere Väter," a symbol of the past, with "deine Kindern und Kindeskindern," a symbol of the future. Perhaps it is this change in temporal context that leads Brahms to rearrange the choral texture when, at the end of no. 3, he brings back the opening material, which is now set for five voices: choir 1 with bass 2 in bars 82–85; choir 2 with bass 1 in bars 85–88.

The closing "Amen" in bars 96–105 extends the new five-voice texture by incorporating soprano 2 into a canon with all of choir 1, while the lower voices of choir 2 add harmonic support. The canonic entries beginning with bass 1 in bar 96 also provide an ultimate realization of the unity amidst diversity that was expressed at the beginning of the opus. As ex. 5.8 illustrates, the seven entries arpeggiate every harmony that belongs to the key of F major (all in first inversion) above a sustained F pedal in bass 2, thus articulating each individual entity within the tonic key (diversity), while the fundamental pitch of that key is constantly sounding (unity).

When the spirit of the *Fest- und Gedenksprüche* is considered in detail, one finds these to be not mere pieces of pomp and nationalistic affirmation but musical works that reflect Brahms's conflicted attitude toward his own patriotism. Whereas the suggested unity of no. 1 finds its realization at many points in no. 3, the cracks in the *Reich* depicted in no. 2 cannot be overlooked and ultimately are not overcome. Brahms seems to have maintained hope in the future, so long as the German *Volk* were willing to remember their past and follow their own "covenant," which had been realized in the founding of the modern *Kaiserreich*. His valuing of the past for the German people as a whole is not unlike his own personal need to be connected to his artistic past. The Bible provided Brahms in op. 109 with an apt historical and cultural symbol with which to represent tradition and law in

Example 5.8   Op. 109, no. 3: seven arpeggiations of harmonies in key of F major.

a way that contemporary patriotic texts could not. Moreover, the division between *Völkisch* and *Staatlich* patriotism at the end of the century had grown out of an earlier religiously inspired nationalism that equated the German people with the very *Volk* referred to in the biblical texts of the *Fest- und Gedenksprüche*. Brahms was not to compose another work on biblical texts before the *Vier ernste Gesänge*, op. 121 of 1896. Those works, whose texts were most likely copied into the pocket notebook of biblical passages shortly before op. 109 was composed, similarly reacted to religious attitudes that grew out of conservative ideological trends in the later nineteenth century.[46] The *Fest- und Gedenksprüche*, however, were his last overt statement on the political ramifications of those trends.

CHAPTER 6

Beyond the End

Reminiscences

Brahms vacillated over the title of op. 109 much as he had with that of his *Deutsches Requiem.* He alternately floated the adjectives "deutsch" and "national" as the first word of the title, as would be fitting for works appropriate to the major national holidays of the *Kaiserreich.*[1] Siegfried Kross supposes (rightly I think) that Brahms decided against such strong adjectives so as not to be politically misunderstood. Kross also finds repugnant the symbolic use to which the National Socialists later subjected op. 109. Specifically, he cites a performance of the *Fest- und Gedenksprüche* by the Berlin Cathedral choir on 21 March 1933 in the Potsdam Garrison Church before former president Hindenburg and Chancellor Adolf Hitler. Kross could not overlook the potentially ominous impact of the closing text of no. 3, "Take care and watch yourselves carefully, so as neither to forget the history your eyes have seen nor to let it slip from your heart all the days of your life." He labels these words, as sung in that context, a "terrifying prophecy."[2]

Kross, born in 1930, reacts as any music lover might (German or not) in the aftermath of World War II. The quotation is drawn from the published version of his thorough and unsurpassed study of Brahms's choral music, which formed his doctoral thesis at the University of Bonn in 1957. As he states in the introduction to that book, Kross felt that his work was part of a new wave of *wissentschaftliche* engagements with Brahms's music after a half century of Brahms biographies that were "so completely random, so un-unified, some of which are so foundationless, that one is never really on firm ground, not even in the purely biographical facts."[3] In other words, Kross believed that he and his contemporaries would have to build a body of Brahms scholarship systematically from the ground up. Those circumstances were not based merely on a failure of scholarship, however. Although here he does not mention the politics of the previous decade, in which he came of age and which engendered his response to the March 1933 performance of op. 109, Kross's later English-language essay on Brahms's choral music for the *American Choral Review* begins with a damning (and telling) critique of choral singing in Germany in the first half of the twentieth century. Reading these lines, one finds it difficult to imagine that the sense of tragedy he felt over the performance of the *Fest- und Gedenksprüche* for Adolf Hitler was not deeply affected by the entire reception of Brahms and his music in the years leading up to Hitler's rise to power:

> A few years before the outbreak of the First World War, new ideals of choral music and choral sound began to take hold in circles of the German Youth Movement. With them a particular attitude towards practices of communal singing arose which found a typical formulation in the silly slogan-like postulate to "de-Brahms" German music (i.e., to cleanse it of Brahmsian influences). With a certain feeling of resignation, one might today raise the question: Which one of the blunders was worse, the blunder to identify—of all forms—the stylized and highly refined madrigal with the ideal of communal singing (mistaking the term musica reservata for "reserved" or non-subjective music), or the blunder to identify Brahms—of all composers—with the type of purely subjective artist?[4]

One gleans from this statement (albeit written twenty-six years later) that Kross despaired in 1957 not at his predecessors' failure to solidify an understanding of Brahms's music, but rather at the concerted effort to distort and misrepresent Brahms by a choral movement that was engulfed in misguided nationalism.

Of course, it was during the years 1933–1945, while the National Socialists were in power, that the reception of Brahms and virtually all of Germany's cultural past came under the heaviest barrage of propaganda-driven historical revisionism. As early as the turn of the century, however, German writers had already begun to shape Brahms's legacy, painting him more and more as an icon of moderation and stability against the rising aura of modernism. By the time the Nazis arrived on the scene, a work such as the *Fest- und Gendenksprüche* was a perfect choice to celebrate the transfer of power in the German state. Thus Karl Laux, writing in 1935, reports on the same event with far different overtones:

> And in the third chorus he expressed the ever-present warning, "That you do not forget the history your eyes have seen nor let it slip from your heart all the days of your life." How weightily the two choirs implore each other; the old technique of the double choir, taken over from the Venetian masters, takes on a particular sense of depth here. And when Brahms allows the choir to celebrate "froh bewegt" at the beginning of this third chorus—"For what other great na-

tion has a god so near to it as the Lord our God is whenever we call to Him?"—this torrent of jubilation storms into our proud German present. And, as Ehrmann rightly says, "perhaps a more meaningful use of the work than the premiere performance itself" when, on 21 March 1933, at the great state ceremony of the German rise to power in the Potsdam Garrison Church, in the presence of the Führer and Reichspresident Hindenburg, the Berlin Cathedral chorus sang this third of the *Fest- und Gedenksprüche* at the conclusion of the ceremony, this time not only a commemorative but rather a true "Festspruch."[5]

One expects such a response from within the National Socialist period. But, as I will show later in this chapter, the seeds for the nationalistic image of "Brahms the German" were sown long before 1933, particularly in some of the best-known books and essays on Brahms from the first third of the twentieth century.

Kross's comments point to the diminished role that Brahms's a cappella choral music came to play in his posthumous reception, not only in comparison with the larger choral-orchestral works but also against the compositions of the 1890s, whose generally somber and nostalgic tone left a lasting impression of the composer and the meaning of his music for a new century. After composing the polychoral works of opp. 109 and 110, Brahms composed nothing further in this medium. In fact, shortly after he completed opp. 109 and 110, he dropped hints that he might cease composing altogether. In a letter of 12 October 1990 Brahms remarked to his publisher Fritz Simrock that upon leaving the resort town of Ischl ten days earlier he had "thrown much ripped-up manuscript paper into the Thun [river]."[6] About a year later, having produced nothing less than the first two of his great chamber works with clarinet for Richard Mühlfeld (the A Minor Trio, op. 114, and the B Minor Quintet, op. 115), Brahms reportedly told his friend Eusebius Mandyczewski: "In the last few years I began various things, symphonies and other works, but nothing came out quite right; it made me think I might already be too old, and decided energetically to write nothing more. I thought to myself that [perhaps] I had been industrious enough all my life, had achieved enough, could have a carefree old age and could now enjoy it in peace. And that made me so happy, so satisfied, so pleased, that it [the writing] started up once again."[7] Brahms would go on to compose two clarinet sonatas (op. 120) for Mühlfeld as well in 1894. Aside from these pieces, however, nearly all of the music Brahms produced during the last seven years of his life was retrospective in some way.

The largest portion of Brahms's output during these last years consisted of twenty piano miniatures published in 1892–93 as opp. 116–119. Although several of these pieces (variously titled Intermezzo, Capriccio, Rhapsodie, etc.) are thought to stem from decades earlier, as a group they clearly display a late style for Brahms.[8] (For the sake of simplicity I refer to them all as "Intermezzi," the term Brahms assigned to fourteen of these twenty works.) The rich and complex harmonic language of such well-known items as the Intermezzi op. 118, no. 2, in A major and op. 119, no. 1, in B minor illustrate Brahms's most highly developed, indeed, his most modern style, not only in technical-analytical terms but also in their world-weary, introspective character. Romantic *Sehnsucht* from Brahms's youth had developed by this point into mature melancholy: these are not the affected musings of the "Junge Kreisler" (the alter ego Brahms created in his youth to concretize his identification with E. T. A. Hoffmann's imaginary *Kapellmeister*), but rather the reflections of an older man. Such sentiment runs throughout the late Intermezzi. Often it is symbolized by musical displacements: harmonies, motives, or gestures which fall outside their proper musical context, thereby suggesting something that is remembered but that can no longer fit comfortably into the context in which it originally occurred.

No piece among the Intermezzi better epitomizes this effect than the E-flat Major Intermezzo, op. 117, no. 1. Brahms provided an epigraph to this piece, the opening lines of a Scottish folk song from Herder's *Stimme der Völker in Liedern*:

> Schlaf sanft, mein Kind, schlaf sanft und schön!
> Mich dauert's sehr, dich weinen sehn.
> [Sleep softly, my child, sleep softly and fine!
> It grieves me greatly to see you cry.]

Herder titled that poem "Wiegenlieder einer unglücklichen Mutter" (Lullaby of an Unhappy Mother), itself a translation of "Lady Anne Bothwell's Lament" from Thomas Percy's *Reliques of Ancient English Poetry*. Brahms copied it and one other "Scottish" poem from Herder's volume, "O weh! o Weh! hinab ins Thal" (Alas! Alas! Down to the Valley), into one of the notebooks of poetic texts discussed in Chapter 2.[9] One can hear the words of Herder's "Wiegenlieder" behind the inner right-hand melody of the first four bars in Brahms's Intermezzo (ex. 6.1). The folklike simplicity of the accompaniment here is a setup: unlike in the urban waltz tune that underlies the op. 49, no. 4, "Wiegenlied," Brahms affects a pastoral tone in this Intermezzo in order to objectify the folk character of the piece. A rustic folk style is depicted by several means here. First, a strumming effect is suggested by the repeated E's in the right hand against the moving melody, which evokes the sound of an open string on a guitar ringing through a melodic phrase. And against this textural effect, the overly plain rhythmic and harmonic profile of the foursquare initial melody contributes to a picture of pastoral simplicity. As he subtly develops that folklike melody in the first section of the piece (bars 1–16), Brahms gradually brings his own (modern) musical language to the fore through the secondary dominants (and other, richer

Example 6.1   Brahms, Intermezzo in E-flat Major, op. 117 no. 1, bars 1–23.

harmonies) engendered by A natural in bars 7–8, 11–12, and so on; the hemiola cross rhythms of bars 13–15; and the recasting of the theme in the minor mode in the codetta of bars 16–20. With each passing device that Brahms applies to the pastoral opening, the folk character of the initial idea is objectified and thus placed at a distance, until the entire middle section of the song, set in the parallel (E-flat) minor, forms a brooding reflection on the pre–cadential turn motive from the initial melody. Brahms restates the F–E–G figure from the middle voice at bar 2 as the hemiola B♭–G–A in octaves in the bass at bar 20, immediately before the figure is inverted as B♭–C–A and as A–B♭–G in the topmost voice at bars 21–22.[10] The folk quality of the opening is rendered not so much an affectation as a memory of something cherished from afar, something over which the ego can reminisce and contemplate—even brood—but which has become distant.

Brahms reportedly referred to the three Intermezzi of op. 117 as "lullabies of my sorrows" ("Wiegenlieder meiner Schmerzen"), a designation that for most commentators has resonated with the generally gloomy nature of the remaining two pieces in op. 117, both of which are cast in minor keys (B-flat and C-sharp).[11] As lullabies connote childhood, one could reasonably conjecture that Brahms's comment to Leyen speaks to his thoughts of his own youth. Accordingly, the distant object of the opening lullaby might be a personal past that Brahms views from his sixties in pastoral imagery. Brahms had owned Herder's *Stimme der Völker in Liedern,* the book from which he drew the epigraph to this piece, for over thirty-five years before he published op. 117. Thus the feeling of reminiscence expressed in this piece might indeed reflect the act of returning to an old valued source and the memories it evoked. It may be significant that Brahms bought the book in 1856, the year of Robert Schumann's death.[12]

We have more concrete evidence that Brahms was looking back through the lens of folk song around this time toward his youth and youthful compositions. In 1894 Brahms revised and published forty-nine settings of *Deutsche Volkslieder* for solo voice(s) and piano (WoO 33) that he had composed throughout his career. In August of that year he wrote to Clara Schumann of the *Volkslieder:* "Has it occurred to you that the last of the songs is in my opus 1? Has something [else] occurred to you as well? It really should say something, it should represent the snake which bites its own tail, thus saying symbolically: the story is now over, the circle closed. . . . Now that I am past sixty, I should like to be as smart as I was before twenty."[13] Brahms is referring to the andante second movement of his Piano Sonata in C Major, op. 1, which forms a set of variations on the song "Verstohlen geht der Mond auf" (The Moon Rises Stealthily), the final song in WoO 33. Brahms deliberately arranged his folk song settings to imply a return to his youth. Indeed, the act was so willful and self-conscious that he pointed it out to Schumann, lest she miss the point.

The forty-nine folk song settings were not Brahms's only bow to youthful endeavors during the last six years of his life. At least two other sets of pieces either drew on earlier compositions or otherwise revived long-dormant genres for Brahms, specifically genres on which he had dwelled during his twenties. Already in 1891 he had published his *Dreizehn Kanons,* op. 113, some of which were composed for the Hamburg Women's Chorus in 1859, and others based on folk songs Brahms had published without opus number in 1858 as solo lieder for the Schumann children. And his *opus ultimo,* the *Elf Choralvorspiele,* op. 122, which Brahms worked on during the summer of 1896, marks a return to an instrument and a genre in which he had rarely worked since the late 1850s.[14] All of these collections that Brahms assembled during his last six years (WoO 33 and opp. 113 and 122) bring together spiritual sentiments with musical types that are strongly associated with German history: folk song, canons, and chorale preludes. At the same time that Brahms was expressing an urge to reminisce, as in the Intermezzi, he was returning to genres with which he had been engaged in his youthful years of intense association with the Schumann family, while simultaneously evoking the more distant German past. In particular, the chorales and many of the folk songs he set in opp. 113, 122, and WoO 33 relate directly to the age of Luther and the rise of a German literary style, and hence the beginnings of modern German culture. Spirituality, it seems, was less ambiguous for Brahms in his sixties than it had been through most of his adult life. Notwithstanding his offhand comments about "heathen texts" and having read too much Schopenhauer to have faith in immortality, Brahms displayed a strong impulse to deal in strictly Christian and overwhelmingly Lutheran texts in his last years. At the end of his life ("the story is now over, the circle is closed"), Brahms was cementing his place in German artistic traditions. He was also strongly connecting his own personal legacy to the German cultural heritage.

As I discussed in Chapter 2, even the philosophically pregnant biblical texts of the *Vier ernste Gesänge,* op. 121, may have been originally chosen with an eye toward unfolding political events in the *Kaiserreich.* Ultimately, however, Brahms chose to dissociate the texts of Ecclesiastes and Ecclesiasticus from themes of sovereign wisdom and nation building, and constructed instead a progression from the depths of existential pessimism (Ecclesiastes 3:19–22; 4:1–3) through an acceptance of death (Ecclesiasticus 41:1–4) to a paean to Christian love (1 Corinthians 13). Whereas many have chosen to focus on the Schopenhauer-like pessimism and dark musical atmosphere of the first two songs, the change of harmonic direction from E minor to its parallel major in the middle of song no. 3 signals a strong move away from the spirit of the first two songs. Then comes the abrupt reversal at the beginning of song no. 4, where the closing high G-sharp of the previous song, the third of an E major harmony, is transformed without warning into a low A-flat, the root note of a subdominant harmony in the entirely distant and fresh tonality of E-flat major. Paul's hymn to love in 1 Corinthians 13 reads as a Romantic manifesto on love. Particularly in his use of the mirror, a metaphor for our incomplete relationship that is completed only through giving ourselves up completely (as in Christian love or in death), Paul finds much resonance in early-nineteenth-century writings on love by Hegel and Hölderlin.[15] Not only, then, do these songs connect to the retrospective genres of the last years through their use of biblical texts, but also in them Brahms achieves a familiar pattern from this time of returning to the heroes of his young adulthood (the German Idealists) and "Junge Kreisler's" spirit of Romanticism. And just as the melancholy reminiscence of the Intermezzi from the 1890s goes far beyond the feigned *Sehnsucht* of Brahms's youthful *Kreislerei,* the depth projected by the musical settings of the biblical texts in op. 121 far exceeds any personal emotional content or philosophical weight of Brahms's youthful biblical settings or other sacred works from the 1850s and 1860s.

Constructing "Brahms the German"

In his 1920 Brahms biography, the Leipzig composer and music critic Walter Niemann avers that Brahms "deepened in his mature years into a resignation which, though still virile, attempts in vain with infinite melancholy to stave off a sense of isolation."[16] To the late Intermezzi in particular Niemann ascribes "a quiet elegiac tone, with a soft, pensive resigned grace, which seems to be smiling through tears. . . . These late [piano] works of Brahms have been appropriately described as 'children of autumn, golden juicy fruit, full of ripe, strong sweetness,' in allusion, above all, to their prevailing mood, which is for the most part deeply resigned, weary and full of pessimistic *Weltschmerz.*"[17] One would be hard-pressed to find any discussion of Brahms's late works that does not refer similarly to the unmistakable mood of resignation and melancholy to which Niemann refers. Commentators frequently point to the rapid series of deaths among Brahms's friends and family between 1892 and 1894 as an impetus for this autumnal mood.[18] Brahms's sister Elise and his longtime friend and confidante Elisabeth von Herzogenberg died in 1892; the singer Hermine Spies, with whom Brahms had developed a close working and personal relationship, died in 1893; musicologist and friend Philipp Spitta, the conductor Hans von Bülow, who coined the notion of the "Three B's," and Theodor Billroth, possibly Brahms's closest Viennese friend, all died in 1894. Coupled with the fact that Brahms turned sixty in 1893, so many personal losses may well have engendered a reflective, even resigned attitude that is conveyed by his music of the time.

Other, less personal causes may also be adduced, however, to account for the widely perceived melancholy tone of Brahms's late music, some of them musical, others cultural. Robert Morgan hears in the *Klavierstücke,* op. 118, the composer's own confrontation with the limits of the tonal language and his coming to terms with the historical passing of the musical era to which he belonged, "that twilight moment in Western music's evolution where the traditional language of post-Renaissance composition is reaching the end of its long blossoming." He concludes that "Brahms's message seems clear: music can continue to exist only by reflecting upon the very difficulty of its continuing existence."[19] By connecting the palpable sense of resignation in Brahms's late piano works ("those qualities of reticence and regret, of melancholy and longing") to the passing of an age, Morgan enters into a stream of Brahms reception from the composer's day down to our own in which Brahms is understood to express a pessimistic reaction to the tenor of his times, musically or otherwise. What has changed over time are the claims of just what it was that Brahms was reacting against. For Morgan, the impetus is strictly musical: the dissolution of common-practice tonality. Niemann's rhetoric seems, at first blush, to be in a similar vein. Yet there is a decisive difference that moves Brahms's response to his world beyond the purely musical sphere; tears born of "pessimistic *Weltschmerz*" imply a deeper and socially more immediate situation as the root of Brahms's resignation. A closer reading of Brahms's place in Niemann's larger understanding of German musical culture in the late nineteenth and early twentieth centuries reveals a strong political slant to this depiction of Brahms.

Niemann's biography was among the most successful in the early-twentieth-century Brahms literature.[20] Not only was his book reprinted fourteen times between its first appearance in 1920 and 1933, but also it appeared in an English translation by Catherine Alison Phillips in 1929, in which form it received seven more reprintings by 1947. This, then, was one of the most widely read Brahms biographies in the first half of the twentieth century. As an epigraph to his book, Niemann chose the closing paragraph of an earlier book on Brahms, Rudolf von der Leyen's *Johannes Brahms als Mensch und Freund* (1905). Leyen was a friend of Brahms, and his book takes the form of a personal reminiscence. In his closing, however, Leyen opens out onto Brahms's larger role in musical and cultural history, a position from which Niemann chose to embark:

> If ever our German nation is passing through a phase of national mourning and tribulation—which God [may] forbid for long years to come, although, as the history of the past teaches us, this becomes necessary in the course of ages, as a result of external and internal enemies, in order to restore national balance— then shall the children of Brahms's muse, like holy angels, droop their lily wands over mankind in its affliction, pouring a healing balm into their wounds, and thus aid in directing our mission in the life of nations toward new and glorious aims. God grant it may be so![21]

Leyen's memoir is full of references to Brahms's patriotism, so his nationalistic flourish in closing comes as little surprise. Writing these words in 1905, Leyen may have sensed the growing European political tensions but could not have foreseen the military catastrophe awaiting Germany in the following decade. Nevertheless, his prescription of Brahms as a "healing balm" is part and parcel of German cultural rhetoric at this time. Bach and Beethoven were the more likely musical remedies, but employing Brahms in this way was soon to become commonplace as well. For example, in a 1907 essay marking the tenth anniversary of Brahms's death, Felix Wilfferodt writes: "Brahms is still the representative of a *non-nervous* artistic language. That [language] sets certain limits, but at the same time has its beneficial side. . . . [I]n Brahms's style of non-nervous musical feelings we have a remedy at hand, which can be useful against the aesthetic confusion of many of the latest compositional trends."[22] When Niemann appropriated Leyen's words in 1920, he was able to take the metaphor one step further: Brahms's music was poised to serve as a cultural model for restoring Germany's "mission in the life of nations" following the defeat in World War I. At the very end of his book, Niemann is explicit about where in the course of that mission Germany then stood. Having asserted that "the old opposition, Brahms *versus* Wagner, . . . has long since been harmoniously resolved in the equation: Brahms *and* Wagner," Niemann writes:

> Wagner was the mightiest culmination and consummation of that pan-Germanicism that collapsed in the World War with the wreck of Bismarck's heritage, of the "German Idea" of Rohrbach, so far as this concerned Germany's position and significance as a world power. . . . But if this "German Idea" is to preserve its inward soundness and vitality, it requires, as a contrast to the vast dramatic power of Wagner, which looks outward, the tranquil, intimate, absolute strength of Brahms, which looks inward.[23]

"Brahms *and* Wagner" is Niemann's way of projecting a unified national German spirit, which, having failed to assert its outward (Wagnerian) character militarily and politically, must now turn inward to heal its wounds. Here Brahms is the model of "absolute strength" for modern Germany.

Niemann's appointment of Brahms to this nation-healing role is a natural extension of the portrait of his subject that he has painted throughout the book. Chapter 18, "Brahms als Mensch," is full of references to Brahms's love of Bismarck and the German *Volk*, his *Niederdeutsch* character, and his deeply Lutheran nature. The label *Niederdeutsch* (or "Low German") is ubiquitous in early-twentieth-century Brahms literature. Although it can be a mere geographical designation, referring to the northwestern region of Germany from Hannover to Hamburg, *Niederdeutsch* also evoked the supposed original Germanic tribe of northwestern Germany on which some ultranationalist writers at the turn of the century pinned their belief in a pure-blooded and culturally superior Teutonic past.[24] And this was not the first time that Niemann had stressed the importance of Brahms's German identity. In an earlier book, *Die Musik der Gegenwart* (1913), Niemann singles out Brahms among the "classicists" of the nineteenth century not only for his strongly stamped national character but for his racial makeup as well.[25] In fact, race surfaces in that book as a central theme for Niemann, who takes national differences among musical styles to be natural and desirable, and attributes those differences directly to racial traits. He devotes the first part of his book to an overview of conservative schools in the mid- to late nineteenth century, dividing them into "Romanticism and Post-Romanticism" and "Classicism," of which Brahms is the central figure. But Brahms's classicism, Niemann immediately points out, is markedly different from that of his Viennese forbears:

> With Johannes Brahms, Romanticism and Classicism provide their first great, truly characteristic modern master. Indeed, that is proved by an external fact. To an ever-increasing degree, as with the great masters of Classicism and Romanticism, one must first come to terms with the personality of the master in order to comprehend his art. That is modern, and it is also modern that the question of lineage and race [Stamm- und Rassenfrage] rises to one of the foremost positions in the estimation of his art. With the great Classical and Romantic masters this had a much stronger effect on the predisposition and development of their personal character than on that of their art; with Brahms—and only with Chopin before him—lineage and race impressed a direct and immediate stamp upon his art. Only with difficulty would one hear from their music that the proudly free and wild Beethoven comes from the sunny lower Rhine; that Mendelssohn, master of Italian beautiful lines, comes from stormy and melancholic Hamburg; or that the deeply inward and impetuously fantastic Schumann comes from soft and friendly Saxony. They speak to all people, to the folk [Volk]. In Brahms's music, conversely, the characteristics of his lineage, of his race, lie directly in all their power also for those who are resolved to know nothing about his personality. Brahms, however, speaks completely clearly only for the people of his stock.[26]

For fifteen pages Niemann goes on to define Brahms's lineage and stock (Stamm) as "Dithmarscher" (referring to the lowlands region north of Hamburg) and "Westholsteiner" (in short, "a compatriot of Hebbel"), and compares Brahms's artistic temperament in turn to that of various other North German literary figures (Theodor Storm, Klaus Groth, and others). Generally, Niemann compares various shades of gray among these artists, noting also their strength, resignation, and pathos.[27]

Supposing nationality as a predictive element for character and behavior does not necessarily carry the extremely negative connotations we are compelled to associate with such assumptions (particularly among German writers) following World War II. Indeed, Niemann's reference to the Volk sounds like a throwback to the benign relativism of Herder; nowhere in these pages does he argue for Brahms's racial superiority, but rather argues for his racial distinction. In the closing section of his book, titled "Nation,

Volk und Stamm," Niemann pursues this line further as he praises each European nationality for its defining features. But two familiar themes in Germanic narratives of music history around this time emerge clearly at the end of the book, belying Niemann's apparently even-handed relativism. First comes the assertion of Germany's privileged role among nationalities, especially in comparison to the French and Italians. "For all the international dissemination of their art," writes Niemann, "in the last analysis we perceive this one as thoroughly French, that one just as sharply as Italian. Only our [i.e., Germany's] classical spirit and role as artistic mediator, only our singular capacity for sympathy that has grown through the centuries, restrain us in this regard."[28] Later Niemann writes of "our nation's position in the nineteenth century as the musical schoolmistress, as the successor to Italy's centuries-long musical hegemony over other nations. Germany has become the catalyst and teacher of national music in foreign lands. One gives, the other receives."[29] For this reason, one presumes, Niemann felt comfortable devoting three quarters of his book overwhelmingly to German music while spending only the fourth part on "National Music."

Niemann's nationalistic outlook sharpened after World War I. In a conclusion that he appended to the book in a 1920 edition, he blames the decline of Romantic nationalist music on the "Neo-Romantics" and "Moderns," who "even before the war pushed everything toward internationalism and cosmopolitanism."[30] The terms "cosmopolitanism" and "modern" often carried anti-Semitic connotations. Whereas his racial attributions lacked any specifically anti-Semitic tone in earlier editions of the book, the new conclusion betrays Niemann's growing distrust for an alleged combination of American and Jewish capitalism that was infecting musical life in Europe:

> Europe groans ever longer and thus heavier under the pressure of American commercial culture [Geschäftskultur]. Art, too, has long been drawn into the general mercantilism and has become a business. . . . Musical life is ruled by the American principle of "objectivism." If a contemporary composer does not work purely for commercial reciprocity, if he does connect himself in some way to a cooperative Strauss-Schillings group, then he can wait in some cases for decades until he is also only "noticed." To an endlessly higher degree the theaters are capitalistic business enterprises. As in the business leadership, so too does business-shrewd Semitedom dominate today's opera and operetta composers. It also dominates the cultural critics of the daily press in the large or at least in the capital cities of every European nation. This is not meant to be a malicious or in any way anti-Semitic reproach; it is merely meant to help explain the spiritual limitations, prevailing tastes, and peculiarities of a musically high-standing and highly gifted race, which taint in many ways the most influential art and music critics as well as the critical-aesthetic penetration of contemporary music and for that reason may not always be to its advantage. Ideals

are not dead, but they live and operate unnoticed; public artistic life has no more room for them.[31]

Niemann's disclaimer notwithstanding ("This is not meant to be a malicious or in any way anti-Semitic reproach"), his segregation of "das Geschäftstüchtige Semitentum" from "ideals" is disturbing, especially after such racial determinism in the first part of the book. Niemann differs from many other conservative writers of the time in that he does not condemn impressionism, expressionism, and futurism outright (he even has some backhanded words of praise for the expressionistic music of Schoenberg—whose "race" he never mentions). But there is no mistaking how the racial distinctions he draws early in his book, and the distinctions he makes between "national musics" and German music, allow for the sort of pigeonholing of Jews into an inartistic, money-centered "race" in counterdistinction to the German "Ideale."[32]

It is here that Niemann's comments about Brahms, both in this book and in his Brahms biography, take on import for German Brahms reception between the wars. For various reasons, it became ever more expedient and necessary for Niemann and his German contemporaries to extol Brahms's Germanness as against a Semitically tainted modernism. As the culture of the Weimar Republic grew ever farther from traditional values, and as postwar Germany struggled economically and politically, it was as easy to assign the blame to the outsiders within as it was urgent to hold up models from the German cultural past who stood for those same values that the modernists seemed to be eroding. As a conservative Romantic, Brahms was a safe bet; his musical style and personal temperament were widely understood as Germanic by his admirers (and detractors), and his music was firmly grounded in traditional aesthetic principles. Moreover, the well-worn comparison between Brahms and his German predecessors Bach and Beethoven allowed him to be plugged into an overarching historical cultural narrative of continuity. Wagner, to be sure, served a similar purpose to some, but his progressive art could too easily be blamed for the excesses of the modernists. The most convenient solution, as Niemann demonstrated at the end of his 1920 biography, was to present Brahms and Wagner as two complementary sides of the German coin; now that the extroverted political aspect of the German nature had run aground, it was time to turn to the "tranquil, intimate, absolute strength of Brahms, which looks inward."

Niemann was hardly alone in presenting Brahms this way: many writers during the first quarter of the twentieth century portray Brahms as a bulwark against modernism, basing their arguments, in part, on his identity as a pure German. Whereas such assertions of German identity and anti-modernism may have been commonplace around this time in writings about icons of German culture, in Brahms reception they mark a departure from the nineteenth-century focus on Brahms as a composer of difficult, cerebral, and intellectual music—all qualities of nineteenth-century modernism. I have already cited Felix Wilfferodt's prescription of Brahms as a "remedy" against modernism. Somewhat later, Willibald Nagel, in his 1923 biography, depicts Brahms as a German in distinction to the cosmopolitan art of Liszt and the New Germans, and he goes on to ascribe to Brahms the culmination of a gradual reunion between artistic and *volkstümlich* expression in the arts during the nineteenth century. Nagel writes, "In Brahms this entire developmental process in German art repeats itself in a concentrated manner insofar as he allowed the large forms of artistic creation to be ever more strongly imbued with the spiritual content of general feelings [*Allgemeinempfindens*]."[33]

Wilfferodt and Nagel represent an important stage in this story and in the transformation of Brahms from a modernist in the nineteenth-century sense (difficult, intellectual, rational) to an antimodernist tool in the twentieth century. In opposing Brahms to modernism, each employs as an essential part of his argument Brahms's supposed German purity: Brahms the "echt Niederdeutscher" for Wilfferodt, and Brahms the embodiment of the reunification of folk and high-art style for Nagel. Both champion Brahms for essentially the same qualities that his Viennese supporters had. But many of those supporters had been among the leading Jewish critics, composers, and music promoters of the city, and they never expressed their support for Brahms in such overtly nationalistic tones. What had changed was Brahms's adaptation to a *völkisch* model of musical conservatism. In some ways this was not a hard sell, given the ample evidence of Brahms's love for German folk song. To Brahms's earlier detractors who had supported Bruckner, however, Brahms's music was too austere, cerebral, and lacking in sympathy with the *Volk* to fulfill any nationalistic function. Later antimodernist writers would turn this outlook on its head. They frequently describe Brahms's personality and music with the words "herb," "knorrig," and "grübelnd" (dry, bony, and brooding), the same sorts of terms that had been used to criticize Brahms's music during his lifetime. Now, however, these were cited as typical *Niederdeutsch* character traits, and thereby as evidence of Brahms's *Niederdeutsch* lineage. In this way they were turned to the composer's advantage.

"Was Brahms a Jew?"

This nationalistically German image of Brahms would be jeopardized were he shown to be anything other than a *Niederdeutscher*. Just such a threat surfaced in the decade following publication of Niemann's Brahms biography, as suspicions circulated that Brahms might be not just less than Aryan but (of all things) a Jew. Brahms reception history has been slow to acknowledge or explore this phenomenon. In fact, the issue had lain dormant since the end of World War II before several German scholars writing on various aspects of music in the Third Reich raised possible connections between the rumor and the Hamburg Reichs-Brahmsfest in May 1933. Peri Arndt suggested in 1997 that the rumor of Brahms's Jewish roots, while never outwardly addressed, forms a backdrop against which to understand seemingly unnecessary protestations of Brahms's Germanness that surfaced in exhibits and news articles surrounding the festival.[34] Like Fred K. Prieberg in his monograph on Wilhelm Furtwängler, *Trial of Strength,* Arndt links the rumor to that festival through published comments by the exiled German-Jewish actor and writer Paul Walter Jacob. Writing in 1934 for a newspaper in Argentina (where he lived in exile), and working from notes written in Amsterdam during his flight from the Nazis, Jacob wrote of "the scandal [that] surrounded the Brahms Festival in 1933, as it was claimed that this ur-*deutsche* musician descended from a Jewish Abrahamson family."[35] Arndt also cites the Zionist leader Leo Motzkin, who went further in his *Black Book: The Position of Jews in Germany* (1934) by claiming that "the great Brahms festival planned by the National Socialists had to be canceled on account of these rumors."[36]

Other sources in the musical press bear witness to the question of Brahms's possible Jewishness. For example, in his article for the third edition of *Grove's Dictionary of Music and Musicians* (1932), John Alexander Fuller-Maitland acknowledges the rumor by doubting its veracity, stating, "An assumption that Brahms was of Jewish origin is extremely unlikely."[37] And Roger Sessions directly cites the rumor in a 1933 article that he wrote upon returning from Germany that fall. Writing about Wilhelm Furtwängler's highly publicized dispute with the new National Socialist regime over whether or not to allow Jewish musicians to play in the Berlin Philharmonic, Sessions lamented the Nazis' influence on musical life in Germany, adding, "It is rumored that even Brahms's music has become suspect on account of a Jewish strain in his ancestry."[38]

In fact, the impetus to defend Brahms's German heritage against the hint of a Semitic strand in his lineage may have roots reaching back to his own lifetime. Specifically, Brahms's close association with Jews and the perception that he belonged to a Jewish brand of cultural elitism in Vienna had colored the reception of his music near the end of the nineteenth century. Margaret Notley has illustrated how completely Brahms's detractors identified the composer with the culturally conservative Jewish elite of the city.[39] Her most poignant example comes from an 1890 article by the music critic Josef Stolzing in which he labeled Brahms himself a Jew: "What a pleasing spectacle awaits us when Hanslick, Hirschfeld, Königstein, and Kalbeck [all music critics associated with the Brahms camp] again offer the palm to their great (?) fellow clansmen Goldmark, Goldschmidt, Brahms, etc., and lead them into the temple of immortality. Long live the music-loving and music-making Jewry!"[40]

Attempts to tie Brahms to Jews came not only in the form of insults from his anti-Semitic detractors, however; they also could come from more sympathetic corners. Most famously, in August 1889 the Jewish satirist Daniel Spitzer wrote a column from Ischl, where Brahms was vacationing, in which he plays up Brahms's socializing with Jews:

> It is Johannes Brahms, who previously had traveled in Jewish circles only now and then, but decided this time to spend a summer exclusively in Ischl. In general company he is very taciturn and only mutters an occasional ironic observation; in intimate circles, however, he actively takes part in the conversation, and since he loves humor and wit, he loves to hear and to tell specifically those splendid anecdotes, in which the Jews so pointedly banter over their own weaknesses, which, unfortunately, they no longer put into circulation, in order not to furnish sterile anti-Semitism with the sharpest weapons to be used against themselves.[41]

Brahms, in Spitzer's depiction, enjoys mingling with Jews as an outsider, even prefers their company to society at large ("größerer Gesellschaft").

For his part, Brahms seems to have enjoyed playing with the perception that he might be Jewish. When in August 1884 Brahms's publisher Fritz Simrock sent the painter Fedor Encke to Brahms's summer retreat of Mürzzuschlag to paint a portrait of the composer, Brahms wrote back to Simrock: "He doesn't want [to paint] me, I look too Jewish to him and would have to shave my beard. But seriously I cannot do it, I have too great an aversion to it and already I have often insulted good painters on this account." The "but seriously" indicates that Brahms found the idea that he looked Jewish to be comical, an impression he reinforced by joking about it again in a subsequent letter: "Encke still drags himself around like a corpse and complains about my Jewish face and my bad character."[42] In light of Stoltzing's attack and Spitzer's ironic remarks, Brahms may have felt a need to cloak Encke's comments in humor, suggesting that he was well aware of the perception that perhaps he associated with Jews too much for some people's taste.

Stolzing's remark notwithstanding, there is little direct evidence from Brahms's own lifetime that anyone actually believed that the composer was of Jewish lineage. Yet the rumor did not spring up only in 1933 and was not merely a by-product of newly unleashed Nazi fanaticism (as both Prieberg and Arndt suggest). At least as early as 1914, the fourth edition of a well-known authority on German name origins, Albert Heintze's *Deutschen*

Familiennamen, suggested as much by listing "Brahms" as a foreshortening of the name "Abraham," which is labeled "mostly Jewish."[43] This derivation is new to the fourth edition, the second to be edited by Paul Cascorbi. Curiously, Cascorbi makes no mention at the point of the entry or in the prefatory material (which is virtually unchanged from the previous edition of 1906) for this new suggested derivation, which he must have realized would raise German eyebrows.

Cascorbi's was not the only book of names to make this suggestion. Several sources from the second quarter of the twentieth century similarly claim that "Brahms" can be a shortened version of the Old Testament name "Abraham." Hans Bahlow makes the same claim in a 1933 book on German names, closely following Cascorbi's entry.[44] Other German authors, however, were less willing to accept Cascorbi's new derivation. In 1935 Gerhard Kessler cites "Brahms" as one foreshortening of "Abraham," but lists it as a typical usurpation of an Old Testament name by German Protestants at the time of the Reformation.[45] Seven years later, at the height of the Nazi period, Konrad Krause puts a more anti-Semitic spin on this line of thinking. In *Die Jüdische Namenwelt*, Krause acknowledges that Jews shortened "Abrahamson" as a means of what he calls "name camouflaging through word mutilation—much beloved by the Jews." But in a defensively worded footnote he adds, "Johannes Brahms's name is as Aryan as the man himself: either Brahms shortened the vestigial Brahmst of the place-name near Hamburg, Brahmstedt, or the name is a genitive patronymic of Bramo, the shortened form of the old single name Brandmar ('Known by the sword')."[46]

One corner of Brahms reception did react to the Jewish rumor, partly because it had a direct stake in settling questions about his roots: studies of Brahms's family and ancestry. *Ahnentafeln*, or family trees, were common during the late nineteenth and early twentieth centuries. Between 1898 and 1938 a number of such articles were published concerning Brahms, and several book-length biographies carried this information as well. Already in the first volume of his biography (1908), Kalbeck laid out much of the known circumstances of Brahms's immediate family going back to his great-grandfather, Peter Hinrich Brahms, a carpenter who relocated from Hannover to Brunsbüttel around 1750 and died in 1782.[47] Much of what followed over the next decades of Brahms studies extended one branch of the family or another back beyond that date: Brahms's mother's side (*née* Nissen) could be traced all the way back to fifteenth-century nobility.[48] Only one of these authors, however, Erwin Freitag, makes a direct connection to a Brahms family line before the mid-eighteenth century. In his 1932 essay "Beitrag zur Geschichte der Familie Brahms," Freitag matter-of-factly connects Peter Hinrich Brahms to a Brahms family line dating back to the early seventeenth century in Horst, north of Hamburg. Some other studies present this family line as one potential origin for the composer's ancestry but find no direct connection. Freitag is also the only *Brahms-Ahnen* author before the National Socialist period who addresses the Jewish question, citing Cascorbi directly: "The family name is written Brahmst, Bramst, and Brahms. In many name books, as in Heintze and Cascorbi, it derives from Abraham, Hebr. "father of the masses" (see 1 Moses 17:5), in that the name is supposedly foreshortened." Freitag goes on to offer other possible derivations found in name books of the day and suggests that the more likely source of the name is the city of Brahmstedt or the Plattdeutsch word *Bram* (bramble), whereafter he dismisses Cascorbi's derivation: "'Abraham' I take here to be completely unlikely."[49] A stronger denial came from Botho Graf von Keyserlingk in his article "Brahms und seine Ahnen" of 1938. After suggesting near the beginning of his essay that Abraham may be a Protestant name, Keyserlingk closes by stating, "It would be absurd to believe that even one drop of foreign blood flowed in the veins of the master."[50]

Defining Brahms at Mid-century

Arnt and Prieberg's focus on 1933 notwithstanding, it appears that the rumor of Brahms's possible Jewish heritage began to circulate earlier in the twentieth century. Even the locale of the 1933 flareup of the rumor is open to question. Although Arndt's essay focused on Hamburg, it is possible that Jacob and Motzkin are referring to some other Brahms festival or to separate instances entirely, since neither identifies where the Brahms festivals to which they refer were meant to take place. It is possible that they are both referring to a series of Brahms concerts that had been planned for Berlin but were canceled because of the Jewish soloists and conductors who had been contracted for the performances (Pablo Casals, Rudolf Serkin, Bruno Walter, Otto Klemperer, Sabine Kelter). These names then surfaced in Vienna as part of a week-long Brahms centennial festival jointly sponsored there by Vienna's Gesellschaft der Musikfreunde and the Berlin-based Deutsche Brahms-Gesellschaft. In place of the Jewish Klemperer, Wilhelm Furtwängler, president of the Deutsche Brahms-Gesellschaft, conducted the orchestral concerts at the festival.[51]

Furtwängler also delivered a (still) much-reprinted inaugural address to the Vienna festival that provides a poignant example of Brahms reception at the time.[52] It is difficult to determine to what extent the rumor of Brahms's Jewish roots affected his speech. Yet it is hard to imagine that Furtwängler, who had been closely involved with the planned Berlin concerts, was unaware of the potential scandal. What is clear is that Furtwängler's essay stands out for its conspicuous references to Brahms's German roots and his place among the greats of German music (so conspicuous, in fact, that Alban Berg, who was present, labeled it a "Nazi-breathed speech [*Naziangehauchte Rede*]").[53] Furtwängler himself was, and remains, a problematic figure for his ambivalent posture toward the Nazi regime. He not only chose to remain in Germany but also served briefly as vice president (under President Richard Strauss) for Göbbel's *Reichsmusikkammer,* and he provided the Nazis with a symbol of cultural legitimacy throughout the war by conducting in both Berlin and Vienna. And although Furtwängler actively sought first protection and then safe passage for many Jewish members of his Berlin Philharmonic, the sheer exercise of influence may have been his prime motivation, more so than compassion for a persecuted group.[54]

Yet Furtwängler was by no one's account a Nazi or even openly anti-Semitic. Rather he believed in an idealized and purely cultural German nation that was beyond the reach of politics and the ideology of the Third Reich. His convictions led him to assert that "there never was a Nazi Germany— only a Germany under the heel of the Nazis."[55] Such statements were familiar enough in the years after the Second World War but are generally regarded nowadays as wishful denial.[56] Acknowledging Furtwängler's vision of Germany helps to explain the conception of Brahms that he sets forth in his centennial essay. Nearly all of Furtwängler's essays on composers from the German canon are laced with references to their German identity, and many focus on this point. From the outset of his 1933 Brahms address, Furtwängler stresses the composer's identity as a German:

> Neither in Vienna nor in the *Reich*—regardless of how our current political masters think about it—should we ever forget that we belong to one and the same cultural world, and that in music, Viennese classical composers have become synonymous with the German classical composers. Nowhere else is solidarity and community so clearly within reach as here; and one would not be far from the truth in saying that Brahms has become the last of the great Viennese musicians, the last of the great German classical composers.

Furtwängler goes on to place Brahms in an explicitly German artistic lineage:

> Brahms belonged to that race of Germanic musical giants, which begins with Bach and Handel, is carried forward by Beethoven, and in which a colossal physical power is combined with the greatest tenderness and sensitivity. His character and stature are thoroughly Nordic. To me he always seemed to be the offspring of the greatest old German or Dutch painters, such as van Eyck or Rembrandt, whose works unify intimacy, fantasy, and fervent, often impetuous vibrancy with a wonderful sense of form. . . . This form is in itself peculiarly characteristic of Germans, which suits Brahms, a form that appears never to be there of its own accord but always for the sake of the "content," a form

sculpted to conform with that content while exhibiting its own individual symmetry and charming clarity. His works are born in a wild, demonic world, and
yet how elegantly and strictly organically are they assembled! Brahms's music is
more qualified than any other to disprove the frequent assertion that German
composers are incapable of writing music that reflects classical forms.[57]

Thus Furtwängler does not merely *present* Brahms as a German but *de-
fends* him as one as well. But against (and for) whom? At first glance one
might assume he is referring to foreign critics and peers among Brahms's
contemporaries. But if one takes Furtwängler's essay in its context—that is,
in the wake of the National Socialist power surge in Germany that year—
those who challenge Germans' ability to write "classically" are more likely
the modernists: Debussy, Stravinsky, and others who rose to prominence in
the two decades after Brahms's death and who outlined distinctly new, anti-
Teutonic criteria for musical aesthetics. (Excluded are German modernists
such as Schoenberg and Hindemith, who never would have challenged German music's classicism. But these figures are the target of Furtwängler's op-
probrium in other essays.)

Furtwängler ultimately traced Brahms's Germanicism to the composer's
unity with the German *Volk*. Brahms, he writes, had "the special ability
to live out and to feel the great suprapersonal community of the folk." And
he accomplished this, according to Furtwängler, through his melodies:
"Brahms . . . had the ability to write melodies that were unmistakably his,
down to the last detail, and which yet sounded like folk songs. . . . Brahms
. . . *was* the folk, *was* the folk song."[58] Little new ground is broken here;
commentators from early on in Brahms's career had identified folk song–
like qualities in his music. Moreover, this has been and continues to be an
enduring and legitimate aspect of Brahms reception. But any focus on an
artist's *völkisch* credentials in 1933 Germany warrants close scrutiny, given
the propagandistic and spiritual value of *das Volk* in Nazi ideology. Accordingly, Furtwängler grabs our attention when he bestows the same connection between folk song and artistic style on a pair of less likely recipients:
"Wagner and Bruckner possessed the same gift, and I have no hesitation in
maintaining that it represents creativity at its highest and constitutes the
mark of a genius." Whereas we are less likely to hear echoes of folk music in
the compositions of these two composers, *völkisch* rhetoric of this type was
to become rampant, especially in the cult of Bruckner that developed during
the later 1930s.[59]

It is revealing to compare Furtwängler's claim of folk qualities in
Bruckner and Wagner to his critique of Gustav Mahler's use of folk melody:
"With Mahler . . . it was quite the reverse. Mahler's relationship to the folk
song was that of a stranger, an outsider, a man who yearned to find refuge in

it, a haven of peace for his restless spirit. Taking it over as it stood, he merely created synthetic folk song."[60] Mahler is likely exhibited here for his status as a modernist as much as for his identity as a Jew. But these two identities were not easily separated at the time in Vienna, where by 1933 a strong strain of anti-Semitism had pervaded the cultural battle against modernism as it had all over Europe.[61] Furtwängler's very need to distinguish Mahler (about whom he makes complimentary remarks in other essays) from "that race of Germanic musical giants" is typical of a nationalistic exclusionary attitude toward the Jews as a separate race. Anti-Semitic music critics as far back as Wagner (in his essays "On the Jewish in Music" [1850] and "What Is German?" [1868]) had accused Jews of merely aping German speech in a futile effort to make themselves sound German, quickly drawing a connection to Jewish attempts to write music in the German tradition. Furtwängler merely omits the first step. And during the early twentieth century, reactionary German ideologues had forged a dichotomy between pure art, which can only spring from *das Volk,* and the empty, derivative art of Jews, which had corrupted an originally folk-based German culture. Modernism came to be the focal point of those discontents.[62]

The last paragraph of Furtwängler's address, presented in full here, sums up this view of antimodernist Germanicism as applied to Brahms, a view that reached its peak and could only have been articulated so bluntly in the political climate that engulfed Austria and Germany in the 1930s:

> The folk, the folk song from which Brahms descends, is German. He was able to accomplish what he did by the strength of his Germanness. And not—this must also be stated—because he *wanted* to be a German, but rather because he *was* a German. He could be nothing else; and if his heart was open to all sorts of inspirations from beyond Germany (also a typically German attitude), his Germanic nature instinctually sought to overcome and subdue these influences. His art, in its bitterness and sweetness, in its apparent exterior hardness and inner resilience, in its imagination and abundance as in its self-discipline and compactness, is German. He was the last musician to reveal to all the world's eyes, with undeniable clarity, the greatness of German music.[63]

However vain his attempt to separate cultural from political nationalism, Furtwängler nevertheless strikes a resonant chord with a constant in Brahms reception from the composer's own day down to the present, namely, the assertion that Brahms's music belongs to an idealized cultural realm that is untouched by the politics not only of its own time but also of the time in which that music is received. One year after the Brahms centennial festival in Vienna, Furtwängler penned another (shorter) piece, this one titled "Brahms and the Crisis of Our Time."[64] While much of his Vienna address is recapitulated and abbreviated in this essay, the notion of Brahms as an objective

composer whose music speaks to posterity is more pronounced now than it
had been a year before. That much is clear from the opening paragraph:

> Great artists, as we have observed more than once, often experience a gradual
> change of attitude toward their environment and their own art, a change that
> begins with middle age and continues thereafter. The complete correspondence
> between the demands of one's environment and the demands of one's own self,
> so easily attainable in youthful exuberance, begins to dissipate as one ages. . . .
> Thus is the way cleared for the most personal and the most universally relevant
> insights which such artists have to confer. We confront this process no matter
> whom we choose as an example, whether we speak of Goethe or Rembrandt,
> Bach or Beethoven. Bound up with this increasing inner insight is a growing
> alienation from one's surroundings, an onset of loneliness, a transcendence of
> one's own time.[65]

Brahms is plucked from his own time in a familiar gambit that links him
more closely to other "timeless" masters than to his contemporaries. As
the essay unfolds, in Furtwängler's view, that from which Brahms would
have dissociated himself becomes clear: "He would relinquish neither himself nor his art to the spiritual crisis which has plagued Europe for the last
fifty years."[66] Read: modernism. In large part, Furtwängler is rehashing his
antimodernist thrust of a year before. But now, instead of pitting Brahms as
a child of the *Volk* in opposition to modernity, he places him above the fray,
as a model to whom contemporary musicians and audiences can look for
guidance out of the "Crisis of Our Time." A side effect of this maneuver—
and perhaps an intentional one on Furtwängler's part—is to render Brahms
apolitical, unsullied by the worldly issues of his day, as well as by its artistic
direction.

For those who sympathize with Furtwängler and accept his denial of
complicity or sympathy with the Nazis, his stance on Brahms as a
superhistorical artist is an easy fit, since it is precisely this view of Brahms's
music that we embrace today. Brahms has maintained down to our day
the same reputation that Furtwängler affords him, as a composer of classical
instincts amid a Romantic musical climate. And Brahms is still regarded as
the "absolute music" composer par excellence. But while we may applaud
Furtwängler for attempting to isolate Brahms's music from the offensively
nationalistic politics of the time, claiming universality and detachment for
Brahms's art is itself a form of cultural nationalism. German intellectuals
and artists had been making such claims about German art (especially music) since the early nineteenth century. Indeed, much of our modern attitude
toward absolute music as an abstract and elevated art form developed from
that philosophical tradition.[67] One may read Furtwängler's comments as
apolitical and therefore disassociated from Nazi ideology, but they speak to
a form of cultural nationalism that could be (and was) exploited by the Na-

zis themselves, that is, the elevated, transcendent, and spiritual status of German art music. In the end it is difficult to separate cultural from political nationalism as Furtwängler wished to do, just as it has been difficult for his biographers and historians to agree on whether and to what degree he was complicit in or resistant to the Nazi agenda.

Perhaps it was Furtwängler's sort of decontextualizing that Paul Bekker had in mind when he simultaneously published quite a different Brahms centennial essay for the April–May 1933 issue of the progressive Viennese music journal *Anbruch*. Bekker, then one of Germany's leading music critics and authors, and best known today for his sociological studies of music, emigrated to the United States later in 1933 under threat of persecution as a socialist and a Jew.[68] Bekker used his essay to offer some Brahms *Rezeptionsgeschichte* of his own. "It is curiously difficult," Bekker begins, "to reach an understanding over Brahms." Noting a distinct sensitivity among the composer's devotees, even an intolerance toward divergent opinions about him, Bekker surmises that the "Brahms orthodoxy" deeply loves a beautiful but dying world for which "Brahms is certainly the last of his stock [*Stamm*]." Comparing such *Sehnsucht* to waiting for "a second coming of gods who, as everyone knows, still carry their character [*Zug*] but no longer their upward-striving power," Bekker asks, "What was it that they had brought us?" and answers:

> The present teaches us with tragic urgency: [those gods brought us] free men, an inherently peaceful personality, the great, glorious liberalism of a democratic worldview. They push forward to the idea of liberating humanity through faith in mankind. This was the immense impulse that they bore and which they will bear, so long as there are people for whom these ideas and this faith are central to existence, that is, people of art, people of culture, people of [inalienable godly grace of personality].[69]

Far from thrusting Brahms into the breach of modernism, Bekker ties him to the liberal culture that had been associated with modernity in the last quarter of the nineteenth century. His position is notable, therefore, as the first stone on the path that would lead to later scholarship that has explored and championed Brahms's identity as a liberal. And whereas Bekker may well equate "Menschlichkeit" with a German form of culture, he makes no vain attempt to separate that cultural world from the politics of his day. Indeed, he invokes politics directly when he comes down squarely in sympathy with a bygone area of liberalism and praises Brahms for representing an "opposing force" to stem the gradual dissipation of liberalism in the nineteenth century. By claiming Brahms for a liberal political sentiment in direct opposition to the fascistic German nationalism of his own day, Bekker presages the process of de-Germanification that would mark Brahms reception after World War II and still dominates our view of the composer today, insofar as these later impulses are generated by a repulsion for German nationalism gone wild in the middle of the twentieth century.

The best-known essay from this period is Schoenberg's "Brahms the Progressive," previously discussed in Chapter 1. This revisionist salvo maintains the centrality of the classical tradition for Brahms's style. As I noted in Chapter 1, Schoenberg favors Brahms's new technique of developing variation as more forward looking than Wagner's ostensibly more progressive musical language, and thereby claims for Brahms a place of privilege in modernist aesthetics of the early twentieth century. And, as I also argued there, the wide acceptance of Schoenberg's view has contributed to the notion of a super-historical, absolute quality in Brahms's style, one that emphasizes the universality of his expression in distinction to a more nationalistically marked tone in Wagner. What is lost, however, in our modern adoption of this viewpoint is Schoenberg's motivation as a nationalistically minded modernist. Recognizing that Wagner's monumental orchestral sound—from which Schoenberg's own earlier style derived—had been overturned by the neoclassical impulse in European music after World War I, Schoenberg sought to ally his own scaled-back and classicized twelve-tone aesthetic with the more austere style of Brahms. Schoenberg thereby provides an anesthetized rendition of Niemann's retreat from the defeated Wagnerianc-extroverted side of German culture to the Brahmsian-reflective side.

As he moves backwards in history to review the development of musical styles that led through Brahms and Wagner to his own compositions, Schoenberg's nationally limited outlook becomes obvious. "The greatest musicians" between Wagner's death (1883) and Brahms's (1897) were Mahler, Strauss, and Reger. Debussy and Puccini receive no mention. Likewise, the preceding aesthetic periods were defined by the music of Germans, of "J. S. Bach on the one hand and of Haydn, Mozart, Beethoven, and Schubert on the other." Between the periods represented by these figures, Bach's contrapuntal art, according to Schoenberg, was eliminated by "ruthless propaganda" from another German triumvirate, Kaiser, Telemann, and Mattheson, who asked composers to "write in the light manner of the French."[70] Brahms's achievement of an asymmetrical (and thus natural) precision and brevity in his art amounted to a reattainment of a Germanic ideal that had been realized in the musical language of an earlier age by Mozart.

In a previous essay, "National Music" (1931), Schoenberg had made his nationalism more explicit. Indeed, his tone at some points in that piece is not far removed from Niemann's: "As soon as some highly developed national art achieves a position of hegemony, one sees the stronghold exerted on art by race and nationality, how convincingly these are expressed by art, and how inseparably the one is tied to the other."[71] Schoenberg went on to identify his music as a focal point of "the battle of German music during the war," adding, "nobody has yet appreciated that my music, produced on German soil, without foreign influences, is a living example of an art able most effectively to oppose Latin and Slav hopes of hegemony and derived through and through from the traditions of German music."[72]

Unlike his "Brahms the Progressive," which was aired as a radio address in 1933 and published in *Style and Idea* in 1950, Schoenberg's handwritten essay "National Music" was not published until the revised 1975 edition of that book. By then the notion of Brahms-the-Progressive exerted a powerful influence on Brahms's historical position. Schoenberg never made the Germanic foundation of his Brahms aesthetic explicit in that essay. Ironically, his omission allowed a postwar musical consciousness that wished (and needed) to downplay Brahms's Germanness to adopt Brahms-the-Progressive as a nationally neutral entity—this despite Schoenberg's own Germanocentric view of music history as expressed beneath the surface of that essay and made explicit in his "National Music." The nationally neutral view of Brahms has largely persisted for over fifty years.

It is interesting to witness the aftereffects of the Nazi period on the next Brahms year, 1947, the fiftieth anniversary of Brahms's death, when the end of the war was still a vivid memory. English-language writers on Brahms are perhaps most conspicuous at this time for their silence on this subject and for their reluctance to acknowledge the recent past. (To be fair, Anglo-American Brahms scholarship had never dwelled on his Germanic identity in any pronounced way.) A striking case appears in the first English-language edition of Karl Geiringer's widely read Brahms biography (translated by H. B. Weiner and Bernard Miall). The translators waste no time in their de-Germanification effort: Geiringer's title, *Johannes Brahms, Leben und Schaffen eines Deutschen Meisters* (Johannes Brahms: Life and Work of a German Master), was rendered *Brahms: His Life and Work* in the first English edition of the book.[73] Most striking, however, is the omission of Geiringer's nationalistic assessment of Brahms as a guardian of German musical traditions, which followed a discussion of the composer's reticence in literary matters. In the original German edition, Geiringer's text reads:

> His innate reserve forbade him [to discuss such things], as did his entire attitude toward music as an absolute art, which one should not be allowed to approach through the indirect path of literature. And whereas the artists of the "New German school" behave like revolutionaries who are obliged to alter and better everything, Brahms, on the contrary, felt himself to be the guardian and preserver of great traditions. *He, who knew himself to be inseparable from the na-*

tionality and religion of his fathers, embraces with warm love every sign of German manner and art from earlier times, and it is his endeavor to be a useful member in the powerful chain of the German spirit.[74]

Weiner and Miall completely strike the final sentence (which I have placed in italics).

As I have touched on already, the origins of the transcendent theme in Brahms reception, including the notion of "absolute music," were rich with Germanic connotations. In the hands of postwar writers, however, the German element was quietly distilled out of the formula. Given the extent to which the Nazis had celebrated Wagner and the difficult associations that surrounded his music directly after the war, foreign admirers of German culture had an even greater stake in preserving the reputation of Brahms, Wagner's antipode. One late-nineteenth-century representative of those "German musical giants" would have to be placed above the cultural traditions that ended in the disaster of the mid-twentieth century, and Brahms was the obvious choice.

The question was more difficult for German writers following the war, and most of them avoided the issue as well. An uncomfortable exception occurs in a 1947 book by Walter and Paula Rehberg. Revisiting the influence of folk song on Brahms's music, the Rehbergs draw conclusions about Brahms's character that differ little from Furtwängler's before the war: "Considered personally, Brahms is typically German, by far the most German composer overall." But then the authors offer a lengthy disclaimer that makes sense only in the context of the times:

> With this statement we wish in no way to give a folk-tempered *limitation*, lest we be guilty of committing the completely false prejudice of valuing a composer according to his national origins [*Bodenständigkeit*]. It remains in principle totally subsidiary to which lineage a creative agent of a world-encompassing and pure art belongs; the personality is always and in every case the deciding factor.[75]

Thereafter the Rehbergs submit a list of nineteenth-century composers from diverse nations, pointing out how each excelled in a genre or style that was foreign to his own land: Mozart as a composer of Italian opera, Rossini as a composer of French opera, Franck (born in Belgium to German parents) as the founder of the "Young French school," and so on. But they cannot help coming back to "the North German in Brahms's manner of being." The authors' contortions become painful to witness as they try to articulate what they hear as Germanic in Brahms's music while remaining sensitive to the dangers of sounding overly nationalistic so soon after the Nazi period:

> In the total assessment, national elements account for absolutely nothing. The North German in Brahms's manner of being is thus to be regarded neither as a

plus nor as a minus. It is there by chance and plays no role in his meaning. But it is a special distinguishing mark of his entire oeuvre. Above all the typically German is sharply stamped in a good sense.[76]

Brahms-the-German: Is he or isn't he? The Rehbergs do not seem comfortable one way or the other. Clearly they could not overlook what they recognized and identified with in Brahms's music as essentially Germanic; but at the same time, they were rightly aware of the historical moment in which they were writing and the limitations it placed on articulating such feelings. Only a few paragraphs later they seek refuge in the newly decontextualized confines of absolute music: "Through a consideration of the complexity of Brahms's manner of being, it becomes especially notable that he was a typical, perhaps the most typical absolute musician, when one limits this idea to music that is self-sufficient, that is not associated with extramusical ideas."[77] Semantic parallels belie the objective status the Rehbergs ascribe to absolute music; just a page earlier Brahms was "typically German, by the far the most German composer overall," and here he is "a typical, perhaps the most typical absolute musician." But ostensibly, the Rehbergs intend to move away from the uncomfortable discussion of Brahms's Germanness by locating him in a less overtly nationalistic category. Thereafter, Brahms's absolute music style is quickly elevated to a transcendent, even a quasi-spiritual sphere: "With the rebirth of the classical forms which [Brahms] executed in his works—by virtue of his own knowledge of their immortal laws—singularly among the great composers of his epoch, he fulfilled a high task and mission."[78]

Just as Bekker's association of Brahms with late-nineteenth-century liberalism bridged Brahms's reputation in his own day with his political identity in ours, the manner in which the Rehbergs used the absolute music label marks a significant point in the transformation of that idea from its deeply Germanic origins to its later neutral meaning. Coming as it does so close on the heels of World War II, the Rehbergs' case highlights the degree to which the impetus for that transformation came from the need to forget the nationalistic associations of absolute music—a maneuver that, until relatively recently, music scholars have been more than happy to replicate under the same inner pressure to dissociate this music (be it by Brahms or some other "German master") from any Germanic connotations.

Brahms has maintained down to our day the same reputation that Niemann, Furtwängler, and Schoenberg afforded him: as a composer of classical instincts amid a Romantic musical climate, and as the absolute music composer par excellence. (Even recent Brahms scholars' increasing focus on allusion in his music does not change this fact: we are still speaking of "music about music.")[79] But while we may applaud Furtwängler for attempting to isolate Brahms's music from the offensively nationalistic politics of the time, or Schoenberg for finding purely musical qualities through which to define Brahms's historical role, claiming universality and detachment for Brahms's art is itself a form of cultural nationalism, as I noted earlier.

In the end, it is difficult to separate cultural from political nationalism as Furtwängler wished to do. Some of our own most common platitudes about Brahms's music—its universality, objectivity, timelessness—derive in part from an earlier long-standing tradition of German cultural chauvinism and, by extension, nationalism. That may (and perhaps should) be hard to accept after World War II. A lot is at stake in admiring Brahms, and specifically in admiring him as a "good" German—to completely subvert the more normal historical meaning of that construction. When viewed against the background of a more openly nationalistic Brahms reception that was practiced in Germany between the wars, Brahms reception later in the twentieth century can be understood as an attempt to neutralize his legacy, an endeavor born of the need to salvage something good, noble, and pure from the German cultural tradition in the wake of National Socialism.

It is unlikely that this state of Brahms reception can change before some more fundamental changes take place in the way we as Westerners understand ourselves and our place in history. A good example of the aftereffects of the Nazi period on Western musical identities came up in the (re)new(ed) German capital Berlin in 2000. A mini-scandal arose when a leading Berlin politician referred to the director of the city's Staatsoper as "the Jew Barenboim."[80] Daniel Barenboim responded with an essay in the *New York Review of Books* in which he questioned whether the politician really understood the multifaceted nature of Jewish identity, "part religion, part tradition, part nation," adding:

> It is hard to deal with, . . . and especially for a country like Germany which has such a common horrible history with the Jews. Sadly, after spending years in Germany, I have a deeper and deeper impression that this part of German history has not been assimilated or understood by many Germans. . . .
> I expect every German not to forget this part of his country's history, and to be especially careful in considering it. Each German will be able to do this, however, only if he has an understanding of his own self and the past that helped to form it: for if you suppress an important element of yourself, you are constrained in your dealings with others.[81]

Although the standpoint and emotional direction of non-Germans vis à vis the National Socialist period in Germany is likely to be quite distinct from that of a German, the repercussions for our cultural identity are not that different. We too will be able to "assimilate or understand" our own reaction to those historical events only if we do not "suppress important elements" of that story. These elements include the ramifications of recognizing nationalistic implications in Brahms's music. We have suppressed that recognition by focusing instead on the "universal" or "absolute" aspects of Brahms's art. But we have done so at the expense of understanding Brahms as a German artist or acknowledging the great extent to which his identity as a German affected his music.

Longer Musical Examples

Example A.1   Brahms, op. 91, no. 2, "Geistliches Wiegenlied," bars 1–93.

Example A.2   Brahms, op. 45, movement one: bars 1–40.

Example A.3   Brahms, op. 45, movement five: bars 1–23.

2

Example A.4   Brahms, op. 45, movement six: bars 1–37.

Notes

1. Introduction

1. *Aufruf zur Errichtung eines Johannes Brahms-Denkmales in Wien* (hereafter *Aufruf*). A copy of this proclamation is found in the Guido Adler archives at the Special Collections Division of the University of Georgia Library, Athens (MS 769 18.51). As listed on the last page of the three-page document, the committee included some of Vienna's leading musical figures (Gustav Mahler, Hans Richter, Eusebius Mandyczewski, and others) and counted among its members a virtual who's who of Brahms's friends in Austro-German musical life. Leon Botstein briefly discusses the monument that was designed by Rudolf Weyr and finished in 1908; see his "Brahms and Nineteenth-Century Painting," *Nineteenth-Century Music* 14 (1990): 154–168.

2. *Aufruf*, 1. In fact, Brahms was buried close *behind* the tombs of Beethoven and Schubert and the Mozart monument, according to Walter Niemann's description of Brahms's funeral procession and burial. Niemann, *Brahms,* trans. Catherine Allison Phillips (New York: Alfred A. Knopf, 1929), 154–157.

3. *Aufruf,* 2.

4. Ibid.

5. The concept of the symphony as society-forming was first articulated by Paul Bekker in *Die Sinfonie von Beethoven bis Mahler* (Berlin: Schuster und Löffler, 1918), 17–18, and later by Theodor Adorno in *Introduction to the Sociology of Music,* trans. F. B. Ashton (New York: Seaburg Press, 1976), 92–95. Walter Frisch has suggested the relevance of Brahms's *Requiem* for the category of society-forming music in *Brahms: The Four Symphonies* (New York: Schirmer Books, 1996), 35–36.

6. Brahms's close friend the composer Heinrich von Herzogenberg wrote of opp. 45 and 55 as "our master's two greatest, in every respect most complete and effective works." See his essay "Johannes Brahms in seinem Verhältnis zur evangelischen Kirchenmusik," *Monatschrift für Gottesdienst und kirchliche Kunst* 2 (1897): 70.

7. First published in Schoenberg, *Style and Idea,* ed. and trans. Dika Newlin (New

York Philosophical Library, 1950), 52–101; reprinted in *Style and Idea: Selected Writings of Arnold Schoenberg,* ed. Leonard Stein (Berkeley: University of California Press, 1975), 398–441.

8. Leon Botstein, intro. to *The Compleat Brahms,* ed. Botstein (New York: Norton, 1999), 23.

9. Pinson, *Pietism as a Factor in the Rise of German Nationalism* (New York: Columbia University Press, 1934).

10. See in particular Botstein, "Brahms and Nineteenth-Century Painting," 154–168; and Notley, "Brahms as Liberal: Genre, Style, and Politics in Late-Nineteenth-Century Vienna," *Nineteenth-Century Music* 17 (1993): 107–123.

11. Greenfeld, *Nationalism: Five Roads to Modernity* (Cambridge, Mass.: Harvard University Press, 1992), 3.

12. Ibid., 7.

13. Language, however, has not always played such a central role in national self-consciousness. E. J. Hobsbawm eloquently argues that before the modern phase of nationalism, language played only a minor role in identifying peoples, and the mythological linguistic unity of a nation was a construct of the modern *völkisch* movements. See his *Nations and Nationalism since 1780: Programme, Myth, Reality* (Cambridge: Cambridge University Press, 1990), 51–63.

14. Adrian Hastings, *The Construction of Nationhood: Ethnicity, Religion, and Nationalism* (Cambridge: Cambridge University Press, 1997), 108–109. Most leading scholars on nationalism discuss the centrality of language. See Benedict Anderson, *Imagined Communities: Reflections on the Origin and Spread of Nationalism,* rev. ed. (London: Verso, 1991), 44–45; and Hobsbawm, *Nations and Nationalism since 1780.* Ernest Gellner addresses the issue throughout his posthumously published *Language and Solitude: Wittgenstein, Malinowski, and the Habsburg Dilemma* (Cambridge: Cambridge University Press, 1998).

15. Schumann, *Gesammelte Schriften über Musik und Musiker,* 5th ed., vol. 1, ed. Martin Kreisig (Leipzig: Breitkopf and Härtel, 1914), 180.

16. See Sanna Pederson, "A. B. Marx, Berlin Concert Life, and German National Identity," *Nineteenth-Century Music* 18 (1994): 87–107. Such associations were not limited to the symphonic tradition. On the national connotations of adagio movements in chamber works, see Margaret Notley, "Late-Nineteenth-Century Chamber Music and the Cult of the Classical Adagio," *Nineteenth-Century Music* 23 (1999): 33–61. Although Notley does not pursue nationalistic conclusions herself, many of the contemporaneous sources she quotes highlight the Germanic element in the tradition.

17. As quoted and translated in Richard Taruskin and Pierro Weiss, eds., *Music in the Western World: A History in Documents* (New York: Schirmer, 1984), 384.

18. Wagner also expressed this formulation in the negative around this time, when in his pseudonymously published 1850 essay "Das Judenthum in der Musik" he asserted that German Jews like Mendelssohn (i.e., German by nurture but not by nature) were incapable of expressing the deeper feeling that stemmed from the soil in the person of the German folk. See Wagner, "Das Judenthum in der Musik," *Neue Zeitschrift für Musik,* 3 and 5 September 1850, 101–107, 109–112, reprinted in Wagner, *Gesammelte Schriften und Dichtungen,* vol. 5 (Leip-

zig: Fritzsch, 1872), 83–108, and translated in *Richard Wagner's Prose Works*, vol. 3, trans. William Ashton Ellis (London: Routledge Keegan and Paul, 1894), 75–122.

19. As quoted and translated in Richard Taruskin and Pierro Weiss, ed., *Music in the Western World: A History in Documents* (New York: Schirmer, 1984), 384. On Brahms, the *Erklärung*, and his relations with Brendel and the *Neudeutsche Schule*, see David Brodbeck, *Brahms: Symphony No. 1* (Cambridge: Cambridge University Press, 1996) 4–5, 8–9.

20. By contrast, Liszt and his disciples Joachim Raff and Peter Cornelius tended to set contemporary poets, including texts from their own pens.

21. I am referring primarily here to two signal studies on the origins of National Socialist ideology that appeared in the early 1960s: Georg Mosse, *The Crisis of German Ideology: Intellectual Origins of the Third Reich* (New York: Grosset's Universal Library, 1964); and Fritz Stern, *The Politics of Cultural Despair* (Berkeley: University of California Press, 1961).

22. Wagner, "Das Judenthum in der Musik"; idem, "Was ist deutsch?" *Bayreuther Blätter* 1 (February 1878): 29–42, reprinted in Wagner, *Gesammelten Schriften*, vol. 10 (1883), 51–74, and translated in *Richard Wagner's Prose Works*, vol. 4, 149–170.

23. Gellner, *Nationalism* (New York: New York University Press, 1997), 59–62, 70 (chap. 8, "The Murderous Virulence of Nationalism").

24. Brahms, *Briefe an P. J. Simrock und Fritz Simrock*, vol. 1, ed. Max Kalbeck, *Johannes Brahms Briefwechsel* (hereafter *Briefe*), vol. 9 (Berlin: Deutsche Brahms-Gesellschaft, 1917), 23.

25. I thank my colleague Mary Rasmussen for directing my attention to this pictorial tradition in German culture.

26. The remaining verses read as follows:

Dein Schoß soll hegen und tragen,
Ein Kindlein zart und klein,
Das Himmel und auch Erden
Einstmals wird nehmen ein.

"Thy womb shall cherish and bear
an infant small and tender,
who will enfold
earth and heaven too."

Maria, die viel reine,
Fiel nieder auf ihre Knie,
Dann sie bat Gott vom Himmel,
Sein Wille geschehen soll.

Mary, the spotless maid,
sank down upon her knees;
then she prayed to God in heaven
that his will might be done.

Dein Will', der soll geschehen
Ohn sonder Pein und Schmerz.
Da empfing sie Jesum Christum
In ihr jungfräulich' Herz.

"Thy will shall be done
without special pain or grief."
Then she conceived Jesus Christ
within her Virgin heart.

27. Brahms's predilection for texts on the Marian legend is also attested by his multiple performances of Eccard's "Übers Gebirg Maria geht" and the many texts on the subject that he copied out of various folk song collections. See Virginia Hancock, *Brahms's Choral Compositions and His Library of Early Music* (Ann Arbor: UMI Research Press, 1983), 114–115.

28. Georg Scherer, *Alte und neve kinderlieder, Fabeln, Sprüche und Räthsel* (Leipzig: Gustav Mayer, 1849), 43–44.

29. The Swiss firm of Rieter-Biedermann published all fourteen in late 1864 without opus number.

30. Printed as "Johannes Brahms: 1931," in Furtwängler, *Ton und Wort: Aufsätze und Vorträge, 1918 bis 1954,* 6th ed. (Wiesbaden: Brockhaus, 1955), 40–52.

31. Of course, this sort of objectified music history was especially popular in the first three decades following the war. But the aura of folk song is so central to Brahms's image that one needs to dig deeper than that in order to explain Morik's approach.

32. *Johannes Brahms im Briefwechsel mit Joseph Joachim,* ed. Andreas Moser, *Briefe,* vol. 2 (Berlin: Deutsche Brahms-Gesellschaft, 1912), 7, 35.

33. "Josef, lieber" is but one of various German translations of "Resonet in Laudibus." Like a few other of these translations, "Josef, lieber" proceeds in a dialogue form between Mary and Joseph, interspersed with lines of the original Latin hymn text. Both the Latin and the various German versions of this song were customarily sung in German mystery plays on Christmas Eve and Christmas Day as far back as the fourteenth century.

34. Corner, *Groß-Catolischen Gesangbuch* (Nuremberg, 1631); Meister, *Das katholische deutsche Kirchenlied in seinen Singweisen von den frühesten Zeiten bis gegen Ende des siebzehnten Jahrhunderts* (Freiburg im Breisgau, 1862). Brahms copied these texts onto a double folio that he eventually included in his manuscript collection "Große Sammlung deutscher, schwedischer, böhmischer u.a. Volkslieder verschiedener Quellen"; see Margit L. McCorkle, *Brahms Thematisch-Bibliographisches Werkverzeichnis* (Munich: Henle Verlag, 1985), app. Va 3.

35. See George Bozarth, "Johannes Brahms und die geistlichen Lieder aus David Gregor Corners Groß-Catholischen Gesangbuch von 1631," in *Brahms-Kongreß Wien 1983: Kongreßbericht,* ed. Susanne Antonicek and Otto Biba (Tutzing: Hans Schneider, 1988), 67–80; idem, "Johannes Brahms und die Liedersammlungen von David Gregor Corner, Karl Severin Meister und Friedrich Wilhelm Arnold," *Die Musikforschung* 36 (1983): 177–199. See also Hancock, *Brahms's Choral Compositions,* 16–17, 82.

36. On all of these manuscript indexes, see McCorkle, *Brahms Werkverzeichnis,* app. Va, "Autograph Collections and Copies," 695–748.

37. Ibid., app. Va 1, "Volkslieder aus verschiedenen Ländern," 695–696; Kalbeck, *Johannes Brahms,* 100.

38. McCorkle, *Brahms Werkverzeichnis,* app. Va 2, "Volksweisen aus verschiedenen Ländern," 697–699. A facsimile of page 3r is provided in Kalbeck, *Johannes Brahms,* between 184 and 185.

39. On Brahms's counterpoint studies in the 1850s, see David Brodbeck, "The Brahms-Joachim Counterpoint Exchange; or, Robert, Clara, and 'the Best Harmony between Jos. and Joh.," in Brodbeck ed., *Brahms Studies,* vol. 1 (Lincoln: University of Nebraska Press, 1994), 30–80.

40. The obbligato lied shows up sporadically in the art song literature of the nineteenth century. Although there are settings with which one can imagine Brahms might have been familiar (examples are found among the lieder of Schubert, Franz Lachner, and Spohr), there is no indication that these served as models. A partial list (based only on extant copies) of nineteenth-century obbligato solo

song can be distilled from Kay Dunlap and Barbara Winchester, *Vocal Chamber Music: A Performer's Guide* (New York: Garland, 1985). The only example (besides Brahms's op. 91) of a song with obbligato viola cited by Dunlap and Winchester is Donizetti's French song "J'aime trop pour être heureux"—not likely a model for Brahms.

41. I thank Bruce Bellingham for bringing this facet of the alto melody to my attention.

42. Jonathan Bellman, "Aus alten Märchen: The Chivalric Style of Schumann and Brahms," *Journal of Musicology* 13 (1995): 117. In pondering the possible reasons for a lack of scholarly discussion on the chivalric style, Bellman rightly suggests that "undue attention to any German glorification of a specifically martial past still provokes discomfort." It is disappointing that Bellman does not pursue this issue any further in his article.

43. Locating Mary or other Madonna-like figures in a medieval setting was hardly uncommon in Romantic poetry and literature. Shortly before he composed the "Geistliches Wiegenlied, Brahms himself had set Josef von Eichendorf's poem "Die Nonne und der Ritter" (The Nun and the Knight), op. 28, no. 1, which, much like Geibel's translation of Vega discussed earlier, is loaded with Romantic imagery in an overtly Christian guise. Just as the "Geistliches Wiegenlied" was composed with the Joachims in mind, the op. 28 duets for alto and baritone, composed between 1860 and 1862 (i.e., around the same time as op. 91, no. 2) were dedicated to Amalie. Brahms uses nearly the same texture, rhythm, and melodic contour there as in his Vega-Geibel setting.

44. Although the rocking arpeggio motion might obscure the effect here, the same progression is repeated in the instrumental interlude that separates the alto's phrase ending in bar 21 from the beginning of her first refrain in bar 23. Now the consecutive thirds in the piano left hand are even less adorned; the notes C–A–F–D occur uninterrupted from bars 21–22, with only the final eighth-note F breaking the progression down to B-flat on the downbeat on bar 23.

45. Botstein, ed., *The Compleat Brahms* (New York: Norton, 1999), 240.

46. The notion that Brahms was a classicist among the Romantics is so widespread as to warrant no specific citation. On the connection between Brahms's historicism and his role as "the first truly modern composer," see J. Peter Burkholder, "Brahms and Twentieth-Century Classical Music," *Nineteenth-Century Music* 8 (1984): 75–83. The personal duality mentioned here is also prevalent in the Brahms literature and forms the main subject (and title) of Peter Ostwald's essay "Johannes Brahms, Solitary Altruist," in *Brahms and His World*, ed. Walter Frisch (Princeton: Princeton University Press, 1990), 23–35. Finally, Brahms's pessimism has been much examined of late, particularly by Reinhold Brinkmann in *Late Idyll: The Second Symphony of Johannes Brahms* (Cambridge, Mass.: Harvard University Press, 1995); and by Leon Botstein in "Time and Memory: Concert Life, Science, and Music in Brahms's Vienna," in Frisch, *Brahms and His World*, 3–22.

2. Religion, Language, and Luther's Bible

1. Suk, "Aus meiner Jugend. Wiener Brahms-Erinnerungen von Joseph Suk," *Der Merker* 2 (1910): 149. The date of this conversation is provided by Oskar

Šourek in *Antonín Dvořák: Letters and Reminiscences,* trans. Roberta Finlayson Samsour (New York: Da Capo Press, 1985), 193.

2. Quoted in Alfred Bock, "Erinnerungen an Clara Simrock und Johannes Brahms," *Zeitschrift für Musik* 98 (1931): 478; cited in Hans Christian Stekel, *Sehnsucht und Distanz: Theologische Aspekte in den wortgebundenen religiösen Kompositionen von Johannes Brahms* (Frankfurt: Peter Lang, 1997), 65.

3. In his last, posthumously published theories of nationalism, Ernest Gellner explains the complicated status of religion as a cultural symbol in the nineteenth century, and suggests the nationalist ramifications of that status as well: "On balance, the Age of Nationalism in Europe is also the Age of Secularism. Nationalists love their culture because they love their culture, not because it is the idiom of their faith. They may value their faith because it is, allegedly, the expression of their national culture or character, or they may be grateful to the Church for having kept the national language alive when otherwise it disappeared from public life; but in the end they value religion as an aid to community, and not so much in itself." Gellner, *Nationalism* (New York: New York University Press, 1997), 76–77.

4. Frederick C. Beiser, ed., *The Early Political Writings of the German Romantics* (Cambridge: Cambridge University Press, 1996), xxii.

5. See Richard Heuberger, *Erinnerungen an Johannes Brahms,* ed. Kurt Hofmann (Tutzing: Hans Schneider, 1971), 34. Heuberger recounts Brahms's own statement about his childhood Bible reading (a quote I return to later in this chapter). Beyond this anecdote, the evidence of Brahms's religious instruction is scanty but adequate to suggest that there was nothing unusual about it. See also Stekel, *Sehnsucht und Distanz,* 15–24.

6. George Bozarth raises this possibility in "Johannes Brahms's Collection of *Deutsche Sprichworte* (German Proverbs)," in *Brahms Studies,* vol. 1, ed. David Brodbeck (Lincoln: University of Nebraska Press, 1994), 2.

7. Ibid., 5.

8. Religious issues continued to engage Brahms, and he sought stability through maintaining some basic socio-religious activities. Christmas Eve away from Hamburg, Stekel notes, was nearly always spent in the home of some other family, and Brahms frequently agreed to be the godparent to his friends' children, including Felix Schumann (1855), Adolf Schubring (1856), and Johannes Joachim (1867).

9. *Johannes Brahms im Briefwechsel mit Heinrich und Elisabet von Herzogenberg,* 2 vols., ed. Max Kalbeck, *Briefe,* vol. 1 (Berlin: Deutsche Brahms-Gesellschaft, 1907), 1:123.

10. Ibid., 1:199–200.

11. Those comments may be found ibid., 2:272; Brahms, *Briefe an Fritz Simrock,* vol. 4 (Berlin: Deutsche Brahms-Gesellschaft, 1919), 195; and Gustav Ophüls, *Erinnerungen an Johannes Brahms* (Berlin: Deutsche Brahms-Gesellschaft, 1921), 44.

12. *Briefwechsel mit Herzogenberg,* 1:200.

13. Stekel, *Sehnsucht und Distanz,* 67.

14. Grimm, *Reden und Abhandlungen,* vol. 1, *Kleinere Schriften,* 2d ed. (Berlin:

Ferdinand Dümmlers Verlagsbuchhandlung, 1879), 219. Joseph Widmann also relates a conversation in which Brahms discussed a theological reform movement in Switzerland at that time, a movement that sought to reconcile the secular tendencies of Strauss and Feuerbach with more orthodox belief. Brahms opined that the reformers would be "unable to satisfy either religious yearnings on the one hand, or a philosophy striving for complete freedom on the other." Whereas his comment is ambiguous and ultimately unilluminating, the fact that he was aware of this movement at all is striking. Widmann, *Johannes Brahms in Erinnerungen* (Berlin: Gebrüder Paetel, 1898), 99–100.

15. On Brahms's markings in his Bible, see Stekel, *Sehnsucht und Distanz*, 65–69; reprinted as "Brahms und die Bibel—historisch-theologische Aspekte," in *Brahms-Studien*, vol. 11, ed. Martin Meyer (Tutzing: Hans Schneider, 1997), 49–54. On the pocket notebook (A-Wst HIN 55.733), see chap. 2 of my "Brahms, the Bible, and Post-Romanticism: Cultural Issues in Johannes Brahms's Later Settings of Biblical Texts, 1877–1896" (Ph.D. diss., Harvard University, 1994), 44–72.

16. Büchner, *Real- und verbal-Bibel-concordance*, 335, §21.5.

17. See Stekel, *Sehnsucht und Distanz*, 65–66.

18. Brahms, *Briefe*, vol. 3, ed. Wilhelm Altmann (1908), 7–8.

19. *Johannes Brahms im Briefwechsel mit Otto Dessoff*, pt. 2, ed. Carl Krebs, *Briefe*, vol. 16 (Berlin: Deutsche Brahms-Gesellschaft, 1922), 184.

20. *Johannes Brahms im Briefe an Widmann et al.*, ed. Max Kalbeck, *Briefe*, vol. 8 (Berlin: Deutsche Brahms-Gesellschaft, 1915), 104–105.

21. Heuberger, *Erinnerungen*, 34.

22. Rudolf von der Leyen, *Johannes Brahms als Mensch und Freund* (Düsseldorf: Karl Robert Langeweische, 1905), 31–32.

23. Abell, "Brahms as I Knew Him," *Etude* 49 (1931): 852. Unfortunately, Abell is not an altogether trustworthy source; in a later book, *Talks with Great Composers* (London: Spiritualist Press, 1955), he offers accounts of meetings with several important turn-of-the-century composers (Brahms and Joachim among them) that are highly fanciful and probably have little if any basis in reality. Nevertheless, Abell's comments about Brahms and Schumann in the 1931 *Etude* article resonate with the quotation from Leyen and bear none of the fantastical flavor of his later book.

24. Niemann, *Brahms*, trans. Catherine Alison Phillips (New York: Alfred A. Knopf, 1929), 420. For a similar conflation of the Heuberger and Leyen quotations, see Rudolf Gerber, "Das 'Deutsche Requiem' als Dokument Brahmsscher Frömmigkeit," *Das Musikleben* 2 (1949): 182.

25. Stekel has also assembled convincing evidence that Schumann's illness heightened his spiritual awareness (and delusions). He further makes the interesting and important observation that in an *Erinnerungsbüchlein* he kept for his children, Schumann wrote, "Studiously [read] the Bible, especially Job and Ecclesiastes" (*Sehnsucht und Distanz*, 33). These two books were among those that Brahms most heavily marked in his Luther Bible.

26. Schumann, "Neue Bahnen," *Neue Zeitschrift für Musik*, 28 October 1853, 185–186.

27. Christopher Reynolds, "A Choral Symphony by Brahms?" *Nineteenth-Century*

Music 9 (1985): 3–25. Reynolds provides the most up-to-date and thorough account of the symphony/sonata/concerto that Brahms wrote in response to Schumann's attempted suicide, and its reuse in the First Piano Concerto, op. 15, and in the *Requiem*.

28. John Daverio, *Crossing Paths: Schubert, Schumann, and Brahms* (New York: Oxford University Press, 2002), 184–190.

29. Ibid., 186.

30. Hernried, "Brahms und das Christentum," *Musica* 3 (1949): 18–21; Gerber, "Das 'Deutsche Requiem' als Dokument Brahmsscher Frömmigkeit," 181. Kalbeck, *Johannes Brahms*, 2:234.

31. On the surface there might seem to be a contradiction at work here, for Brahms was deeply committed to the laws of tonal harmony and classical form, an aesthetic disposition that defined him for better or worse in distinction to the New Germans. Yet even in such matters, Brahms avoided becoming the head of an orthodox school. He declined various offers to take faculty positions in conservatories (indeed, he took on few composition pupils during his career) and resisted committing his ideas about music into writing. Form and tonality were less a set of rules to Brahms than a great tradition to which he felt he belonged. More specifically, they were part of a German cultural tradition, as were Protestantism and many other aspects of the North German society in which he was reared.

32. Brahms, *Briefe,* vol. 3, 7–8.

33. Ibid, 10.

34. Arndt, *Meine Wanderungen und Wandelungen mit dem Reichsfreiherrn Heinrich Karl Friedrich von Stein* (Berlin: Weidmann, 1869), 202. Arndt's book was not published until 1869. Brahms purchased the book secondhand at some unknown date, making it difficult to know whether he marked Arndt's remark during the years around 1870, when those comments would have had special resonance, or at a later date.

35. Fichte, *Addresses to the German Nation,* trans. R. F. Jones and G. H. Turnbull, ed. George Armstrong Kelly (New York: Harper and Row, 1968), 47–48.

36. Ibid., 59.

37. Townson, *Mother-Tongue and Fatherland: Language and Politics in German* (Manchester: Manchester University Press, 1992), 92.

38. Scherer, *Geschichte der deutschen Literatur* (Berlin: Knaur, 1885).

39. Brahms owned two posthumous publications of Scherer's (1841–1886), each apparently sent to Brahms by Scherer's daughter Maria, who inscribed the books "in herzlicher Verehrung" and "mit herzlichsten Grüßen," respectively. The books are *Kleine Schriften* (Berlin: Weidmann, 1893) and *Karl Müllenhoff: Ein Lebensbild* (Berlin: Weidmann, 1893). See Kurt Hofmann, *Die Bibliothek von Johannes Brahms: Bücher und Musikalienverzeichnis* (Hamburg: Karl Dieter Wagner, 1974), 100. Many thanks to Rose Mauro, who brought to my attention the connections among Brahms, Billroth, Scherer, and the philologian Erich Schmidt.

40. Scherer, "Die deutsche Spracheinheit," in *Vorträge und Aufsätze zur Geschichte des geistigen Lebens in Deutschland und Österreich* (Berlin: Weidmann, 1874), 45; quoted in Claus Ahlzweig, *Muttersprache-Vaterland: die deutsche Nation und ihre Sprache* (Opladen: Westdeutscher Verlag, 1994), 159. Ahlzweig sees in

Scherer (among other nineteenth-century *Sprachwissenschaftler*) "all the elements of linguistic nationalism."

41. Scherer, *Geschichte der deutschen Literatur,* 9th ed. (Berlin: Weidmannsche Buchhandlung, 1902), 278.

42. Ibid., 276.

43. Ibid., 36.

44. Gellner, *Nationalism,* 77. See also Gellner's earlier *Nations and Nationalism* (Ithaca: Cornell University Press, 1983).

45. Of further interest on this point is Benedict Anderson's notion of "imagined communities," whose origins he specifically traces to the advent of capitalist print media in Europe around 1500. Anderson even singles out Martin Luther as "the first best-selling author." See Anderson, *Imagined Communities: Reflections on the Origin and Spread of Nationalism* (London: Verso, 1983), 43.

46. Hofmann, *Die Bibliothek von Johannes Brahms,* 10–11. H. 63, the 1885 Plattdeutsch New Testament, now belongs to a private collection in Hannover. See ibid., xxxii.

47. Hofmann does not list the 1526 Pentateuch, which Brahms listed in his own "Fair Copy" catalog (A-Wst Ia 67.338), made sometime around 1890 according to George Bozarth in "Brahms's Lieder Inventory of 1859–60 and Other Documents of His Life and Work," *Fontes Artis Musicae* 30 (1983): 107. Read from one end, this notebook contains an inventory of the books Brahms owned; read from the other, it is an inventory of his musical scores. Four Bibles are listed on the "B" page of the book inventory in the following order: H. 59, H. 63, the 1526 Plattdeutsch edition, and H. 61.

48. And among those nine, two are barely marked (Psalms 1 and 8 merely have their headings underlined, with no specific passages marked), and two more are texts he set to music (Psalm 51 of the motet "Schaffe in mir, Gott, ein rein Herz," op. 29, no. 2; and Psalm 126:5–6 from *Ein deutsches Requiem,* movement two).

49. OT here stands for "Old Testament," indexing the separate run of page numbers for the three parts of his Luther Bible. Accordingly, AP stands for pages of the Apocrypha and NT for those of the New Testament.

50. On the *Missa* and its relationship to op. 74, no. 1, see Robert Pascall, "Brahms's *Missa Canonica* and Its Recomposition in His 'Warum,' Op. 74, No. 1," in *Brahms Studies,* vol. 2, ed. Michael Musgrave (Cambridge: Cambridge University Press, 1985), 111–136. The other texts in the motet are Lamentations 3:41, James 5:11, and Luther's chorale "Mit Fried und Freud ich fahr dahin."

51. At this point it must be noted that the close connections between the notebook and Brahms's markings in his 1833 Bible (many of the same passages are referenced in each) are not shared by Brahms's copy of the Büchner concordance and his markings therein. Although there may be some general overlap in subject matter, none of the entries marked by Brahms in Büchner refer to specific passages that he also marked or copied in his Bible and notebook respectively. Nor for that matter do the marked Büchner entries correspond to any biblical passages that Brahms set to music. All of this suggests that Brahms did not use the concordance as a tool for finding texts in the Bible to set to music or to facilitate his Bible reading. He seems instead to have read entries in Büchner for their own sake, as yet another source that shed light on religious issues.

52. These notebooks are located at the Vienna Stadt- und Landesbibliothek, where their shelf numbers are (poetic notebooks) HIN 55.734, Ia 79.563, Ia 79.564, and (biblical notebook) HIN 55.733. For a rough list of the contents from all four notebooks, see Bozarth, "Brahms's Lieder Inventory," 109–112. These four notebooks were only some of many such text collections maintained by Brahms; others include the collection of sayings by poets, philosophers, and others (mostly from among the Romantics) titled "Des jungen Kreislers Schatzkästlein," and a collection of "Deutsche Sprichworte" (not to mention the previously discussed collections of melodies and texts to German folk songs that Brahms copied throughout his life). Four notebooks made up the "Schatzkästlein"; of these, we know the whereabouts of only one (A Wst, Ia 79.562). See Carl Krebs, ed., *Des Jungen Kreislers Schatzkästlein. Aussprüche von Dichtern, Philosophen und Künstlern. Zusammengetragen durch Johannes Brahms* (Berlin: Deutsche Brahms-Gesellschaft, 1909).

53. There was clearly writing on the first twelve pages; each contains partial letters and word fragments, none of which, unfortunately, I found intelligible upon examining the document. See also Bozarth, "Brahms's Lieder Inventory," 109–110.

54. The fourth and final text was not biblical: Luther's chorale "Mit Fried' und Freud ich fahr dahin."

55. "Let us therefore approach the throne of grace with boldness, so that we may receive mercy and find grace to help in time of need."

56.

Wisdom of Solomon 2:4	Unser Leben fähret dahin, als wäre eine Wolke da gewesen
Jeremiah 8:20	Die Ernte ist vergangen, der Sommer ist dahin
Psalm 35:14	Ich ging traurig, wie einer, der Leid trägt über seine Mütter
2 Corinthians 7:4	Ich bin erfüllet mit Trost, ich bin überschwänglich in Freuden, in aller unserer Trübsal.

57. Brahms marked only two texts with *Trost* themes in his Bible: Psalm 51:14 ("Tröste mich wieder mit deiner Hülfe, und der freudige Geist enthalte mich") from the third part of the motet "Schafe in mir Gott," op. 29, no. 2, and Ecclesiastes 4:1 ("und siehe, da waren Tränen derer, die Unrecht litten, und hatten keinen Tröster; und die ihnen Unrecht täten, waren zu mächtig, daß sie keinen Tröster haben konnten") from the second of the *Vier ernste Gesänge*, op. 121, no. 2. Thus, with the exception of the three *Trost* texts on folio 14v of his notebook, Brahms marked only those *Trost* texts in his Bible that he eventually set to music. In other words, this theme seems to have appealed to his musical instincts, beyond its biblical ramifications.

58. In the case of some of the texts cited here, Brahms marked more than the verse or verses quoted here.

59. Brahms also marked three passages under the entry "Bauen" in the Büchner Bible Concordance, all of which adhere to these conventional uses of the house metaphor (Büchner, *Real- und Verbal-Bibel-Concordanz*, 129). The passages are Proverbs 24:3 ("A house is built through wisdom and maintained through un-

derstanding"); 1 Peter 2:5 ("And like living stones, let yourself too be built into a spiritual house"); and Psalm 127:1 ("Unless the Lord builds the house, those who build it labor in vain").

60. That reference is apparent in such thoughts as Ecclesiasticus 41:8–11 (5–7) (which Brahms did not copy into his notebook): "⁵The children of sinners are abominable children, and they frequent the haunts of the ungodly. ⁶The inheritance of sinners' children shall perish, and their posterity shall have a perpetual reproach. ⁷The children will complain of an ungodly father, because they shall be reproached for his sake."

62. The actual citation at the bottom of 16v reads "NB Weisheit Salomos/Kap. 8 Gebet eines Königs." The chapter listed there (8) is clearly a mistake and should read 9. Chapter 8 does not contain a "prayer" but rather closes with the words "so I appealed to the Lord and implored him, and with my whole heart I said . . ." Immediately thereupon follows the "Gebet" as it is copied (with the correct citation of chapter 9) on folios 18v–19r.

63. Kalbeck, *Johannes Brahms,* 4:111.

64. Ibid., 444–445.

65. I have argued elsewhere that Brahms used this text in op. 121 to overturn the Schopenhauerian pessimism of the bleak statements from Ecclesiastes in songs 1 and 2, all in a reaffirmation of his youthful Romantic outlook. See my "Brahms on Schopenhauer: The *Vier ernste Gesänge,* op. 121, and Late-Nineteenth-Century Pessimism," in Brodbeck, *Brahms Studies,* 1:170–188.

66. On Brahms's political outlook toward Vienna and the Austro-Hungarian Empire, see Margaret Notley, "Brahms as Liberal: Genre, Style, and Politics in Late-Nineteenth-Century Vienna," *Nineteenth-Century Music* 17 (1993): 107–123.

3. Ein deutsches Requiem, Op. 45

1. MacDonald, *Brahms* (New York: Schirmer, 1990), 196.

2. See the discussion of a possible chronology for the notebook HIN 55.733 in Chapter 2.

3. Suffice it for now to mention that the ambiguous status of C-sharp in these bars—now descending to C natural as if a flat six (bars 37–40), now rising to D natural as if a leading tone (bar 42)—is no localized matter; it relates strongly and directly to some of the most significant harmonic, formal, and expressive points in the *Requiem.* I return to these later in the chapter.

4. These notions are covered by Michael Musgrave in *Brahms: A German Requiem* (Cambridge: Cambridge University Press, 1996), 24–34. The identification of the "hidden" chorale originated with Siegfried Ochs in his preface to the Eulenberg Edition score of op. 45 (page iv). There, Ochs reported that Brahms had mentioned to him the presence of a "well-known" chorale melody in the first two movements of op. 45. According to Ochs, Brahms also said: "If you can't hear it, it doesn't matter much. You can find it in the first measures and in the second movement." Ochs deduced that Brahms was referring to the chorale "Wer nun den lieben Gott läßt walten," which shares several characteristics with the passages to which Brahms alluded. Many years later, in his published recollections, Ochs embellished this account: "[Brahms] also called my attention to

the fact that the chorale 'Wer nun den lieben Gott läßt walten' lay at the root of the entire work." Ochs, *Geschehenes, Gesehenes* [Leipzig: Grethlein, 1922), 302. For a divergent idea on the chorale's identity, see Christopher Reynolds, "A Choral Symphony by Brahms?" *Nineteenth-Century Music* 9 (1985): 3–26. The so-called "selig" motive was first postulated by William Newman in "A Basic Motive in Brahms's 'German Requiem,'" *Music Review* 24 (1963): 190–194, and was further developed by Michael Musgrave in "Historical Influences on Brahms's Requiem," *Music and Letters* 53 (1973): 3–17. See also Walter Westafer, "Overall Unity and Contrast in Brahms's *German Requiem* (Ph.D. diss., University of North Carolina, 1973).

5. An autograph text page (26.9 × 34.3 cm) for op. 45 has been widely interpreted as a preexisting blueprint for its musical composition, because the opposite side of the sheet contains a sketch to the song "Liebe kam aus fernen Landen," op. 33, no. 4, composed in 1861. As this sheet contains the texts for all seven movements of the *Requiem,* that date suggests that the entire text was planned long before the first completed music to the piece, the fourth movement which Brahms mentioned to Clara Schumann in April 1865. This theory was first proposed by Kalbeck, who supposed the text had been partially collected by Brahms, put away and lost after a walking tour of the Harz Mountains in 1861, and rediscovered by the composer while staying in Hamburg in 1865 following his mother's funeral (*Johannes Brahms,* 2: 258–261). Siegfried Kross, however, has argued convincingly that the sheet was probably compiled after the first six movements were composed (its physical proximity to the sketch of op. 33, no. 4, notwithstanding), and that rather the texts were written down by Brahms at the time he composed movement five as an aid in determining where to place this added movement. Kross, *Die Chorwerke von Johannes Brahms* (Berlin: Max Hesses Verlag, 1958), 221–222.

6. To wit: excepting the brief *mezzo forte* passage at bars 33–34 in the strings, the dynamic range is never marked above *piano* (and frequently at *pianissimo*); the tempo is *Langsam* throughout; and the frequent solo wind phrases and pizzicato string figures convey a sense of chamber music at many points in the movement.

7. One cannot speak of a modulation here; only the viola's C-sharp in bar 18 hints at D major, but this is too brief and localized to sound like more than a secondary vii^{o7} harmony within a still strong G major.

8. Note that the soprano has just repeated the tritone C–F♯ within a D dominant harmony only a few bars before (14–16), a defining marker for the key of G.

9. On the recapitulatory overlap in Brahms's music, see Peter H. Smith, "Liquidation, Augmentation, and Brahms's Recapitulatory Overlaps," *Nineteenth-Century Music* 18 (1994): 237–261.

10. Steinberg, "*Ein deutsches Requiem* for Soloists, Chorus, and Orchestra, Op. 45," in *The Compleat Brahms,* ed. Leon Botstein (New York: W. W. Norton, 1999), 375–376.

11. Ibid., 378.

12. Brahms to Clara Schumann, April 1865, in *Clara Schumann-Johannes Brahms Briefe,* ed. Berthold Litzmann, vol. 1 (1853–1871) (Leipzig: Breitkopf and Härtel, 1927), 504; the comment to Dietrich is recounted in his *Erinnerungen an*

Johannes Brahms in Briefen besonders aus seiner Jugendzeit (Leipzig: Otto Wigand, 1898), 60.

13. Levi is quoted by Max Kalbeck in *Johannes Brahms*, 3d expanded ed. (1921; reprint, Tutzing: Hans Schneider, 1976), 2:220. Accounts of the *Requiem*'s *Entstehungsgeschichte* are numerous. Michael Musgrave summarizes the details clearly and succinctly in *Brahms: A German Requiem*, 4–13. Following the lead of Kalbeck, most scholars believe the *Requiem* originated sometime in the 1850s, was substantially planned out by 1861, and was brought to completion between 1865 and 1867. See Kalbeck, *Johannes Brahms*, 2:214–232; Kross, *Die Chorwerke von Johannes Brahms*, 1958), 208–218; and Klaus Blum, *Hundert Jahre Ein deutsches Requiem von Johannes Brahms* (Tutzing: Hans Schneider, 1971), 91–108.

14. Letter of January 1866, quoted in Alfred Orel, *Johannes Brahms und Julius Allgeyer: Eine Künstlerfreundschaft in Briefen* (Tützing: Hans Schneider, 1964), 39.

15. Kalbeck, *Johannes Brahms*, 2:218.

16. "I dispute that in no. 3 the themes of the various sections have something to do with one another. (With the exception of [one] little motive.) If it is indeed so (I cannot recall anything intentional): for this I want no praise, rather I confess that my thoughts do not take flight far enough in my work, and thus frequently return unintentionally to the same ideas." *Johannes Brahms im Briefwechsel* vol. 9, ed. Max Kalbeck (Berlin: Deutsche Brahms-Gesellschaft, 1915), 213–214.

17. Abrams, *Natural Supernaturalism: Tradition and Revolution in Romantic Literature* (New York: W. W. Norton, 1971), 36.

18. Ibid., 37.

19. Kermode, "Apocalypse and the Modern," in *Visions of the Apocalypse: End or Rebirth?* ed. Saul Friedlander et al. (New York: Holmes and Meier, 1985), 84.

20. Abrams, *Natural Supernaturalism*, 64.

21. Hoffmann "Review of Beethoven's Fifth Symphony," in *E. T. A. Hoffmann's Musical Writings: "Kreisleriana," "The Poet and the Composer," "Musical Criticism,"* ed. David Charlton, trans. Martyn Clark (Cambridge: Cambridge University Press, 1989), 234–252. See also Carl Dahlhaus, *The Idea of Absolute Music*, trans. Roger Lustig (Chicago: University of Chicago Press, 1989), 42–46.

22. Frank Kermode, *The Sense of an Ending: Studies in the Theory of Fiction* (Oxford: Oxford University Press, 1967), 12.

23. Ibid., 7.

24. Carl Dahlhaus, "Zur Entstehung der romantischen Bach-Deutung," in *Klassische und romantische Musikästhetik* (Laaber: Laaber Verlag, 1988), 124.

25. For an example, see Musgrave, *Brahms: A German Requiem*, 23–26.

26. It is worth noting that here, more than anywhere else in the *Requiem*, one hears an audible connection to J. S. Bach's cantata BWV 106, *Gottes Zeit ist die allerbeste Zeit*, a work that is often cited as a precursor and potential model for op. 45. Amid a less chromatic musical language and steadier harmonic direction, Bach too begins with repeated notes in the bass and suspensions in middle-range strings (viola da gambas) in a work that is more overtly concerned with time, as the word "Zeit" in its title suggests.

27. Although that pitch is actually present in the horn, it is too far removed timbrally to serve as the head of the descending line carried out by cellos 1 and 2.

28. Schubring, *Schumanniana*, 12, as cited in Blum, *Hundert Jahre Ein deutsches Requiem*, 81.

29. Interestingly, Mendelssohn's Fifth, though composed in 1828–1830, was only published posthumously in 1868, the very year of the *Requiem*'s official premiere. Thus it could not have served as a model for the opening of op. 45; the two works merely partake similarly of the use of musico-religious symbolism.

30. Even after the complete cadence to the tonic F in bar 13, D-flat doggedly persists, now as an upper neighbor to C in viola 2, turning what would otherwise be an unremarkable (albeit darkly scored) V^7 harmony into a prolonged vii^{o7} suspended above the tonic F pedal. In the primarily diatonic choral material that follows, D-flat is introduced as a minor-mode inflection of a IV chord in bar 34. It then hangs on, re-spelled as a C-sharp in bars 37 and 39, producing an unfulfilled dominant of D, the relative minor, a function it only realizes in bar 42 (now as part of a passing vii^{o7} over a tonic F pedal).

31. There is a conventional cadence to the tonic in bar 73, during the baritone's reprise of the opening line, but this comes at mid-phrase, where the same melodic close to D had been weakened by a B-flat major (VI) harmony in bar 8.

32. Although the beginning of movement four is more stable, the descending melody in the winds at bars 1–4 is an inverted version of the soprano's initial phrase in bars 4–8, thus slightly confusing the sense of where the movement starts (albeit in an abstract way), or at least lessening the strong sense of a beginning.

33. The defining element in this sequence is the descending tetrachord in the second and third trombones. The model for the sequence is therefore prefigured by the first violas in the previous phrase, at bars 62–64.

34. Tovey, *Essays in Musical Analysis: Concertos and Choral Works* (London: Oxford University Press, 1981), 304–305. In a parenthetical note Tovey opines, "The resemblance of its preamble to the main theme of Ex. 8 [the movement 2 fugue] is accidental: a theme cannot purposely refer across five [sic] intervening movements to a declamatory formula without collateral evidence in the context."

35. In his Bible, Brahms drew lines in (or otherwise marked) substantial portions of chapters 40–55 in Isaiah, particularly 40–45.

36. The length of this section precludes reproducing a musical example. Rather, the reader is encouraged to consult the published score.

37. For example, the augmentation that begins motet op. 29, no. 2 ("Schaffe in mir, Gott"); the double canon at the ninth in the "Geistliches Lied," op. 30, for chorus and organ; or the various augmentations and inversions in the concluding fugue to the *Variations on a Theme of Handel*, op. 24.

38. *Allgemeine musikalische Zeitung* 12, no. 40 (4 and 11 July 1810): 630–642, 625–659; translated by F. John Adams and reprinted as "Review of the Fifth Symphony," in *Beethoven: Symphony No. 5 in C Minor*, ed. Eliot Forbes, Norton Critical Score (New York: W. W. Norton, 1971), 150–163 (quote 161).

39. Ibid., 152. This phrase in particular found resonance in Schumann's "Neue Bahnen" essay of 1853: "If he directs his magic wand where the power and masses of the choir and orchestra can lend him their strength, then we will have

before us wonderful glimpses into the secrets of the spiritual realm."
Schumann's addition of the chorus to the instrumental forces Hoffmann had in
mind is especially felicitous for relating the C major breakthrough from movement six of the *Requiem* to the same moment in Beethoven's Fifth Symphony.
Robert Schumann, "Neue Bahnen," *Neue Zeitschrift für Musik,* 28 October
1853, 185–186.
40. Gesellschaft der Musikfreunde A 116. A facsimile of this side of the sheet appears in Robert Haven Schauffler, *The Unknown Brahms: His Life, Character,*
and Works (New York: Dodd, Mead, 1933), opp. 348.
41. M. H. Abrams offers a concise discussion of the destruction and renewal theme
and apocalyptic traits in the Book of Daniel and Revelations. See Abrams, *Natu-*
ral Supernaturalism: Tradition and Revolution in Romantic Literature (New
York: Norton, 1971), 37–46.
42. Ibid., 36.
43. Kermode, *The Sense of an Ending,* 100.
44. Abrams, *Natural Supernaturalism,* 36.

4. The Triumphlied, Op. 55

1. This was a two-room apartment at Postgasse 6. Max Kalbeck, *Johannes*
Brahms, 2:227.
2. Ibid., 406–407. One cannot speak of Brahms "furnishing" his apartment; that
was done by his landlady, Frau Celestine Truxa.
3. Viktor Miller zu Aichholz, ed., *Ein Brahms-Bilderbuch,* with explanatory text
by Max Kalbeck (Vienna: R. Lechner, 1905), 69–89. For these pages, Kalbeck's
commentary closely matches the relevant passages from his Brahms biography
of 1904–1912. The other pictorial record can be found in Maria Fellinger,
Brahms-Bilder (Leipzig: Breitkopf and Härtel, 1900).
4. The room that eventually served as the library had originally been Brahms's bedroom until he had his collection of books and scores sent from Hamburg in
1877. At that time he acquired the third room, which became his new bedroom.
Kalbeck, *Brahms,* 2:408.
5. Indeed, in the context of Aichholz's book, this is "The End" for Brahms; the remainder of the book is given over to images from his funeral and burial.
6. Kalbeck, who meticulously catalogues the art in the other rooms of the apartment, mentions only Cornelius's drawing in the library. Aichholz, *Ein Brahms-*
Bilderbuch, 88.
7. Herman Riegel, *Cornelius: Der Meister der deutschen Malerei,* 2d ed.
(Hannover: Carl Rümpler, 1870), 419.
8. Josef Viktor Widmann relates Brahms's remarks about the *Triumphlied* when
it was performed for the consecration of the new Zurich Tonhalle on 20 October 1895. "The joyous satisfaction that the successful performance brought
[Brahms]," writes Widmann, "was so great that on the way home from the concert he himself began to speak about this one of his creations, which occurred
very rarely with him. He drew my attention to details in the work and asked me,
among other things, whether I had correctly heard how, in the second chorus
[i.e., movement], at the sounding of the melody: 'Nun danket alle Gott' the vic-

tory was pronounced by all the bells, and a celebratory Te Deum swept over the land?" Widman, *Erinnerungen an Johannes Brahms* (Berlin: Gebrüder Paetel, 1898), 111.

9. Kretschmar, "Neue Werke von J. Brahms," *Musikalische Wochenblatt* 9 (1874): 148.

10. Krummacher, "Eine meiner politischen Trachtungen über dies Jahr: Eschatologische Visionen im Triumphlied von Brahms," in *Studien zur Musikgeschichte: Eine Festschrift für Ludwig Finscher*, ed. Annegrit Laubenthal (Kassel: Bärenreiter, 1995), 640.

11. Siegfried Kross, in his landmark study *Die Chorwerke von Johannes Brahms* (Berlin: Max Hesses Verlag, 1963), holds the *Triumphlied*, and Brahms's only other overtly patriotic work, the *Fünf Gesänge für Männerchor*, op. 41, in singularly low esteem (148–161 and 315–333). He blames Brahms's ambivalence toward op. 55 for the composer's decision to take up the project of the *Schicksalslied* at the expense of completing the *Triumphlied* for over a year. Klaus Häfner, one of the *Triumphlied*'s more recent champions, writes of Kross's stance as the "predisposition of the postwar German toward his history, above all his recent history, which he rejects and denies, and thereby takes every sort of patriotism for unpleasant chauvinism." Häfner, "Das *Triumphlied*, op. 55, ein vergessene Komposition von Johannes Brahms," in *Johannes Brahms in Baden-Baden und Karlsruhe* (Karlsruhe: Badischen Landesbibliothek Karlsruhe, 1983), 84.

12. See Krummacher, "Eine meiner politischen Trachtungen."

13. Kalbeck discusses the *Triumphlied* in *Johannes Brahms*, 2:343–359.

14. Ibid., 349. Krummacher is particularly unconvinced of Scholz's authority on the matter, since Kalbeck only added this corroborating story as a footnote in the second edition of his biography. Krummacher, "Eine meiner politischen Trachtungen," 638. In fact, Kalbeck did get it wrong, but not in a manner that negates his point. Peter Petersen offers a strong rebuttal to Krummacher's thinking on the "great whore" issue, arguing convincingly that, despite botching the evidence, Kalbeck's claim was correct, and the missing line from Revelation 19:2 does indeed fit Brahms's orchestral figure at bar 70, rather than the recurrence of that theme at bar 79, as Kalbeck suggests, a mistake on which Krummacher's argument rests. See Petersen, "Über das 'Triumphlied' von Johannes Brahms," *Die Musikforschung* 51 (1998): 462–466.

15. Kalbeck, *Johannes Brahms*, 2:348.

16. Alexander, "Byzantium and the Migration of Literary Works and Motifs: The Legend of the Last Roman Emperor," *Medievalia et Humanistica*, n.s. 2 (1971): 49.

17. Krummacher, "Eine meiner politischen Trachtungen," 639.

18. Ibid.

19. Petersen, "Über das 'Triumphlied' von Johannes Brahms." See also Sabine Giesbrecht-Schutte, "Gründerzeitliche Festkultur—die 'Bismarckhymne' von Karl Reinthaler und ihre Beziehung zum *Triumphlied* von Johannes Brahms," *Die Musikforschung* 52 (1999): 70–88.

20. Alings, *Die Berliner Siegessäule: Vom Geschichtsbild zum Bild der Geschichte* (Berlin: Parthos Verlag, 2000), 87; translation from Alings, *The Column of Victory in Berlin* (Berlin: Bezirksamt Tiergarten von Berlin, 1994), 31.

21. Krummacher, "Eine meiner politischen Trachtungen," 643, citing Spitta, "Johannes Brahms," in *Zur Musik* (Berlin: Gebrüder Paetel, 1892), 413.

22. The title page is reproduced in Kurt Hofmann, ed., *Die Erstdrucke der Werke von Johannes Brahms* (Tutzing: Schneider, 1975), 114. Franz Pyllemann, in reviewing the Viennese premiere of op. 55, simply states, "The composer drew the text from the 'Apocalypse'"; see his "Erste Aufführung von Johannes Brahms' 'Triumphlied' in Wien," *Allgemeine Musikalische Zeitung* 7 (25 December 1872): 827.

23. *Brahms Briefe an P. J. Simrock und Fritz Simrock*, vol. 1, ed. Max Kalbeck, *Briefe*, vol. 9 (Berlin: Deutsche Brahms-Gesellschaft, 1917), 98.

24. *Brahms im Briefwechsel mit Karl Reinthaler*, ed. Wilhelm Altmann, *Briefe*, vol. 3 (Berlin: Deutsche Brahms-Gesellschaft, 1908), 30, 32.

25. Contemporaries' critiques of the *Triumphlied* are summarized in Angelika Horstmann, *Untersuchungen zur Brahms-Rezeption der Jahre 1860–1880* (Hamburg: Wagner, 1986), 199–206.

26. Davies, *Humanism* (London: Routledge, 1997), 11.

27. William Vaughan writes: "It has that sense of power and control that one associates with truly heroic art. The maelstrom of panic is held in balance by the circular design. This superb handling of a dramatic theme makes one wish that [Cornelius's] other designs had more action and less exposition in them." Vaughan, *German Romantic Painting* (New Haven: Yale University Press, 1980), 221.

28. Grimm, "Berlin und Peter von Cornelius (1859)," in *Zehn ausgewählte Essays zur Einführung in das Studium der Modernen Kunst* (Berlin: Ferd. Dümmler, 1871), 277.

29. Grimm, "Die Cartons von Peter von Cornelius," ibid., 308. Brahms's copy, published as a separate pamphlet, bears the longer title "Die Cartons von Peter Cornelius in den Sälen der königl. Akademie der Kunste zu Berlin" (Berlin: Verlag von Wilhelm Hertz, 1859). Brahms owned five separate writings by Grimm (one in manuscript), all dating from 1854–1863. This roughly reflects the important connection of Joseph Joachim with Brahms and Grimm. These same years mark the most intense years of the friendship between Brahms and Joachim, up to Joseph's marriage to Amalie in 1864. During the mid-1850s, Joachim courted Ghisela von Arnim (daughter of Bettina) in Berlin. Grimm had been a close friend of von Arnim through adolescence and became Joachim's rival for her affections. Although Joachim lost (Grimm and von Arnim wed in 1859), the three remained close friends for the rest of their lives. I thank Rose Mauro and Robert Eschbach for drawing my attention to these relationships.

30. Riegel, *Cornelius: Der Meister der deutschen Malerei*, 2d ed. (Hannover: Carl Rümpler, 1870), 269.

31. Dahlhaus, *Ludwig van Beethoven: Approaches to His Music*, trans. Mary Whittall (London: Oxford University Press, 1991), 77, 78.

32. Bekker, *Die Sinfonie von Beethoven bis Mahler* (Berlin: Schuster und Löffler, 1918), 18. I return to Bekker's idea of the symphony as "society forming" in Chapter 5.

33. Dahlhaus, *Ludwig van Beethoven*, 80.

34. In Schering, *Von großen Meistern der Musik* (Leipzig: Koehler and Amelang, 1940). Unfortunately (as the date of the essay might suggest), Schering's

thoughts must be treated with circumspection. All too predictably for German music-historical literature of this time, Schering discerns separate types of monumentality according to nationalities. And, not surprisingly, he finds English and (especially) German monumentality to be more moral, edifying, and spiritually rich than their Italian and French counterparts. In the first part of his essay, however, he manages to discuss musical monumentality in broad historical terms, and for this, his national bias notwithstanding, Schering's treatment of monumentality is quite valuable.

35. At least one early reviewer of the *Triumphlied* likened its monumental effect to that of architecture: "[The *Triumphlied*] so fully makes an impression of the 'monumental' that when hearing it one completely forgets to ask by whom or when it was created, just as it never occurs to the onlooker, when one views an immense [*mächtig*] building, to inquire as to the original builder." Pyllemann, "Erste Aufführung von Johannes Brahms' *'Triumphlied,'* 827–828.

36. Perhaps of relevance is Brahms's comment when thanking Theodor Billroth for a gift of a silver goblet, which the latter sent in lieu of attending the premiere of the *Triumphlied* at Karlsruhe on 5 June 1872. Brahms wrote, "One cannot accompany thanks by trumpets and timpani, on the contrary, the warmer they are, the softer they get." As translated by Josef Eisinger and Styra Avins in Avins, *Johannes Brahms: Life and Letters* (Oxford: Oxford University Press, 1997), 441.

37. Giesbrecht-Schutte, "Gründerzeitliche Festkultur." She draws her data on "Nun danket alle Gott" from Adolf Brüssau, *Martin Rinckart, 1586–1649, und sein Lied Nun danket alle Gott,* Welt des Gesangbuchs, vol. 10 (Leipzig: Gustav Schoessmann, 1936).

38. That performance never materialized, nor did any other during 1830. The work was finally premiered at Berlin in 1832, only to be shelved by Mendelssohn for the rest of his life. It was published posthumously in 1868.

39. Brinkmann, *Late Idyll: The Second Symphony of Johannes Brahms,* trans. Peter Palmer (Cambridge, Mass.: Harvard University Press, 1995), 220–226. For reactions to Brinkmann's view, see Leon Botstein, "Embracing the Gift of Life," *Times Literary Supplement* 19 (January 1996): 20; Walter Frisch, *Brahms: The Four Symphonies* (New York: Schirmer Books, 1996), 64; and David Brodbeck, *Brahms, Symphony No. 1* (Cambridge: Cambridge University Press, 1997), 68–70.

40. See Brinkmann, *Late Idyll,* 126–131, and my own "The Great 'Warum'? Job, Christ, and Bach in a Brahms Motet," *Nineteenth-Century Music* 19 (1996): 231–251.

41. Krummacher, "Eine meiner politischen Trachtungen," 651.

42. Brahms went further still, however, and sent an effusive dedication letter to Wilhelm along with the published score:

> Most eminent, most powerful,
>   most gracious Kaiser and Lord!
> The attainments of recent years are so great and glorious, that to one who was not granted the opportunity to take part in the mighty war for Germany's greatness there is all the more a heartfelt need to say and to demonstrate how fortunate he feels to have lived through this great time.

Thoroughly driven by these feelings of thanks and joy, I have tried to give them expression through the composition of this *Triumphlied*.

My music is based on text from Revelation, and in order not to overlook what it celebrates, I cannot suppress the desire to name the special occasion and purpose of this work, if possible, through the placement of Your Majesty's name.

Thus I presume most reverently to express the request for permission to respectfully dedicate the *Triumphlied* to Your Majesty upon its appearance in print.

To your Imperial and Royal Majesty
   most humbly
      Johannes Brahms

Translated from Kalbeck, *Johannes Brahms,* 3:351.
43. Nipperdey, "Nationalidee und Nationaldenkmal in Deutschland im 19. jahrhundert," *Historische Zeitschrift* 206 (1968): 543.
44. Begun in 1865 to commemorate the Austro-Prussian defeat of Denmark in the preceding year, the *Siegessäule* was not completed until 1876, by which time it had assumed the role of commemorating the Austro-Prussian War of 1866 as well as the Franco-Prussian War and German unification in 1870–71. Alings, *Berliner Siegessäule,* 35–55.
45. Ibid., 90.
46. If anything, the first sixteen beats (the two-beat pickup bar through beat two of bar 5) sound like four bars in common time. Beyond that point all meter breaks down until the choirs enter.
47. Some commentators hear this theme as yet another kingly chorale, "Heil dir im Siegerkranz," a late-eighteenth-century German adaptation of the English hymn "God Save the Queen." Hermann Kretschmar, who penned the only contemporaneous review of the published score and was the first to note the similarity among the opening orchestral motive, the choirs' initial "Hallelujah," and the tune of this "universal national anthem" *(Allerweltsnationalhymne),* discounted the likelihood that Brahms meant to impart any meaning through his simple three-note theme. To bolster his doubt, Kretschmar cites Brahms's alteration of the hymn's triple meter into duple here, which would render the "symbolism intelligible to only the most gifted diviner." Kretschmar, "Neue Werke von J. Brahms," 148n. See also Kalbeck, *Johannes Brahms,* 2:352–353.
48. One exception might be that the brass are absent for much of the first section of movement two. But Brahms does not even exploit this feature to create contrasting timbral episodes: the brass are gone for so long and so completely (they enter only at the *più forte* arrival at rehearsal E, bar 85), that when they enter it sounds only as part of the dynamic intensification that began back at bar 73 and continues through to the *fortissimo* "Lebhaft" section at bar 95.
49. In describing this passage Karl Geiringer writes, "Shortly before the final climax a *tranquillo* passage reveals the gentle and reflective Brahms—one might also say the *true* Brahms." Geiringer, *Brahms: His Life and Work,* 2d rev. ed. (New York: Anchor Books, 1961), 288. It is a curious remark since Geiringer's assessment of the *Triumphlied* is entirely positive. Even a fan of the work, it seems,

finds it necessary to distance its bombastic tone from our image of Brahms, reserving that distinction for the few "tranquillo" passages in the piece.

50. On the ending of the *Schicksalslied,* see John Daverio, "*Die Wechsel der Töne* in Brahms's *Schicksalslied,*" *Journal of the American Musicological Society* 46 (1993): 84–113.
51. Kross, *Die Chorwerke von Brahms,* 63.

5. Gebet Einer König

1. Cited in Kalbeck, *Johannes Brahms,* 4:487–488.
2. Personal communication. For a more purely musical explanation, see Walter Frisch, *Brahms: The Four Symphonies* (New York: Schirmer Books, 1996), 5–17.
3. Bekker, *Die Sinfonie von Beethoven bis Mahler* (Berlin: Schuster and Löffler, 1918).
4. On Germans' associations between classical humanism and their own nation, see Tony Davies, *Humanism* (London: Routledge, 1997).
5. Adorno, *Introduction to the Sociology of Music,* trans. E. B. Ashton (New York: Seabury Press, 1976), 94.
6. Ibid., 160.
7. Carl Dahlhaus developed the idea of the "Second Age of the Symphony" in his *Nineteenth-Century Music,* trans. Bradford Robinson (Berkeley: University of California Press, 1989), 265–276.
8. Frisch, *Brahms: The Four Symphonies,* 36.
9. The origins of op. 74, no. 1, are discussed in Chapter 2. Most commentators believe that no. 2 was composed at least as early as 1870 and perhaps earlier. See Margit L. McCorkle, *Brahms Thematisch-Bibliographisches Werkverzeichnis* (Munich: Henle, 1985), 314–315.
10. The word *Haus* can be understood to connote the community of a state if we consider the division of the Hapsburg Empire into various families or "houses."
11. *Johannes Brahms im Briefwechsel mit Franz Wüllner* ed. Ernst Wolff, *Briefe,* vol. 15 (Berlin: Deutsche Brahms-Gesellschaft, 1921), 158. Wüllner writes: "Soon I will publish a continuation of my *Chorübung,* a collection of more-than-four-voice pieces (five to sixteen), old Italian and old German; but also modern, i.e., Mendelssohn and Schumann. Do you not have something for this collection? I am not so bold as to ask you for one or the other of your new eight-voice pieces." That collection appeared as part three of *Chorübungen der Münchner Musikschule, Neue Folge, Mustersammlung fünf bis sechszehnstimmiger Gesänge aus dem sechzehnten, siebzehnten und achtzehnten Jahrhundert* (Munich: Theodor Ackermann, 1893–94). It is unclear to which of the motets Wüllner is referring when he says "one or the other" ("eines oder das andere"). If he is referring to entire groups of pieces (presumably unaware that op. 110 contained one single-choir motet), then Wüllner's request indicates that very early on, Brahms had discussed the two sets as a pair. If, however, he is referring to two individual works, he most likely means op. 110, nos. 1 and 3.
12. Johannes Brahms, *Briefe an P. J. und Fritz Simrock,* vol. 3 ed. Max Kalbeck,

Briefe, vol. 11 (Berlin: Deutsche Brahms-Gesellschaft, 1917), 219–224; vol. 4 (*Briefe,* vol. 12), 10, 15–18. The origins of op. 109 and 110 are discussed more completely by Margit McCorkle in *Brahms Werkverzeichnis,* 428 and 432, and by Siegfried Kross in *Die Chorwerke von Johannes Brahms* (Berlin: Max Hesses Verlag, 1958), 438–441 and 454–458.

13. Kross, *Die Chorwerke,* 438–439.

14. For instance, the texts he chose for the three sets of lieder that he published in 1888 (opp. 105–107) are almost all tinged with melancholy or bitter irony.

15. See *Johannes Brahms im Briefwechsel mit Breitkopf und Härtel, Bartolf Senff, J. Rieter Biedermann et al.,* ed. Wilhelm Altmann, *Briefe,* vol. 14 (Berlin: Deutsches Brahms-Gesellschaft, 1920), 289. Before 1885, his last documented interest in Schütz's works was in May 1878, the year in which the op. 74 motets were completed. At that time he requested Wüllner's edition of three polychoral psalm settings by Schütz (Psalms 6, 130, and 98) from Edmund Astor at the publisher J. Rieter-Biedermann.

16. These *Abschriften* are contained on bifolio 23–24 of Gesellschaft der Musikfreunde A 130. Virginia Hancock describes that entire collection and others left by Brahms in *Brahms's Choral Compositions and His Library of Early Music* (Ann Arbor: UMI Research Press, 1983), 11–68; the Schütz passages are discussed on pages 30–33. See also Hancock, "Brahms and Early Music: Evidence from His Library and His Choral Compositions," in *Brahms Studies: Analytical and Historical Perspectives,* ed. George Bozarth (Oxford: Oxford University Press, 1990), 40–48; and McCorkle, *Brahms Werkverzeichnis,* 720–721), listing the specific passages that Brahms copied from the Schütz *Werke.*

17. Hancock, *Brahms's Choral Compositions,* 135–146.

18. Hancock even points out that the declamatory style of the first choir in these bars closely resembles some of the passages from Schütz's *Psalmen Davids* that Brahms had copied into A 130, leaving no doubt about the psalmodic implications of the texture (*Brahms's Choral Composition,* 144–145).

19. Brahms's letter to Hans von Bülow is quoted by Kalbeck in *Johannes Brahms,* 4:184. On possible further evidence of Brahms's intention for these pieces to be sung at the festivals mentioned in this letter, see Kurt Hofmann's essay "Brahmsiana der Familie Petersen. Erinnerungen und Briefe," in *Brahms Studien,* vol. 3, ed. Kurt and Renate Hofmann (Hamburg: Johannes Brahms-Gesellschaft, 1979), 71–72. The most thorough discussion of *Fest- und Gedenksprüche*'s occasional purpose comes from Ryan Mark Minor, "National Memory, Public Music: Commemoration and Consecration in Nineteenth Century Choral Works" (Ph.D. diss., University of Chicago, 2004).

20. The development of *völkisch* ideology throughout the nineteenth century is covered at length in George L. Mosse, *The Crisis of German Ideology: Intellectual Origins of the Third Reich* (New York: Grosset's Universal Library, 1964). As the title of his book suggests, Mosse is ultimately concerned with the modern implications of nineteenth-century political and ideological developments. Nevertheless, chaps. 1 and 2 ("From Romanticism to the Volk" and "A Germanic Faith") offer thorough accounts and thoughtful interpretations of *völkisch* trends in the nineteenth century.

21. For exhaustive essays on the complex history of the terms *Reich, Staat, Nation,*

and *Volk*, see the entries under those words in *Geschichtliche Grundbegriffe: Historisches Lexikon zur politisch-sozialen Sprache in Deutschland*, ed. Otto Brunner, Werner Conze, and Reinhart Koselleck (Stuttgart: Klett-Cotta, 1984). In particular see the entry under *Reich*, pts. 5–6 (6:487–505). For a considerably condensed discussion of these terms, see Liah Greenfeld, *Nationalism: Five Roads to Modernity* (Cambridge, Mass.: Harvard University Press, 1992), 364.

22. Greenfeld outlines the Pietists' influence on Romanticism and German national-ism in *Nationalism*, 314–322. Her work updates Koppel S. Pinson's extensive discussion of this topic in *Pietism as a Factor in the Rise of German Nationalism* (New York: Columbia University Press, 1934).

23. Lagarde develops these ideas throughout his *Schriften für das deutschen Volk* (Munich: J. F. Lehmanns Verlag, 1937). His ideas on nationalism and religion are covered at length by Fritz Stern in *The Politics of Cultural Despair* (Berkeley: University of California Press, 1961). See also Mosse, *German Ideology*, 31–39; William John Bossenbrook, *The German Mind* (Detroit: Wayne State University Press, 1961), 346–349; and Wolfgang Tilgner, "Volk, Nation und Vaterland im protestantischen Denken zwischen Kaiserreich und Nationalsozialismus (ca. 1870–1933)," in *Volk-Nation-Vaterland*, ed. Horst Zilleßen (Gütersloh: Gerd Mohn, 1970), 146–149.

24. The same cannot be said for the annotations in his 1833 Luther Bible, where Brahms marked no passages (other than Wisdom of Solomon 9) that touch on this theme. One might take this for evidence of a chronological separation be-tween his Bible markings and his entry of the texts on folios 15–19 of his note-book.

25. Both Isaac and the word of God make the passing of the covenant explicit earlier in that chapter. Genesis 28:3–4 [Isaac]: "May God almighty bless you and make you fruitful and numerous, that you may become a company of peoples. May he give to you the blessing of Abraham, to you and to your offspring with you"; Genesis 28:12–13: "And he [Jacob] dreamed that there was a ladder set up on the earth, the top of it reaching to heaven; and the Angels of God were ascending and descending on it. And the Lord stood beside him and said, 'I am the Lord, the God of Abraham your father and the God of Isaac; the land on which you lie I will give to you and to your offspring.'"

26. Bossenbrook, *The German Mind*, 343. For a more thorough discussion of Treitschke and Sybel and other historians at this time, see George G. Iggers, *The German Conception of History: The National Tradition of Historical Thought from Herder to the Present*, rev. ed. (Middletown, Conn.: Wesleyan University Press, 1983), 116–120. See also *Geschichtliche Grundbegriffe*, 5:498–504.

27. As listed in Kurt Hofmann, *Die Bibliothek von Johannes Brahms: Bücher und Musikalienverzeichnis*, Schriftenreihe zur Musik (Hamburg: Dieter Wagner, 1974), 117.

28. Quoted in Kalbeck, *Johannes Brahms*, 4:376.

29. There are several in-depth studies of German national festivals in the nineteenth century, including Dieter Dülding, Peter Friedmann, and Paul Münsch, eds., *Öffentliche Festkultur: Politische Feste in Deutschland von der Aufklärung bis zum Ersten Weltkrieg* (Reinbeck bei Hamburg: Rowohlts, 1988); George L. Mosse, *The Nationalization of the Masses: Political Symbolism and Mass Move-*

ments in Germany from the Napoleonic Wars through the Third Reich (Ithaca: Cornell University Press, 1975); Fritz Schellack, *Nationalfeiertage in Deutschland von 1871 bis 1945* (Frankfurt am Main: Peter Lang, 1990); and Theodore Schieder, *Das Deutsche Kaiserreich von 1871 als Nationalstaat,* Wissenschaftliche Abhandlungen der Arbeitsgemeinschaft für Forschung des Landes Nordrhein-Westfalen, vol. 20 (Cologne: Westdeutscher Verlag, 1961), 71–87.

30. Mosse, *Nationalization of the Masses,* 73–76.

31. Ibid., 132–133.

32. Ryan Minor interprets Brahms's remark in the opposite manner; the composer, Minor argues, did not wish the works to be limited to the three holidays in question, but rather hoped they could be performed more frequently for a wider variety of festivals. See Minor, "National Memory, Public Music."

33. The program is reproduced by Fritz Schellack in "Sedan- und Kaisergeburtstagfeste," in Dülding, Friedmann, and Münsch, *Öffentliche Festkultur,* 283.

34. Kalbeck, *Johannes Brahms,* 3:400.

35. Although these pieces were not published until 1867, they were probably composed five or more years earlier. See McCorkle, *Brahms Werkverzeichnis,* 148.

36. See Mosse, *Nationalization of the Masses,* 137.

37. A note entered by a chorister in one of the part books of the Hamburg *Frauenchor* claiming that the S S A A version Brahms arranged for that group in 1860 was "originally written for four men's voices" led Sophie Drinker to surmise that Brahms set the T T B B version as far back as the summer of 1847, when he assembled a men's chorus in the town of Winsen. See Drinker, *Brahms and His Women Choruses* (Merion, Pa.: Masurgia Publishers, 1952), 95; Kalbeck, *Johannes Brahms,* 1:47; and Hancock, *Brahms's Choral Compositions,* 115–116. The idea that this setting originated in Brahms's youth gains credence through the unusually austere imitation of "early" music displayed here. Not only do the voices move in absolutely like rhythms up until the final extended cadence of each strophe in bars 32–36, but also the song is set entirely in root-position harmonies. Missing are the trademark intricacies of rhythm and voice-leading that normally mark Brahms's emulation of German styles from the sixteenth and seventeenth centuries. Although the utter simplicity of "Ich schwing mein Horn" might be understood as a character piece that carries parameters of rhythm and harmony to extremes in order to evoke a Gothic aura, it is also possible that this setting predates the intense study of earlier musical styles that Brahms undertook in the 1850s.

38. Kross argues that the scarcity of *Männerchor* works in Brahms's oeuvre was due to the lack of situations Brahms encountered that would have called for such pieces—as compared with the large number of works he composed for women's chorus—and to Brahms's possible distaste for the lower culture for which the men's chorus movement was partially responsible in the nineteenth century (*Die Chorwerke,* 149).

39. Hugo Riemann, writing in 1882, says, "More recently the term hymn designates vocal works of various forms, mostly, however, referring to works with grand effect, for large choir with brass accompaniment, on sacred as well as secular subjects." *Musik-Lexikon von Dr. Hugo Riemann* (Leipzig: Verlag des Bibliographischen Instituts, 1882), 409–410.

40. Hans Michael Beuerle makes an especially thorough comparison of the piece's two ends. See Beuerle, *Johannes Brahms: Untersuchungen zu den A-cappella-Kompositionen* (Tutzing: Hans Schneider, 1971), 210–211.

41. Even the basses become unstuck at the word "anrufen" (bars 31–32), misplacing their accent on the second syllable as the other six voices do.

42. When Wüllner—whose advice Brahms solicited in conjunction with opp. 109 and 110—objected to this detail, Brahms refused to waver. Brahms writes: "For every NB I am thankful to you—even when it wasn't useable! I cannot give you f♯–F natural, for example in no. 2" (*Briefwechsel mit Franz Wüllner,* 164). Of course, had he altered anything, it would have been to change the F-sharp to an F natural and thus make all of bar 21 a D minor harmony.

43. Hancock, *Brahms's Choral Compositions,* 150–151.

44. The only dynamic marking other than *forte* in the opus before the middle section of no. 3 is the *piano* in bars 36–40 of no. 2, which occurs at the pictorial setting of the words "das wird wüßte."

45. Bernhard W. Anderson, "Deuteronomy," in the *New Oxford Annotated Bible,* ed. Bruce M. Metzger and Roland E. Murphy (New York: Oxford University Press, 1991), 217 OT (Old Testament). Robert Polzin has explored this aspect of Deuteronomy more deeply by analyzing the literary relationship between Moses and the "Deuteronomist." Polzin, "Deuteronomy," in *The Literary Guide to the Bible,* ed. Robert Alter and Frank Kermode (Cambridge, Mass.: Harvard University Press, 1987), 92–94.

46. See my "Brahms on Schopenhauer: The *Vier ernste Gesänge,* op. 121, and Late-Nineteenth-Century Pessimism," in *Brahms Studies* vol. 1, ed. David Brodbeck (Lincoln: University of Nebraska Press, 1994), 170–188.

6. Beyond the End

1. Brahms wrote to his publisher Fritz Simrock on 7 June 1889: "I am giving the three choruses [op. 109] as one work, but I am not sure about the title. . . . The title will be something like: 'German Festival and Commemorative Sayings [*Deutsche Fest- und Gedenksprüche*],' and I am tempted, in case you should suggest it, to give a second title for other countries (Switzerland, England): 'National' etc. Will that work?" Johannes Brahms, *Briefe an P. J. Simrock und Fritz Simrock,* vol. 3, 3d ed., ed. Max Kalbeck *Briefe,* vol. 11 (Berlin: Deutsche Brahms-Gesellschaft, 1917), 219.

2. Kross, *Die Chorwerke von Johannes Brahms* (Berlin: Max Hesses Verlag, 1958), 434.

3. Ibid., 3.

4. Kross, "The Choral Music of Johannes Brahms," *American Choral Review* (special issue) 25 (1994): 5. Kross's later remarks begin to explain why Brahms's music, though still quite prevalent during the Third Reich, was not put to as much public use as it might have been: he was never a favorite with the farthest right wing in German politics.

5. Karl Laux, *Der Einsame: Johannes Brahms Leben und Werk* (Graz: Verlag Anton Pustet, 1944), 341–342. See also Alfred von Ehrmann, *Johannes Brahms: Weg, Werk und Welt* (Leipzig: Breitkopf und Härtel, 1933), 417–418.

6. Brahms, *Briefe an Fritz Simrock*, vol. 4, ed. Max Kalbeck, *Briefe*, vol. 12 (Berlin: Deutsche Brahms-Gesellschaft, 1919), 30.

7. As quoted in Kalbeck, *Johannes Brahms*, 4:247, n. 2.

8. On the possible inclusion of earlier material in the late Intermezzi, see ibid., 277.

9. A Wst Ia 79.564, fol. 7r. See George Bozarth, "Brahms's Lieder Inventory of 1859–60 and Other Documents of His Life and Work," *Fontes Artis Musicae* 30 (1983): 111. (Bozarth incorrectly cites the folio on which Brahms copied the texts as 7 *verso*.) See also Dillon Parmer's interpretation in "Brahms and the Poetic Motto: A Hermeneutical Aid?" *Journal of Musicology* 15 (1997): 367–379.

10. In fact, the three-note motive is developed immediately in the supporting voices at bar 5: A–F–G on top against C–A–B♭ in the "tenor" (upper left hand).

11. Rudolf von der Leyen, *Johannes Brahms als Mensch und Freund* (Düsseldorf: Karl Robert Langeweische, 1905), 82–83.

12. The book appears as volume 8 of Herder's *Sämmtliche Werke. Zur schönen Literatur und Kunst*, 20 parts published in 9 instead of 10 vols. (Stuttgart: J. G. Cottaschen Buchhandlung, 1827–1830). According to Kurt Hofmann's index of Brahms's library, "On the end paper [*Vorsatz*] of the third part the ownership notice 'J. Brahms 1856.'" Hofmann, *Die Bibliothek von Johannes Brahms: Bücher- und Musikalienverzeichnis* (Hamburg: Verlag Karl Dieter Wagner, 1974), 51.

13. *Clara Schumann–Johannes Brahms: Briefe aus den Jahren 1853–1896*, vol. 2, ed. Berthold Litzmann (Leipzig: Breitkopf und Härtel, 1927), 562, cited in Malcolm MacDonald, *Brahms* (New York: Schirmer, 1990), 292.

14. Leon Botstein suggests that op. 122 may be "based on material [Brahms] worked on at several points in his life before 1896." Botstein, ed., *The Compleat Brahms* (New York: Norton, 1999), 205. There is, however, no indication that any of these chorale preludes were composed before June 1896. See George Bozarth's preface to his ur-text edition of op. 122, Johannes Brahms, *Werke für Orgel*, ed. George Bozarth (Munich: Henle, 1987), vi–vii.

15. See G. W. F. Hegel, "Two Fragments on Love," trans. H. S. Harris and Cyrus Hamlin, *Clio* 8 (1987): 261–262; and Dieter Henrich, "Hegel and Hölderlin," *Idealistic Studies* 2 (1972): 151–173. See also my "Brahms on Schopenhauer: The *Vier ernste Gesänge*, op. 121, and Late-Nineteenth-Century Pessimism," in *Brahms Studies*, vol. 1, ed. David Brodbeck (Lincoln: University of Nebraska Press, 1994), 174–177.

16. Walter Niemann, *Brahms* (1920), trans. Catherine Alison Phillips (New York: Alfred A. Knopf, 1929), 212.

17. Ibid., 241.

18. Karl Geiringer's formulation is typical: "A gentle tranquility, combined with a certain unworldliness, increasingly took possession of the aging man; even when the circle around him grew smaller, as death robbed him of some of his nearest friends, this mood was essentially unshaken." Geiringer, *Brahms: His Life and Work*, trans. H. B. Weiner and Bernard Miall (Boston: Houghton Mifflin, 1936), 167.

19. Morgan, "Six Piano Pieces, Opus 118," in Botstein, *The Compleat Brahms* 194–195.

20. Niemann, *Brahms* (Berlin: Schuster and Loeffler, 1920).

21. Ibid., v, citing Leyen, *Johannes Brahms als Mensch und Freund*, 98–99.

22. Wilfferodt, "Zum zehn jährigen Todestage von Johannes Brahms," *Musikalisches Wochenblatt / Neue Zeitschrift für Musik* 28, no. 13/14 (1907): 314. Also, Walter Frisch has discussed how both Bach and Brahms were posited as healing agents; see his "Bach, Brahms, and the Emergence of Musical Modernism," in *Bach Perspectives*, vol. 3, *Creative Responses to Bach from Mozart to Hindemith*, ed. Michael Marissen (Lincoln: University of Nebraska Press, 1998), 109–131.

23. Niemann, *Brahms*, 445.

24. Fritz Stern, in his seminal study of German nationalist ideology, *The Politics of Cultural Despair: A Study in the Rise of Germanic Ideology* (Berkeley: University of California Press, 1961), outlines the centrality of *Niederdeutschland* in the work of one such writer, Julius Langbehn, whose book *Rembrandt als Erzieher, von einem Deutschen* (Leipzig: C. L. Hirschfeld, 1890) enjoyed immense popularity in the 1890s and again in the 1920s (120, 147). Langbehn wrote of *Niederdeutschland* as the repository of true German *Volkstümlichkeit*, as opposed to Prussian culture, which had been racially compromised through intermingling with Jews, Slavs, and Frenchmen.

25. Niemann, *Die Musik der Gegenwart und der Letzten Vergangenheit bis zu den Romantikern, Klassizisten und Neudeutschen*, 9th–12th eds. (Berlin: Schuster and Loeffler, 1920).

26. Ibid., 32.

27. A "racial" fingerprint is so pronounced in Brahms's style, says Niemann, that one can distinguish his music from that of his "prophet," Robert Schumann: "Brahms's character differentiation from Schumann is easiest to grasp from a racial standpoint. As a *Niederdeutscher*, Brahms took on Schumann's heavy, serious, melancholy side, that doom [*Verhängnis*] which slumbered deep within his inner self. That which was Saxon in the charming disposition of Schumann, the smoothly folklike, naïve, and happy character of his sunniest themes, showed itself from the beginning in blooming lyricism. The middle-class character of German Romantic art was also not lacking, finally, . . . in Brahms. As one of a harsh, manly, and Beethovenian nature, however, he favored serious epic pathos. So in general the woman supported Schumann, the man supported Brahms." Niemann, *Die Musik der Gegenwart*, 43.

28. Ibid., 275.

29. Ibid., 277.

30. Ibid., 289.

31. Ibid., 295–296. Niemann had lodged similar complaints about the Americanization, mercantilization, and industrialization of music elsewhere in the book.

32. One can see the two stereotypes butt heads in Niemann's discussion of Gustav Mahler, whose "brilliant, decorative, and fresco-like effect" Niemann attributes to the "characteristic tendency of an Austrian who grew up in a healthy artistic sensuality," but whose "coarsest deficiencies . . . rest in the monstrous extravagance of the elementary sound phenomena of a Simon Mayr, a Meyerbeer, and Berlioz." And, Niemann adds, these speak to "his often outrageous, strongly marked Semitic race." Niemann, *Musik der Gegenwart*, 147–148. Yet, when his complete statement on Mahler is considered, it is clear that Niemann does not

perceive his own racial stereotyping to be anti-Semitic. He closes by chiding the "blind and foolish Jew hatred of [Mahler's] opponents" (149).

33. Willibald Nagel, *Johannes Brahms* (Stuttgart: J. Eingelhorns Nach f[olger]., 1923), 10–11.

34. Arndt, "Exkurs: Das Gerücht über Brahms' jüdische Abstammung," in *Das "Reichs-Brahmsfest" 1933 in Hamburg: Rekonstruktion und Dokumentation,* ed. Arbeitsgruppe Exilmusik am Musikwissenschaftlichen Institut der Universität Hamburg (Hamburg: Bockel Verlag, 1997), 119–120.

35. P. Walter Jacob, *Musica Prohibida/Verbotene Musik: Ein Vortrag im Exil,* ed. with commentary by Fritz Pohle (Hamburg: Hamburger Arbeitsstelle für deutsche Exilliteratur, 1991), 14. For his part, Jacob never locates the tainted *Brahmsfest* in question. Rather, it is Pohle who draws this connection in an editor's note (54, n. 81).

36. Motzkin, *Das Schwarzbuch: Tatsachen und Dokumente: Die Lage der Juden in Deutschland 1933* (Paris: Comité des Délégations Juives, 1934), 14. Motzkin offers this comment as a footnote to a reprint of an interview with the Prussian culture minister Hans Hinkel in the *Frankfurter Zeitung* of 6 April 1933. Like Jacob, Motzkin does not specify where the canceled festival was to have taken place.

37. Fuller-Maitland, "Brahms," in *Grove's Dictionary of Music and Musicians* 3d ed., vol. 1, ed. Fuller-Maitland (London: Macmillan, 1921), 444.

38. Sessions, "Music and Nationalism: Some Notes on Dr. Göbbel's Letter to Furtwängler," *Modern Music* 11 (1933): 4.

39. Margaret Notley, "Brahms as Liberal: Genre, Style, and Politics in Late-Nineteenth-Century Vienna," *Nineteenth-Century Music* 17 (1993): 107–123. See also Leon Botstein, "Brahms and Nineteenth-Century Painting," *Nineteenth-Century Music* 14 (1990): 154–168.

40. Stolzing, *Ostdeutsche Rundschau,* 19 October 1890, cited in Notley, "Brahms as Liberal," 122. Notley does not provide a title or page number for Stolzing's remark.

41. Spitzer, *Lezte Wiener Spaziergänge* (Vienna, 1894), 266–267; quoted in Kalbeck, *Brahms,* 4:175–176.

42. Kalbeck, *Brahms,* 4:438–439.

43. Albert Heintze, *Die Deutschen Familiennamen: geschichtlich, geographisch, sprachlich,* 4th improved and enlarged ed., ed. P[aul] Cascorbi (Halle: Buchhandlung des Waisenshauses, 1914), 7.

44. Bahlow, *Deutsches Namenbuch: Ein Führer durch Deutschlands Familiennamen* (Neumeister in Holstein: Wachholtz, 1933), 57. The first entry under part "1b: Familiennamen aus Kirchlichen Taufnamen," reads: "**Abraham.** Biblisch / jud. *Abraham; Abram* (ursprüngl. Form). *Abrahamso(h)n. / Obromeit (littauisch). Aberle* (jüd in Mannheim). / Slaw. Abresch, Abrusch. / ostfried. *Abrahams; Abrams. Brahms.* (vgl. Zunz S. 53)." The Zunz reference is to Ludwig Zunz, "Namen der Juden (1836, Dezember)," in *Gesammelte Schriften,* vol. 2, ed. Curators of the Zunz Foundation (Berlin: Louis Gerschel, 1876), 53. Zunz lists "Brahim" as a Jewish first name.

45. Kessler, *Die Familiennamen der Juden in Deutschland* (Leipzig: Zentralstelle für Deutsche Personen- und Familiengeschichte, 1935), 17: "The Reformation bat-

tled with ardent zeal against medieval saint worship, and the storm against Catholic relics and images in the churches was followed by efforts to root out saints' names from families. From the second half of the sixteenth century, one began to introduce Old Testament names as substitutes for the saints' names among the Protestant population. . . . To this Protestant group and time belong also Christian German family names like Abraham (Brahms)."

46. Krause, *Die Jüdische Namenwelt* (Essen: Essener Verlagsanstalt, 1942), 33; 151n24.

47. Kalbeck, *Johannes Brahms,* 1:1–13.

48. Franz Brenner, "Über die aus Tondern stammenden Ahnen des Komponisten Johannes Brahms," *Die Heimat* (Kiel) 39 (1929): 275, 279.

49. Erwin Freitag, "Beitrag zur Geschichte der Familie Brahms," *Ditmarschen* (Kiel) 8 (1932): 80–81. The anonymous author of an article in *Hamburger Fremdenblatt* of 25 May 1933 (in connection with the Hamburg "Reichs-Brahmsfest") titled "Johannes Brahms' Vaterhaus" may have been directly echoing Freitag in stating: "Family names such as Braahmstädt, Brahmste, Brahmst, or Brahms are quite common in northwest Germany. Other meanings are absurd." The article is cited by Arndt, "Das Gerücht über Brahms," 119.

50. *Signale der Musikalische Welt* 96 (1938): 26.

51. The events surrounding the Vienna Brahms-Fest are recounted in Fred K. Prieberg, *Trial of Strength: Wilhelm Furtwängler and the Third Reich,* trans. Christopher Dolan (London: Quartet Books, 1991), 64–66; and in Albrecht Dümling, ed., *Verteidigung des Musikalischen Fortschritts: Brahms und Schoenberg* (Hamburg: Argument Verlag, 1990), 45–49.

52. Printed as "Johannes Brahms: 1931," in Furtwängler, *Ton und Wort: Aufsätze und Vorträge, 1918 bis 1954,* 6th ed. (Wiesbaden: Brockhaus, 1955), 40–52. The date 1931 is apparently an error, or it may refer to some earlier, unrecorded venue for the same speech.

53. In a letter from Berg to his wife, 17 May 1933, quoted in Dümling, *Verteidigung des Musikalischen Fortschritts,* 56.

54. As Michael Kater points out, Furtwängler also aided "anti-Semites, Nazis, and musicians sympathetic with the Nazi cause," and concludes that "this much meddling, whether for a positive or a negative purpose, suggests that Furtwängler was not an altruist but a man obsessed with personal connections, who always had to be at the center of things." Kater, *The Twisted Muse: Musicians and Their Music in the Third Reich* (New York: Oxford University Press, 1997), 196. Kater's approach to Furtwängler might best be described as a sympathetic thrashing. Prieberg's account in *Trial of Strength* is far more apologetic.

55. Furtwängler, *Notebooks, 1924–54,* trans. Shaun Whiteside, ed. Michael Tanner (London: Quartet Books, 1989), 161. This is only one of many such remarks in Furtwängler's notebooks, particularly from 1945 (155–163).

56. See Peter Gay, *Freud, Jews, and Other Germans: Masters and Victims in Modernist Culture* (New York: Oxford University Press, 1978), 3–10.

57. Furtwängler, "Brahms: 1931," 48.

58. Ibid., 51–52.

59. Ibid., 51. For an account of the Nazi Bruckner program, see Benjamin Marcus Korstvedt, "Anton Bruckner in the Third Reich and After (An Essay on Ideology

and Bruckner Reception)," *Musical Quarterly* 80 (1996): 132–160. See also Korstvedt's "'Return to the Pure Sources': The Ideology and Text-Critical Legacy of the First Bruckner *Gesamtausgabe*," in *Bruckner Studies*, ed. Timothy L. Jackson and Paul Hawkshaw (Cambridge: Cambridge University Press, 1997), 91–109.

60. Furtwängler, "Brahms: 1931," 51.

61. On Mahler's encounters with anti-Semitism and antimodernism in Vienna, see Karen Painter, "The Sensuality of Timbre: Responses to Mahler and Modernity at the Fin de Siècle," and K. M. Knittle, "'Ein hypermoderner Dirigent': Mahler and Anti-Semitism in Fin de Siècle Vienna," *Nineteenth-Century Music* 18 (1995): 236–256 and 257–276.

62. On this point, see Richard Taruskin, "Back to Whom? Neoclassicism as Ideology," *Nineteenth-Century Music* 16 (1993): 286–302; and idem, "The Darker Side of Modern Music," *New Republic* 5 (1988): 28–34.

63. Furtwängler, "Brahms: 1931," 52.

64. Furtwängler, "Brahms und die Krise unserer Zeit: 1934," in *Ton und Wort: Aufsätze und Vorträge, 1918 bis 1954,* 6th ed. (Wiesbaden: Brockhaus, 1955), 86–90.

65. Ibid., 86.

66. Ibid., 90.

67. Richard Taruskin has tackled the question of "Teutonic universalism" head-on in his introduction to *Repercussions* 5 (1996): 5–20.

68. On Bekker's career, see Christopher Hailey, "The Paul Bekker Collection in the Yale University Music Library," *Notes* 51 (1994): 13–21. Michael Kater mentions Bekker's religion in relation to Hans Pfitzner's anti-Semitic slurs against the critic in *The Twisted Muse,* 213.

69. Bekker, "Brahms," *Anbruch* 15, no. 4/5 (April–May 1933): 56, 57–58.

70. Schoenberg, "Brahms the Progressive," in *Style and Idea: Selected Writings of Arnold Schoenberg,* ed. Leonard Stein (Berkeley: University of California Press, 1975), 399–409.

71. Schoenberg, "National Music (1)," ibid., 169.

72. Schoenberg, "National Music (2)," ibid., 173.

73. Geiringer, *Johannes Brahms, Leben und Schaffen eines deutschen Meisters* (Vienna: Adolf M. Roher, 1934); in English, *Brahms: His Life and Work,* trans. Weiner and Miall (see note 18).

74. Geiringer, *Johannes Brahms,* 306–307. By 1955 Geiringer himself, while moved to adopt the English title in his second German edition, let the quoted passage stand in full. Geiringer, *Johannes Brahms, Sein Leben und Schaffen,* 2d enlarged and improved ed. (Zurich, 1955); pocket edition (Kassel: Bärenreiter, 1974), 359.

75. Walter Rehberg and Paula Rehberg, *Johannes Brahms, sein Leben und Werk* (Zürich: Artemis-Verlag, 1947), 394–395.

76. Ibid., 395–396.

77. Ibid., 397.

78. Ibid., 398.

79. Brahms scholarship that focuses on allusion includes the Bozarth and Parmer essays mentioned in note 9, as well as David Brodbeck, "Brahms, the Third Sym-

phony, and the New German School," in *Brahms and His World,* ed. Walter Frisch (Princeton: Princeton University Press, 1990), 65–80; idem, *Brahms: Symphony No. 1* (Cambridge: Cambridge University Press, 1997); Kenneth Hull, "Brahms the Allusive: Extracompositional Reference in the Instrumental Music of Johannes Brahms" (Ph.D. diss., Princeton University, 1989); and Raymond Knapp, *Brahms and the Challenge of the Symphony* (Stuyvesant, N.Y.: Pendragon Press, 1997).

80. The politician was Klaus Landowsky, head of the Christian Democratic Union in the Berlin Senate.

81. Barenboim, "Germans, Jews, and Music," *New York Review of Books* 48 (29 March 2001): 50–51.

Index

Abell, Arthur M., 39, 215n23
Abrams, M. H., 78–79, 96
Absolute music, 186, 188, 190–193
Adorno, Theodor, 134
Alexander, Paul J., 104
Alings, Reinhard, 104, 135
Allgeyer, Julius, 76
Anderson, Benedict, 217n45
Anti-Semitism, 176–177, 179–180, 181, 185
Apocalypse, 77–80, 126, 144; and French
    Revolution, 78. *See also* Brahms, Works,
    Ein deutsches Requiem; Brahms, Works,
    Triumphlied
Arndt, Ernst Moritz, 24, 43–44; "Des
    deutschen Vaterland," 43; *Meine
    Wanderungen und Wandelungen,* 43–44
Arndt, Peri, 179, 180, 182
Arnim, Achim von and Clemens Brentano,
    Das Knaben Wunderhorn, 15
Austro-Prussian War, 76–77

Bach, Johann Sebastian, 9, 99, 102, 114, 135
Bahlow, Hans, 181
Barbarossa, Friedrich, 104
Barenboim, Daniel, 192
Beckerath, Laura von, 146–147, 148
Beethoven, Ludwig van, 1, 8–9, 98–99, 110,
    134, 175, 186, 187; Symphony no. 5 in C
    minor, op. 67, 91, 92; Symphony no. 9 in
    D minor, op. 125, 9, 114–116, 127
Beiser, Frederick C., 32
Bekker, Paul, 110, 111, 134–135, 187, 191
Bellman, Jonathan, 26–27
Berg, Alban, 183
Beuerle, Hans Michael, 156

Bible, 2, 4, 10, 37–41, 65, 75, 77–78, 96, 97,
    117, 145–147, 163; Brahms's baptismal
    Bible, 35, 37, 47–53, 55, 60, 89; specific
    passages: Wisdom 9, 48–50, 59–63, 65;
    Job 3:20–23, 52–53, 55; 1 Kings 8, 59–60;
    1 Kings 6:11–12, 60–63; Psalm 51, 52;
    Psalm 126:5–6, 50, 68; 1 Corinthians 13,
    62, 64; Revelation 6, 99–101; Revelation
    19, 102–103, 105. *See also* Brahms, note-
    book of biblical texts
Billroth, Theodor, 45, 136, 172, 226n36
Bismarck, Otto von, 4, 76, 98–99, 133, 137,
    146
Botstein, Leon, 6, 29
Bozarth, George, 23
Brahms, Johannes: Vienna monument to, 1–
    3; as liberal, 4, 6, 102, 146, 187, 191; pa-
    triotism, 4, 98, 102, 104, 118, 132, 133,
    137, 143–151, 163–164; "Erklärung"
    [Declaration] against New German
    School, 10; and folksong, 12–18; study of
    early music, 24, 69, 139–140, 162; collec-
    tion of *Deutsche Sprichworte,* 33; religious
    attitudes, 24–25, 31, 33–37, 41–43, 64,
    76–78, 90, 144–145, 147, 164, 171; note-
    book of biblical texts, 35, 48–50, 53–63,
    66–67, 137–139, 143, 145; apartment at
    Karlgasse 4, Vienna, 98–101; possible Jew-
    ish origins of name, 178–182; as godfa-
    ther, 214n8
WORKS:
"Abenddämmerung," op. 49, no. 5, 29
"Ach lieber Herre Jesu Christ," WoO 34,
    no. 6, 16, 149
Agnus Dei, WoO 18, 52–53

Brahms *(continued)*

Alto Rhapsody, op. 53, 105, 128, 149

Ave Maria, op. 12, 15

"Die Nonne und der Ritter," op. 28, no. 1, 213n43

Ein deutsches Requiem, op 45, 1–2, 34, 40–43, 50, 65–98, 106, 119, 131, 135, 165; German Language in, 43, 46, 77, 78, 90, 94, 97; "Trost" (comfort), as a theme, 57, 65–70, 73, 75, 80; temporality in, 68–70, 73, 75, 79–81, 93, 96–97; apocalypticism in, 84–97, 126–127, 128–129; text autograph, 220n5

Eleven Chorale Preludes, op. 122, 171

Fest- und Gedenksprüche, op. 109, 38, 57–58, 63, 77–78, 118, 135–167; polychoral techniques in, 135–136, 139–143, 151–153, 157–159; prayerfulness in, 137–139, 144, 151–156, 161–162

Five songs for Men's Chorus, op. 41, 149–151

"Geistliches Wiegenlied," op. 91, no. 2, 18–30

Gesang der Parzen, op. 89, 34–35, 128, 131

"Gestillte Sehnsucht," op. 91, no. 1, 28

"Herbstgefühl," op. 48, no. 7, 29

Intermezzo in E-flat major, op. 117, no. 1, 168–170

Marienlieder, op. 22, 12–15

"O Heiland, reiß die Himmel auf," op. 74, no. 2, 135

Piano Concerto No. 1 in D minor, op. 15, 65

Piano Sonata in C major, op. 1, 170

Rinaldo, op. 50, 27, 149

Romances on Tieck's Magelone, op. 33, 27

"Schaffe in mir, Gott, ein rein Herz" op. 29, no. 2, 52

Schicksalslied, op. 54, 106, 128, 131

Six Piano Pieces, op. 118, 172–173

Symphony No. 1 in C minor, op. 68, 91, 115–116, 134

Symphony No. 2 in D major, op. 73, 134

Thirteen Canons for Women's Voices, op. 113, 170–171

Three Motets, op. 110, 135–143, 167; "Ich aber bin elend," no. 1, 54–56

Triumphlied, op. 55, 1–2, 63, 76, 94, 101–108, 111–133, 143, 144; monumentality in, 101, 105, 108, anti-French sentiment in, 102–105; apocalypticism in, 105, 126–127; cho-rale "Nun danket alle Gott" in, 111–118

Twelve Lieder and Romances for Women's Chorus, op. 44, 149

Variations and Fugue on a Theme by Handel, op. 24, 5

"Vergangen ist mir Glück und Heil," op. 48, no. 6, 29

"Verstohlen geht der Mond auf," WoO 33, no. 49, 170

Vier ernste Gesänge, op. 121, 34, 36, 61, 63–64, 66, 164, 171–172

"Warum ist das Licht gegeben dem Mühseligen?", op. 74, no. 1, 38, 51–56, 66, 116, 135, 138

"Wiegenlied," op. 49, no. 4, 15–16, 29, 168

Brahms, Christiane (mother), 33, 65, 72, 75

Brahms, Elise (sister), 172

Brahms, Peter Hinrich (great-grandfather), 181

Brahms-Wagner dichotomy. See Wagner, Richard

Brendel, (Karl) Franz, 9–10

Brinkmann, Reinhold, 116, 134

Büchner, Gottfried, Real- und verbal-Bibel-concordance, 35–36

Bülow, Hans von, 136, 143, 147, 172

Burckhardt, Jakob, 108

Campe, Joachim Heinrich, 44

Cascorbi, Paul, 181–182

Cherubini, Luigi, 98–99

Chorale, 114–116. See also "Ein feste Burg ist unser Gott"; Haydn, "Gott erhalte unsern Kaiser"; "Nun danket alle Gott"; "Nur wer den lieben Gott läßt walten"

Christianity, 36–37, 41–42; and romanticism, 8, 9, 11–17, 22, 24, 31–33, 41, 64, 171–172; and German nationalism, 144–145

Cornelius, Peter (painter), 108–110; Die Apokalyptischen Reiter, 99–101, 119, 126, 129

Corner, David Gregor, Groß-Catholischem Gesangbuch, 22–24

Dahlhaus, Carl, 110

Daverio, John, 40

Davies, Tony, 108

Dessoff, Otto, 38

Drei-Kaiser-Jahr, 63, 137, 146, 148

Drinker, Sophie, 231n37

Dvořák, Anton, 31

Eichendorff, Johann, 24
"Ein feste Burg ist unser Gott" (chorale), 114
Encke, Fedor, 180

Fichte, Johann Gottlieb, 24; *Reden an die deutsche Nation*, 44
Folk. *See* Volk
Franco-Prussian War, 2, 77–78, 101, 105, 117, 126, 151
Freitag, Erwin, 181–182
French Revolution, 78, 147. *See also* Romanticism
Friedrich Wilhelm IV, King of Prussia, 108–109
Frisch, Walter, 135, 234n22
Fuller-Maitland, John Alexander, 179
Furtwängler, Wilhelm, 18, 179, 182–187, 191–192

Gabrieli, Giovanni, 162
Gay, Peter, 6
Geibel, Emanuel, 19, 22–23, 25, 29
Geiringer, Karl, 189–190
Gellner, Ernest, 12, 46, 214n3
Gerber, Rudolf, 41
German language, 7–8, 43–46; the Volk and, 43–45; Wilhelm Scherer and, 45–46. *See also* Grimm, Jacob
Giesbrecht-Schutte, Sabine, 104, 114
Goethe, Johann Wolfgang von, 10, 35, 40
Greenfeld, Leah, 4, 7
Grimm, Hermann, 109–110
Grimm, Jacob, 35; on German language, 45

Häfner, Klaus, 224n11
Hamburg Reichs-Brahmsfest (1933), 179, 182, 236n49
Hancock, Virginia, 139, 156, 161
Handel, George Frideric, 9, 101–102, 183; Dettingen Te Deum, 102; *Messiah*, 106, 148
Hanslick, Eduard, 5
Hassler, Hans Leo, 24
Hastings, Adrian, 7–8
Haydn, Franz Josef, "Gott erhalte unsern Kaiser," 77
Hebbel, Christian Friedrich, 175
Hegel, Georg Wilhelm Friedrich, 171
Heintze, Albert, *Die deutschen Familiennamen*, 180–182
Helst, Barthel van der, *Friedensschluß zu Münster*, 99
Herder, Johann Gottfried von, 168, 170, 175
Hernried, Robert, 41
Herzogenberg, Elisabet von, 34, 172

Herzogenberg, Heinrich von, 34, 209n6
Heuberger, Richard, 38–39
Hindemith, Paul, 184
Hitler, Adolf, 102, 165–166
Hobsbawm, Eric J., 11, 210n13
Hoffmann, E. T. A., 79, 92, 168
Hofmann, Kurt, 47
Hölderlin, Johann Christian Friedrich, 10, 35, 78, 128, 171
Humboldt, Wilhelm von, 109

Jacob, Paul Walter, 179, 182
Joachim, Amalie, 22, 25
Joachim, Josef, 22, 25, 34, 45
Jochmann, Carl Gustav, 44
"Josef, lieber Josef mein" (hymn), 19, 21–23, 25–30

Kalbeck, Max, 23, 41–42, 63, 102–104, 117, 133, 137, 143, 147, 148, 181
Kater, Michael, 236n54
Kermode, Frank, 78, 79, 97
Kessler, Gerhard, 181
Keyserlingk, Botho Graf von, 182
Kleist, Heinrich von, 24
Klemperer, Otto, 182
Krause, Konrad, 181
Kretschmar, Hermann, 101, 227n47
Kretzschmer, August and Wilhelm Florentin von Zuccalmaglio, *Deutsche Volkslieder mit Ihren Original-Weisen*, 23
Kross, Siegfried, 132, 138, 165–167, 224n11
Krummacher, Friedhelm, 102–105, 116

Lagarde, Paul de, 145–146, 147, 162
Langbehn, Julius, 234n24
Laux, Karl, 166
Lemcke, Carl, 149–150
Levi, Hermann, 106, 126
Leyen, Rudolf von der, 38–40, 170, 173–174
Liszt, Franz, 9, 12, 42, 178
Lope de Vega, Garcia, 19, 22–23, 29
Luther, Martin, 45–46, 114–115

MacDonald, Malcolm, 65
Mahler, Gustav, 184–185, 234n32
Mandyczewski, Eusebius, 167
Mann, Thomas, *Doktor Faustus*, 116
Marx, Adolf Bernhard, 8
Meister, Karl Severin, *Das Katholische Kirchenlied*, 22–23
Mendelssohn-Bartholdy, Felix, 40, 175; Symphony no. 5 in D ("Reformation"), 8, 82, 114–115
Men's choruses, 149–151, 152–153

Miall, Bernard, 189–190
Miller zu Aichholz, Viktor von, *Brahms-Bilderbuch*, 98–99, 101
Minor, Ryan M., 229n19
Modernism, 3, 11, 30, 166, 177–178, 184–188
Monumentality, 110–111, 114–118. *See also* Brahms, Works, *Triumphlied*
Morgan, Robert P., 172–173
Morik, Werner, 18
Mosse, George L., 147
Motzkin, Leo, *Blackbook: The Position of Jews in Germany*, 179, 182
Mühlfeld, Richard, 167

Nagel, Willibald, 178
National festivals, 143, 145, 147–149, 151
Nationalism, German, 3–9, 32–33, 102, 103–104, 109–110, 117–118, 134, 147–148, 166, 187–193; distinction from patriotism, 4; cultural, 8–11, 45, 46, 78, 185–187; *völkisch*, 11–12, 118, 144, 145, 147, 178. *See also* Romanticism
National Socialist Party (Nazis), 2, 5, 11, 102, 165–167, 179, 180, 183, 184, 186–187, 190, 192
Nazarene painters, 109
Neudeutsche Schule (New German School), 9–10, 12, 178, 189
Niederdeutsch (low German), 174–175, 178
Niederwald Denkmal, 147–148
Niemann, Walter, 172–178, 188, 191
Nipperdey, Thomas, 118
Notley, Margaret, 6, 179, 210n16
Novalis (Hardenberg, Friedrich Leopold von), 8, 24, 32
"Nun danket alle Gott" (chorale), 148. *See also* Brahms, Works, *Triumphlied*
"Nur wer den lieben Gott läßt walten" (chorale), 69

Ochs, Siegfried, 219n4

Palestrina, Giovanni Pierluigi da, 24
Percy, Thomas, *Reliques of Ancient English Poetry*, 168
Petersen, Peter, 104, 224n14
Pietism, 4, 11
Pinson, Koppel S., 4
Prieberg, Fred K., 179, 180, 182

Raphael (Raffaelo Sanzio), *Sistine Madonna*, 98–99
Rehberg, Walter and Paula, 190–191
Reinthaler, Karl, 37, 42–43, 76, 90, 94, 106

"Resonet in Laudibus" (hymn), 19, 22, 29
Reynolds, Christopher, 40
Riegel, Herman, 109–110
Romanticism: fascination with past, 8, 11, 16, 22, 24, 26–27, 30; and German language, 43, 45, 90; and French Revolution, 78, 103–104; and German nationalism, 151. *See also* Christianity
Rückert, Friedrich, 25

Schack, Adolf Friedrich von, 29
Scherer, Georg, 15–16
Scherer, Wilhelm. *See* German language
Schering, Arnold, 111
Schiller, Friedrich, 35, 108
Schinkel, Karl Friedrich, 108
Schleiermacher, Friedrich Daniel Ernst, 32, 144
Schoenberg, Arnold, 177, 184; "Brahms the Progressive," 3, 5, 188–189; "National Music," 188–189
Scholz, Bernhard, 103
Schopenhauer, Arthur, 31, 171
Schubert, Franz, 1; "Der Lindenbaum," 13
Schubring, Adolf, 77, 82
Schumann, Clara, 24, 33–34, 64, 76, 170
Schumann, Robert, 8, 10, 26, 33–34, 38–41, 65, 170, 175, 234n27; "Neue Bahnen," 40, 134; *Requiem für Mignon*, 40
Schütz, Heinrich, 69, 75, 139–140, 162
Sedantag, 147–148
Sessions, Roger, 179
Siegessäule (monument), 118–119, 126
Signale für die musikalische Welt, 10
Simrock, Clara, 31, 133
Simrock, Fritz, 31, 106, 133, 136, 167, 180
Spies, Hermine, 172
Spitta, Philipp, 105, 139, 172
Spitzer, Daniel, 180
Steinberg, Michael P., 75
Stekel, Hanns Christian, 33–35
Stolzing, Josef, 179–180
Strauß, Richard, 183
Suk, Joseph, 31
Sybel, Heinrich von, 146–147
Symphony, community forming function, 2, 115–116, 133–135

Third Reich. *See* National Socialist Party (Nazis)
Thirty Years' War, 76, 99
Tovey, Donald Francis, 89
Townson, Michael, 44–45
Treitschke, Heinrich von, 146–147

Vaughan, William, 225n27
Volk, the, 9, 11–18, 24–25, 29–30, 151, 152, 162–164, 174–176, 178, 184–185. See also German language

Wagner, Richard, 9–10, 11–12, 16–17, 42, 79, 102, 116, 131, 132, 184, 185; Brahms-Wagner dichotomy, 3, 4–6, 131, 174, 177, 188, 190
Weiner, H. B., 189–190

Werner, Anton von: fresco for the Siegessäule monument, 118–119, 126; Proclamation of the Empire at Versailles, 119
Widmann, Josef Viktor, 38, 151, 215n14, 223n8
Wilfferodt, Felix, 174, 178
Wilhelm I, German Kaiser, 63, 76, 101, 105, 116, 118, 137, 148, 226n42
Wilhelm II, German Kaiser, 63, 118, 137
Wüllner, Franz, 136, 228n11